TRADE AMONG MULTINATIONALS
Intra-Industry Trade and National Competitiveness

Many developed countries are increasingly tempted to improve their national competitiveness by adopting protectionist policies. This book demonstrates that such policies would be mistaken and would do serious damage to industries in the countries concerned.

As worldwide trade has become more free in recent decades, manufacturers in developed economies have found themselves at a cost disadvantage compared to foreign competitors, particularly to those in newly industrialising countries. In order to regain cost advantage many manufacturers have adapted by undertaking more specialised production through the contracting-out, often abroad, of small-run component production and by increasing the scale of their overall production through exporting. These two connected processes have led to the growth of both imports and exports. This two-way trade in similar products has been termed intra-industry trade (IIT). The large growth of IIT has surprised economists who were expecting simply increased imports in sectors with comparative disadvantages and increased exports in sectors with comparative advantages. This book, based on extensive original research, explores these important issues. It disaggregates import and export data and matches up imports and exports at the firm level. It thereby provides important empirical evidence concerning the proportion of all trade which is intra-industry trade; concerning the key role of multinationals in the growth of intra-industry trade; and concerning the contrasting response — particularly between those companies which are multinational parents and those which are multinational subsidiaries — to the changing competitive conditions.

Donald C. MacCharles is Professor of Economics at the University of New Brunswick, Canada

A volume in the *Croom Helm Series in International Business* edited by Alan M. Rugman

THE CROOM HELM SERIES IN
INTERNATIONAL BUSINESS
Academic Editor: Alan M. Rugman,
Dalhousie University

— TRADE AMONG MULTINATIONALS: — Intra-Industry Trade and National Competitiveness

Donald C. MacCharles

CROOM HELM
London ● New York ● Sydney

© 1987 D. C. MacCharles
Croom Helm Ltd, Provident House, Burrell Row,
Beckenham, Kent BR3 1AT
Croom Helm Australia, 44–50 Waterloo Road,
North Ryde, 2113, New South Wales

British Library Cataloguing in Publication Data

MacCharles, D. C.
    Trade among multinationals: intra-industry
    trade and national competitiveness. —
    (The Croom Helm series in international
    business)
    1. International business enterprises
    I. Title
    338.8′8   HD2755.5
    ISBN 0-7099-4618-X

Published in the USA by
Croom Helm
in association with Methuen, Inc.
29 West 35th Street
New York, NY 10001

Library of Congress Cataloging-in-Publication Data

MacCharles, D.C. (Donald C.), 1935–
    Trade among multinationals.

    (The Croom Helm series in international business)
    Bibliography: p.
    Includes index.
    1. Commercial policy. 2. Competition, International.
3. International business enterprises. 4. Canada —
Commercial policy. I. Title. II. Title: Intra-industry
trade and national competitiveness. III. Series.
HF1411.M2325 1987   382′.3   87-9077
ISBN 0-7099-4618-X

Printed and bound in Great Britain
by Billing & Sons Limited, Worcester.

Contents

List of Tables

About the Author

Dr Donald C. MacCharles is Professor of Economics in the Division of Social Sciences, University of New Brunswick, Saint John, New Brunswick, Canada. He holds a PhD in economics from the University of Toronto, and is a Fellow of the Certified General Accountants' Association of Canada. He has management experience in finance and accounting with several Canadian manufacturing and banking firms. His research has focused on the role of international corporations in transferring technology, knowledge and management expertise to Canada, and the impact of the transfer on productivity. In publications, he has applied economic and accounting concepts to the areas of international trade and industrial policy with emphasis on decision-making in the public and private sectors.

Acknowledgements

I would like to acknowledge the assistance of Professor Bernard M. Wolf of York University, Toronto, Canada, in this study. His review of the first draft of the manuscript and earlier involvement in the development of the study provided many helpful ideas, comments and suggestions on both its form and substance. I also would like to acknowledge the assistance of J. McVey and J. Lacroix of the MNE section in the Financial Flows group of Statistics Canada. They were diligent in assembling the data and providing suggestions about sources of information. My intellectual debt to Professor D. J. Daly of York University, Toronto, Canada, is apparent throughout the study. I would also like to acknowledge the help of H. Krauklis in Canada's Department of Regional Industrial Expansion (DRIE) in supporting the study and attending to the bureaucratic details necessary for its completion. The financial assistance of DRIE is gratefully acknowledged since it was a prerequisite to doing the study. Finally, credit is due to the Policy Section of DRIE for appreciating the importance of a current analysis of intra-industry trade and its relationship to improved competitiveness and to industrial and commercial policy. However, any errors and misinterpretations of the data and ideas remain solely the responsibility of the author.

Preface

The industrial nations have experienced high levels of unemployment over the past decade compared to the historic norm since the Second World War. In part, this is due to the freer trade environment and reduced tariffs as a result of GATT negotiations. It is also partly attributable to an increase in efficient manufacturing capacity on a worldwide basis and in the Pacific-Rim countries in particular. The increased competition resulting from these factors has led to pressure from established producers for increased protection, often in the form of non-tariff barriers. This book demonstrates that such commercial policies are harmful since the barriers impede the adjustments on an international basis that are necessary to improve the competitiveness of the established producers.

The mistaken nature of protectionist policies is a problem especially for the smaller industrial nations. They can only achieve cost-competitiveness by becoming more specialised in their products and production activities and by increasing the scale of their operations. To specialise, it is necessary to contract-out production to large and more efficient specialist suppliers, many of whom are in other countries. To achieve greater scale it is necessary to export. These two activities cause an increase on a two-way basis in the imports and exports of similar goods for many industries. This type of trade is called intra-industry trade to distinguish it from the more familiar inter-industry trade in which imports increase in industries with comparative disadvantages and exports increase in industries with comparative advantages.

The large growth in international trade for manufactured goods since the Second World War has mainly been of the intra-industry type. It reflects the international rationalisation of resources as manufacturers attempt to improve productivity and lower costs to meet increased competition. The extent of intra-industry trade has surprised economists who were expecting the growth in international trade to be of the more traditional variety of inter-industry trade.

A major problem is created for firms attempting to rationalise when protectionist commercial policies are introduced by governments. Manufacturers find it more difficult to export in order to increase their scale. And they also find it more difficult to specialise by importing from foreign suppliers. Protectionism is particularly a problem for manufacturers in nations where domestic markets are too small for the efficient support of home-country producers that are large in scale and highly specialised. Consequently, it is producers in smaller nations and newly industrialising countries whose potential for improved competitiveness is harmed the most by increased protectionism.

Protectionist commercial policies also affect the international flow of direct investment by multinational firms. Manufacturers build factories behind barriers to trade, especially in countries with large markets, in order to gain access to them with their products. Thus, direct investment is a substitute for denied trade and it flows towards the protected, developed economies at the expense of the less efficient, smaller ones. The result is declining production capacity in the smaller countries which further adds to their cost and employment problems.

This book, based on extensive original research, explores these important issues using Canada as a case study. It analyses the extent of intra-industry trade by matching import and export data for manufactured goods, disaggregated to the level of the firm. This provides important empirical evidence concerning: the proportion of all trade which is of the intra-industry type; the key role that multinationals have in the pattern and growth of intra-industry trade; and the contrast in responses (particularly between multinational subsidiaries and domestic firms) to the changing international competitive conditions in the form of increased international and domestic intra-industry trade.

1

Introduction

INTERNATIONAL CROSS-TRADE IN MANUFACTURED GOODS

The volume of international trade in manufactured goods has increased significantly since the Second World War, both in absolute terms and relative to trade in resources and primary materials. Within manufactured goods, cross-trade has grown even more quickly and now dominates the total as firms increasingly became involved in the simultaneous export and import of products manufactured in their individual industries. It is estimated that cross-trade now represents more than 60 per cent of the total international trade in manufactured goods.[1] A considerable portion of this international trade is intra-firm, between the various national subsidiaries of multinational enterprises (MNEs). The existence and growth of intra-firm cross-trade is not adequately explained by the traditional trade paradigms and for this reason alone the phenomenon needs further exploration. This is such an exploration and analysis of cross-trade by MNEs, using Canada as a case study.

The increase in cross-trade raises three major paradoxes. The first one is that while real growth in the international trade of manufactured goods has been substantial, both relative and total employment in the manufacturing sectors of the industrial countries has remained static, with some countries even recording declines.[2] At the same time, domestic production and consumption of manufactured goods has grown less rapidly than cross-trade.

The second paradox is that the conventional Heckscher-Ohlin-

1

Samuelson (HOS) trade model predicts international trade should be between firms and industries, which is at variance with the large volume of international cross-trade actually taking place within both industries and firms. According to the HOS model, firms in each industry of a country should either export goods if they are produced with a comparative cost advantage or import them if there is no such advantage. This would result in the international trade of dissimilar goods between countries, with each country specialising in the production and export of outputs from industries different than those of its trade partners, while importing goods produced by the partners' industries.

The third paradox is that the HOS model of trade relies on differences between countries in the relative availability of various factors of production to explain why trade takes place. Relative differences in the level of factor endowments between countries cause international price variations for the factors of production. In turn, the price variations cause differences in costs of production between countries that lead to goods flowing from low- to high-cost countries. Each country eventually specialises in the production of those goods produced in industries that intensively utilise the lower-priced factors of production. However, much of the increase in trade of manufactured goods since the Second World War has been between industrial nations that have very similar factor-endowment ratios.[3] Thus, differences in factor-endowment levels and prices do not adequately explain the growth in trade between the industrial countries.

Differences do exist in factor-endowment ratios between the developing and industrial countries. But this is decreasingly true, especially for goods produced in export sectors. There are several reasons for this. Firstly, large and increasing flows occur on an international basis of financial capital, technology, management practices and intermediate and capital goods. These exist even for the industrial countries and reduce any significant difference between them in the ratios. Secondly, many nations have industrial, education and labour-training policies designed to speed up the growth in stocks of critical factors of production and narrow any gaps with competitor countries. Such policies have been successfully used by the developing countries, including those in the Pacific-Rim, and they help to explain their success in penetrating the international markets for high-technology goods in recent years.[4] Also, industry-level cost advantages achieved from the availability of key factors of production may not be as important as advantages developed or acquired by individual firms. Therefore, continuing significant differences in relative factor-endowment ratios are unlikely to exist for long periods between the industrial nations nor will they be primary in determining which manufactured products are imported and exported. Indeed, firm-specific advantages (often held by MNEs) may be more important in determining which products are traded. Firm-specific advantages such as technological leads, marketing skills and advanced management practices are not necessarily based on country-specific differences in factor-endowment ratios.

CROSS-TRADE AND THE INTRA-INDUSTRY TRADE PARADIGM

What is clear is that the post-Second World War pattern of international trade in manufactured products has been shaped by influences other than those normally allowed for in the traditional inter-industry trade model which emphasises the influence of availability and price of factors of production. What does appear to be important, and especially so for smaller countries, is the existence of international differences in the efficiency of production and changes to it over time. A different trade paradigm, called the intra-industry trade (IIT) model, provides a better construct for understanding this and explaining its connection to the growth in cross-trade of manufactured goods. The IIT model also provides an explanation for the apparent paradoxes of the HOS model.

The IIT model puts emphasis on dynamic changes to production conditions between countries, spurred by increasing competition as the economic environment is subjected to freer trade and growth in manufacturing capacity. The adjustment by firms towards more internationally efficient production causes changes in trade flows that result in the growth of cross-trade in similar goods. This adjustment explains the paradoxes evident between the trade data and the HOS model. With more efficient production conditions, domestic production, employment and consumption can remain stable while the increased output stemming from enhanced efficiency serves to increase trade flows.

Also, the greater incidence of contracting-out raises the value of trade flows even though net output is unchanged.

The necessary conditions in the IIT model for cross-trade have certainly existed in the trade environment since the Second World War. Trade has become much freer under the various GATT-inspired reductions in tariff and non-tariff barriers to trade. There has also been a significant increase in the number of large trading blocs with free movement of goods internally as a result of multilateral trade arrangements between smaller groups of nations independent of GATT. At the same time, there has been an increase in manufacturing capacity worldwide as the developing countries and Japan entered international markets with their products. The net result has been a significant rise in the level of competition, both in domestic and international markets, for established producers in the industrial nations. This competition became particularly acute after the early-1970s when the impact of the various GATT tariff reductions negotiated since the Second World War became cumulatively significant while at the same time Japanese producers became cost-competitive and entered world markets on an unprecedented scale.

In order to remain competitive, profitable or simply to survive, high-cost manufacturers in smaller countries had to reduce unit costs, since the usual practice when markets were more protected of raising prices to cover high costs was no longer possible. The only alternative in such a case was to lower costs by rationalising production systems. This involves reducing diversity and increasing the scale of output by contracting-out the manufacture of semi-finished materials, services and components to more efficient suppliers both at home and abroad (vertical specialisation), producing fewer products in plants (horizontal specialisation), and increasing the scale of output of remaining products by exporting them. Manufacturers usually specialise horizontally in those products that intensively utilise their firm-specific skills as well as any country-specific advantages that may exist (e.g. a relatively large endowment of resources). Often the products are differentiated to command a share of international market niches.[5] At the same time, similar but differentiated products are imported from manufacturers in other countries who are also rationalising and improving their competitiveness. These products replace the less competitive products dropped by domestic manufacturers as they specialise.

Such a rationalisation process, carried out across the manufacturing sector of a nation, improves efficiency in production as firms benefit from the associated product- and plant-specific economies of scale.[6]

Rationalisation also affects the trade flows for a nation, measured at the level of individual industries. Increased vertical specialisation causes imports to rise while increased horizontal specialisation and scale causes exports to rise. It is this type of increased international trade, resulting from the quest for improvements to production efficiency, that has been called intra-industry trade. It is in distinction to the inter-industry trade flows arising from comparative cost advantages due to factor price differences between countries. In the latter case, freer trade and increased competition would cause firms in an industry making products under an international cost disadvantage to close down so that exports would decline and imports increase for such an industry. An industry with firms making products with a comparative cost advantage would thrive and grow so that its imports would decline and exports increase. That is, unlike the IIT case, trade for individual industries would be one-way rather than two-way.

The HOS model proves troublesome when trying to explain cross-trade because of its restrictive assumptions. Three of them are particularly important. One is the assumption that capital is immobile between countries. Yet one of the significant developments since the Second World War has been the large and growing international flow of direct foreign investment of which Canada has been a major recipient. Accompanying this investment are significant, continuous transfers of management expertise and technological information on an intra-firm basis. The extent of international capital flows casts some doubt on a key assumption of the HOS model that trade is due to major differences in relative factor endowment ratios between countries. In fact, there have been major levellings of such differences, due partly to these capital flows and partly to government policies (as will be discussed in Chapter 2). At least for the industrial nations, significant differences in factor endowment ratios do not exist and the access each has to the other's factor stocks of physical and intellectual capital through direct foreign investment, international trade shows, conferences etc. reduces even further the meaningfulness of this idea. At the same time, trade continues to grow between these countries.

The other two inappropriate assumptions normally used in the HOS model are that uniform production conditions and product homogeneity exist internationally. The assumption of uniform production conditions means unit costs cannot vary from country to country because of differences in productivity between plant locations and because production methods for a product use identical, homogeneous inputs of labour and capital with constant returns to increased scale of output no matter where they are produced. Uniform goods are ensured by the assumption of product homogeneity no matter what firm or country produces them. It is in terms of these two key assumptions about production conditions and product homogeneity that the IIT model differs most from the HOS model.

The assumption of uniform productivity in the HOS model is particularly inappropriate for analyses of the Canadian trade situation. One of the major causes of unit cost differences between countries (see Table 2.1) is the wide variation between them in productivity. In particular, Canada has had a persistent productivity gap with the US and, more recently, with other countries such as Japan. This is attributed to Canada having small markets set within a protected trade environment which led to the development of small firms with high levels of diversity. The European nations also had a similar problem. Given a situation in which there is not uniform productivity, the introduction of trade liberalisation and increased competition would force firms to specialise and increase their scale through exports if they wished to survive. It is this connection between the need for improved productivity and changes in trade data that is the important point of the IIT model and which the HOS model is not normally designed to handle.

The assumption of product homogeneity is also troublesome in a world where, apart from basic industrial goods, a large proportion of products are highly differentiated. This differentiation is important in determining which firms will be able to specialise and survive. A move towards increased specialisation usually requires firms to select products in which they have firm-specific advantages that can be used to acquire a share of export markets. The product differentiation could be based on any of several things, including the design and quality of the product, innovative management or some special skill in production (i.e. firm-specific advantages). They can also be based on a national advantage that is generally available to all firms. An abundant

6

availability of some low-cost primary material is an example of a country-specific advantage. But country-specific advantages explain product and export success only at the industry level and not at the level of the firm. Firm-specific product differentiation is an important determinant of which products and firms within an industry will thrive and export.[7]

Product differentiation alone can explain some IIT, although the model would be more limited in its explanatory power than when it also allows for rationalisation through increased scale and specialisation. For instance, the firms in an industry could be specialised, large-scale producers with world-efficient unit costs. The basic trade balance for an industry would be determined by such firms and their ability to capitalise upon some comparative cost advantage arising from a relatively abundant and cheap factor of production which is a major input into their products. In the case of Canada, products using capital or materials and resources intensively would have such cost advantages and be exported. Other industries producing products that did not use relatively low-cost Canadian inputs to any extent would be subject to competition from imports. The result in this case would be trade of the inter-industry type.

But with product differentiation, IIT could develop. Firms would specialise in serving a particular market niche large enough for them to capture plant and product-specific economies of scale. Cross-trade would then take place between countries in the various differentiated products manufactured within an industry with firms in different countries specialising and exporting those products in which they have successfully differentiated themselves. Similar, but differentiated, products would be imported.

A first-mover advantage can also be an important determinant of success. Firms that first combine country and firm advantages can erect entry barriers and benefit from market power.[8] A firm could engage in specialisation and be at the appropriate scale so that it would be competitive in international markets. But without some advantage, its products would be homogenous with those of competitors and would have to compete for market share on the basis of price alone. While such markets may be easier to enter, it is usually difficult to make a profit in them because of the need to maintain productivity and costs at international levels while subject to the discipline of price. But the price discipline and competition is less severe for first-mover firms with differentiated products and other advantages.

RESOURCE REALLOCATION IN THE MODELS

The two models also have different processes of resource reallocation. The distinctions become important when setting public policy to ameliorate the disruptions in resource allocation associated with freer trade and increased competition. The resource reallocation in the inter-industry trade model is between industries as labour and other factors of production leave uncompetitive industries with firms going into decline and even out of business under the pressure of increased imports. The factors of production are required to move to competitive firms and industries that are growing with increased exports. This is a very expensive and traumatic process.

In the IIT model the resource reallocation is within firms in each industry as they rationalise production methods, improve capital stock and internally retrain labour so that it can acquire the new skills and adapt to the new jobs required by changes in production conditions. The cost of adjustment in this case is considerably less than for the inter-industry case because it is intra-firm rather than inter-industry.[9] And the cost is largely borne by employers rather than labour and governments.

Also, since the IIT model puts increased emphasis on the role of the firm in the adjustment process along with greater recognition that competitiveness can be a result of firm-specific rather than just country-specific factors, it has some advantages over the traditional model for coming to an understanding of the role played by MNEs in the adjustment to freer trade. Firm-specific advantages provide a major reason for the existence of MNEs[10] and they help to explain why the MNEs are major international traders.

Because of these connections between increased competition, technical change, IIT and trade and industrial policies, it is important to establish the relevance of the IIT model, the extent of IIT in international trade and the degree to which MNEs are involved in it.

APPROPRIATE USE OF EACH MODEL

It is not meant to suggest that the inter-industry model of trade is incorrect or unimportant. The point being made, instead, is that it is not wholly appropriate to the situation of smaller countries in the post-World War Two era in which their highly protected and inefficient manufacturing sectors were being subjected to increasing competition and considerable rationalisation of production systems. Also, the inter-industry model is less appropriate for explaining the significant amount of imperfectly competitive international, intra-firm trade by large MNEs, based as it is on the assumptions of perfect competition.

Without doubt, the inter-industry model is appropriate for explaining trade in resource products where factor-endowment ratios are clearly important. It may also be appropriate in the longer run for explaining trade in manufactured goods when a common level of international production efficiency is achieved by the smaller countries and between the plants of MNEs. At such a time, further trade improvements could well depend upon international cost advantages and disadvantages at the country level based on national differences in the prices for factors of production. Yet, even then, the uneven diffusion between countries of dynamic changes in production conditions could still exist since some countries tend to lag behind others in the adoption of new technologies and management practices. But until a state of equilibrium is achieved with all nations having the same level of efficiency in production, the IIT model seems an appropriate construct through which to view the world because of its ability to explain actual developments in world trade of manufactured products resulting from changes to production conditions on an international basis.

At the same time, it is recognised that the IIT model is not wholly appropriate to all international trade in manufactured products. It is mainly relevant to smaller economies. Prior to, and immediately after, the Second World War, most of the industrial nations had highly protected domestic markets as a result of the depression in the 1930s and the erection of trade barriers to maintain domestic levels of employment. In the case of each of the European nations and Canada, the individual national market was small relative to the rate of output which could be produced by a world-scale production facility. Consequently, manufacturers in these countries were relegated to producing in small runs that were suited to the small size of their domestic markets. Such production could be in small-scale plants. But this is inefficient and costly due to plant-specific diseconomies of scale. Alternatively, production could be in larger, more efficient plants. However, that would require diversification both horizontally and vertically in order to fully utilise plant capacity. Such diversification creates inefficiencies and high costs because of the product-specific diseconomies of scale.[11] It is this type of industrial structure in those smaller industrial countries which contain both small and diversified manufacturers operating in an increasingly competitive environment that has resulted in the worldwide growth of intra-industry trade as increased competition forced firms to rationalise their production systems.

The US did not develop this type of industrial structure because of its internally large domestic markets with free trade and high levels of competition. US markets could support producers that were specialised and able to manufacture at large rates of output without having to rely to the same extent as smaller counties, such as Canada, on less accessible export markets.[12] The greater degree of scale and specialisation of US manufacturers allowed them to be more efficient much earlier in comparison to producers in many other industrial nations. It helped to account for the much-discussed technological superiority of US producers up to the 1970s, at which time this superiority began to erode under the pressure of freer trade, increased competition and consequent improved productivity on a worldwide basis.

Japan also had a relatively large national market so the producers there could move towards higher levels of scale and specialisation and lower unit costs without having to resort to external trade to the same extent as smaller countries. The Japanese experience is similar to that for the US and helps to explain why both countries have much lower levels of cross-trade than Canada and individual European countries. The relative lack of cross-trade by Japanese producers is also attributable to the logistical problems associated with their use of offshore suppliers because of just-in-time inventory practices. This prevented Japanese manufacturers from extensively contracting-out components to distant foreign suppliers, thereby reducing the growth of imports by many industries as their exports increased.

10

The Western European nations moved towards larger market size and free trade internally some time ago with the introduction of the European Economic Community (EEC) and other common market groups. Producers in these nations thereby achieved a higher degree of scale and specialisation along with lower unit costs closer to those achieved earlier by US producers. It also explains the earlier development in the Western European countries of cross-trade in similar products relative to Canada. Only now is Canada considering improved access to the larger US market with the recent decision to seek a common market arrangement between the two countries.

CANADIAN CROSS-TRADE

The lag by Canadian manufacturers, compared to those in the rest of the industrial nations, to adopt increased scale and specialisation unfavourably affected comparative costs of production. This is evidenced by the large number of smaller manufacturers who have continuing lower productivity and higher costs relative to US producers. The productivity difference has ranged between 20 and 40 per cent for several decades.[13] Its chronic nature reflects the difference in production conditions between the two countries, attributable to contrasting degrees of scale and specialisation as well as different qualities of management and Canada's slower adoption of state-of-the-art technologies.[14] There has been some increase in the degree of scale and specialisation throughout the 1970s, stemming from the freer trade environment. This adjustment has continued into the 1980s.[15] Nevertheless, Canada still has much to gain relative to the other industrial nations from improved productivity, unit costs and real incomes through greater rationalisation achieved by increased scale, specialisation and two-way trade.[16]

The more recent movement towards greater rationalisation of production systems makes Canada a good prototype on which to base a case study of the adjustments to a freer trade environment by smaller countries, especially since it has a high level of direct investment by foreign MNEs in its manufacturing sector. Chapter 2 outlines in greater detail the trade environment which led to Canada having a high-cost environment for its manufacturers. Chapter 3 reviews in an international context the literature and prior studies on IIT as they apply to the Canadian

11

situation. Canadian trade flows are assessed in Chapter 4 from the perspective of the domestic and international situation, using the IIT model as a paradigm for guiding the analysis. In Chapter 5 some conclusions are then drawn from the analysis, relating them to international developments and outlining some of the policy issues arising from IIT.

NOTES

1. Laroisière, J. de, 'Persistent Structural Rigidities Must be Tackled For Industrial World To Break Grip of Stagflation', *IMF Survey* (February 1982); and Greenaway, D. and C. Milner, 'On the Measurement of Intra-Industry Trade', *Economic Journal*, no. 93 (December 1983), pp. 900–8.

2. Based on data made available from CHELEM, 1984, a French government database using information collected from OECD and other sources and purged for statistical irregularities between countries. The data for the statements in the text and the supporting tables in this note were made available under the auspices of Professors J. Fleck and J. D'Cruz at the University of Toronto, who acquired it from the Centre for the Study of Productivity and International Industry (CEPII), Paris, France.

Table 1.1: Indices of Total International Trade for Canada and other Selected Industrial Nations, based on US Dollar Values in Current Prices, Selected Years, 1967 to 1982 (1980 = 1.00)

Year	Canada	France	Exports West Germany	Japan	US	UK
1967	0.17	0.10	0.11	0.08	0.15	0.13
1970	0.27	0.15	0.18	0.15	0.21	0.18
1975	0.48	0.46	0.47	0.42	0.49	0.42
1980	1.00	1.00	1.00	1.00	1.00	1.00
1982	1.10	0.84	0.91	1.05	0.99	1.05

Year	Canada	France	Imports West Germany	Japan	US	UK
1967	0.09	0.09	0.08	0.09	0.13	0.12
1970	0.25	0.15	0.16	0.16	0.21	0.16
1975	0.61	0.40	0.40	0.39	0.43	0.40
1980	1.00	1.00	1.00	1.00	1.00	1.00
1982	0.94	0.87	0.84	0.97	1.08	1.01

Source: Datafrance.

Table 1.2: Indices of Employment Levels for Canada and other Selected Industrial Nations Using Indices for Manufacturing and for Total Employment, Selected Years, 1960 to 1982 (1980 = 1.00)

Year	Manufacturing to total employment					
	Canada	France	West Germany	Japan	US	UK
1960	1.40	1.04	1.01	0.83	1.25	1.29
1965	1.42	1.01	1.05	0.99	1.24	1.25
1967	1.37	1.01	1.02	1.04	1.28	1.23
1970	1.29	1.02	1.14	1.10	1.20	1.24
1975	1.13	1.03	1.05	1.04	1.04	1.10
1980	1.00	1.00	1.00	1.00	1.00	1.00
1982	0.92	0.98	0.97	0.99	0.93	0.90

Year	Manufacturing employment					
	Canada	France	West Germany	Japan	US	UK
1960	0.78	1.03	1.05	0.67	0.83	1.23
1965	0.91	1.07	1.07	0.85	0.89	1.25
1967	0.95	1.05	1.00	0.92	0.96	1.21
1970	0.95	1.07	1.15	1.01	0.95	1.22
1975	0.98	1.08	1.03	0.98	0.90	1.09
1980	1.00	1.00	1.00	1.00	1.00	1.00
1982	0.91	0.94	0.94	1.01	0.93	0.84

Source: Datafrance.

3. US Department of Labor, *Report of the President on US Competitiveness* (US Government Printing Office, Washington, September 1980), Tables V-1, V-2 and V-5.

4. See Scott, B. and G. C. Lodge (eds), *US Competitiveness in the World Economy* (Harvard Business School University Press, Boston, 1984); and Abernathy, W. J., Kim B. Clark and Alan Kantrow, *Industrial Renaissance* (Basic Books, New York, 1983).

5. Daly, D. J. and D. C. MacCharles, *Canadian Manufactured Exports: Constraints and Opportunities* (The Institute for Research on Public Policy, Montreal, 1986), Chs. 4 and 5.

6. Daly, D. J., B. A. Keyes and E. J. Spence, *Scale and Specialization in Canadian Manufacturing* (Economic Council of Canada, Ottawa, 1968), Staff Study no. 21; and Daly, D. J. and D. MacCharles, *Canadian Manufactured Exports*, Ch. 2 and Appendix 2.

7. There has been much discussion in the literature of the concept of firm-specific, or acquired, advantages with much of it developing in the 1970s using the concept of internalisation. In this, firms that have advantages use internal markets to utilise them rather than sales to third parties or exports because of the potential loss for the advantage when it moves outside the control of the firm. This concept is developed, for instance, by Rugman, A., *Inside the Multinationals* (Croom Helm, London, 1981). An early statement of this concept as it relates to IIT is

13

in Brown, W., 'Market Segmentation and International Competitiveness: Trade Theory and Practices Reexamined', *Nebraska Journal of Economics and Business* (Summer 1972), pp. 33–48.

8. Williamson, O., *Markets and Hierarchies: Analysis and Antitrust Implications* (The Free Press, New York, 1985).

9. Harris, Richard G. with David Cox, *Trade, Industrial Policy, and Canadian Manufacturing* (Ontario Economic Council, Toronto, 1983); and also as reported in *Au courant*, vol. 4, no. 3 (1983), p. 8. This study reports that with complete multilateral free trade by Canada there would be an increase in the size and specialisation of manufacturers that would significantly improve productivity, increase real incomes and boost the output of manufactured goods. At the same time, the volume of trade would almost double due to the increase in two-way trade as both imports and exports increased as a result of increased specialisation and greater contracting-out, while the cost of adjustment would be only 6 per cent of the total resources requiring reallocation.

10. See, for instance, Buckley, P., 'The Modern Theory of the Multinational Enterprise' in *Management Bibliographies and Reviews* (1979), pp. 171–85; and MacCharles, D. C., *The Cost of Administrative Organizations in Canadian Secondary Manufacturing Industries* (University of Toronto, Department of Political Economy, 1978), dissertation; and Rugman, Alan, *Inside the Multinationals* (Croom Helm, London, 1981).

11. Daly, Keyes and Spence, *Scale and Specialization*; and Daly, D. J. and S. Globerman, *Tariff and Science Policies: applications of a model of nationalism* (University of Toronto Press, 1976).

12. Caves, R. E., *Diversification, Foreign Investment and Scale in North American Manufacturing Industries* (Economic Council of Canada, Ottawa, 1975).

13. Daly, D. J. and D. C. MacCharles, *Canadian Manufactured Exports*, Ch. 2; and Daly, D. J. and D. C. MacCharles, *Focus on Real Wage Unemployment* (The Fraser Institute, Vancouver, 1986).

14. Daly, D. J., 'Canadian Management: Past Recruitment Practices and Future Training Needs' in Max von Zur-Muehlen (ed.), *Highlights and Background Studies* (Canadian Federation of Deans of Management and Administrative Studies, Ottawa, 1979); and Daly, D. J., 'Natural Science and Human Science Research — Does Research Funding Match Canada's Problem Areas?' in Social Science Federation of Canada, *Cahiers No. 9* (Ottawa, 1983); and MacCharles, D. C., *Summary of Ownership and Performance Differences: Non-Production Costs and Manufacturing Productivity* (University of New Brunswick, Saint John, 1982), mimeograph; this latter item is summarised in MacCharles, D. C., 'Knowledge, Productivity and Industrial Policy', *Cost and Management* (January–February 1983).

15. Baldwin, J. R. and P. K. Gorecki with J. McVey and J. Crysdale, *The Relationship Between Plant Scale and Product Diversity in Canadian Manufacturing Industries* (Economic Council of Canada, Ottawa, August 1983), Discussion Paper no. 237; and, by the same authors, *Trade, Tariffs and Relative Plant Scale in Canadian Manufacturing Industries: 1970–1979* (Economic Council of Canada, Ottawa,

May 1983), Discussion Paper no. 232.

16. Daly and MacCharles, *Canadian Manufactured Exports*; and Harris with Cox, *Trade, Industrial Policy*.

2

The Canadian Economic and Trade Environment

THE CHANGING ENVIRONMENT FOR MANUFACTURERS

In 1984, the latest year for which data are available, Canadian manufacturers on average had a unit-cost disadvantage of about 20 per cent compared to their counterparts in the US, on an exchange-rate-adjusted basis. It reflects Canada's lower productivity, which historically has been about 30 per cent less than in the US, and high real wages (stated in domestic currency) that are about equal to those in the US despite the productivity gap. This cost difference is significant, given the geographic closeness of the two countries and their economic similarities. Furthermore, Canada depends on sales to US markets for a significant proportion of its exports and GDP. Canadian manufacturers also have a large unit-cost disadvantage, at about 50 per cent in the US market, compared to Japanese producers. This too is a serious disadvantage, since Japanese producers are the major foreign competitors to Canadians in the US market.[1]

Canada has had a higher rate of inflation since the mid-1970s than the US and Japan. Cumulatively, it amounted to a differential increase in unit costs of about 35 per cent compared to both countries.[2] The differential cost increase accounts for a major part of the devaluation of the Canadian dollar relative to the US dollar since the mid-1970s which served to offset the higher Canadian cost escalation and maintain purchase power parity with US and Japanese competitors. At the same time, Canadian manufacturers ranked below those in the US and Japan in productivity improvement over the past decade and were near the bottom of the list of all the industrial nations on this key economic factor. This is in contrast to earlier periods when Canadian productivity improvement typically exceeded that of the US, although starting from a lower absolute level. The net result of Canadian cost and wage growth outstripping productivity improvement is that its unit costs of production for manufactured goods are now among the highest in the industrial world (stated in terms of the common currency unit of the US dollar) even after allowing for the devaluation of the Canadian relative to the US dollar. The unit-cost comparisons are shown in Table 2.1.

Table 2.1: Unit Labour Costs, Manufacturing; Major Industrialised Countries, Selected Years (US = 100 and in US dollars)

Country	Unit Cost Level		
	1970	1980	1984
United Kingdom	89	198	118
Canada	108	113	116
US	100	100	100
Italy	85	132	95
Sweden	97	168	92
Germany	70	139	82
France	70	127	77
Japan	49	75	59

Source: Daly & MacCharles, *Focus on Real Wage Unemployment*, Tables 3.2 and A.4.

The deteriorating competitiveness of Canadian manufacturers both at home and in export markets occurred at the same time as the trade environment became more competitive. For instance, the successive tariff reductions achieved by GATT under the Dillon, Kennedy and Tokyo Rounds reduced Canadian tariffs to about 15 per cent of their pre-1950 level and non-tariff barriers have also been reduced. Almost one-half of Canadian imports are now free of import duties. The average tariff on the remaining dutiable items, at 8 per cent, is about one-half the level that existed at the beginning of the 1980s.

Since the 1960s, there has been a considerable increase in manufacturing capacity on a world-wide basis. Products from large and efficient producers (particularly MNEs in the Pacific-Rim countries) now enter domestic and world markets served by Canadian manufacturers, considerably increasing the degree of competition. This increased capacity was created at about the same time economic growth rates over the 1970s were halved for the industrial world, reducing the pressure of demand against capacity. This eroded the ability of Canadian manufacturers to raise prices as costs increased, a practice they had been accustomed to in the past. Also, technical change in the transportation and communication sectors lowered the costs of these traditional barriers to trade, further adding to the competitiveness of the trade environment. The impact of these changes on the trade environment seriously increased competition for Canadian manufacturers, particularly from the early-1970s onwards when they cumulatively became very significant.

The relatively high cost of goods manufactured in Canada combined with increased capacity and competition have put Canadian producers in the position of striving just to survive. For instance, the 1981–2 recession was about 50 per cent steeper in Canada than in the US, measured in terms of GDP, and the recovery has been much more sluggish. This is the first time in this century a recession has displayed these characteristics. Typically, because of the similarities between the two economies, the timing of recessions is coincident with the Canadian economy having less severe changes in output. This is because of the high dependency of the Canadian economy on imports which take the brunt of any slack rather than domestic production. The recession was also more severe in Canada than almost every other industrial nation. The reduced demand during the recession further increased the degree of price competition with disastrous effects on profits and unemployment, the latter going to a post-Second World War high.

Low profits in the manufacturing sector reduced rates of return on investment (ROI) in physical assets. Profits and ROIs had already been declining since the early-1970s in both nominal and real terms under the pressure of increased competition, but fell to negative values in the trough of the recession after adjustment for inflation.[3] They have now recovered from their recession lows but are still low in relation to their historical values and those currently prevailing in the US. In turn, their low values have seriously reduced the incentive, and the cash flow available, for manufacturers to invest in new equipment. This is evident in the reduced spending on fixed capital investment since 1981. While some recovery in business investment spending has taken place, it still remains below its 1981 level in real terms.[4]

Other indicators also exist of the impact of increased

competition on high-cost Canadian manufacturers. It shows up in Canada's declining share of the world market for manufactured goods.[5] It also shows up in the large trade deficit on manufactured goods.[6] The deficit would be even greater more recently if the normal timing of the recovery in Canada had prevailed. The relatively faster US recovery increased Canadian exports while the slower Canadian recovery depressed imports. And, contrary to the historical experience, there now is a large and growing deficit on direct investment flows in the balance of payments. The proportion of world direct investment flows coming into Canada have declined while there has been a dramatic increase in outflows by Canadian businesses.[7] This deficit exists in spite of Canada's need for development capital and mainly reflects the high-cost, low-profit opportunities available to investors.

The exchange rate has not been able to adjust for the cost disadvantage on manufactured goods. This is partly because Canada has a large comparative advantage in agricultural products, fish, resources and primary materials.[8] The per-capita exports of these products is high, acting to stabilise the exchange rate. However, current fiscal and monetary policy is also preventing the foreign exchange rate from fully offsetting the high costs of Canadian manufacturers.[9] Since the Second World War Canadian governments have had 'loose' fiscal policies as they accommodated increased pressure for social and income redistribution programmes. The current government of Prime Minister Mulroney is not prepared to change this emphasis, in spite of its large majority and mandate for change. This has forced the central bank to have a 'tight' monetary policy. Such a policy is necessary partly to offset the inflation-inducing fiscal spending. But it is also necessary to finance the programmes with foreign capital attracted by the high interest rates created by the tight monetary policy. Such interest rates also help to stabilise the exchange rate at a level higher than what is needed for improved export competitiveness and employment in the manufacturing sector.

CANADA AND WORLD TRADE DEVELOPMENTS

It was noted in Chapter 1 that a major feature of trade in manufactured goods since the Second World War has been the growth in cross-trade of similar items (i.e. differentiated but closely sub-stitutable products) between the industrial nations. Yet total employment in the manufacturing sectors of the industrial nations remained comparatively static. This general feature of trade in manufactured goods also applies to Canada. Both the import and export propensities for manufactured goods in-creased by 50 per cent between 1966 and 1979 (and this simul-taneous growth in both propensities was also observed for many individual industries). This represents a significant growth in international trade for Canada relative to domestic production and consumption.[10] But employment in manufacturing increased by only 7 per cent. The growth in international trade was paral-leled by a similar change in levels of domestic trade, as measured by the ratio of purchased material to value-added. Between 1966 and 1979, this ratio increased by 20 per cent for the manufac-turing sector in Canada.[11]

The Western European nations moved toward larger market size and freer trade internally some time ago with the introduc-tion of the European Economic Community (EEC) and other common market groups. This allowed the producers in these nations to achieve increased scale and specialisation with lower unit costs closer to those achieved earlier by US producers. It also explains the earlier development by individual countries in Europe, relative to Canada, of cross-trade in similar products. The US and Japan had much larger national markets than Canada which allowed their producers to move towards higher levels of scale and specialisation with lower unit costs without having to resort to external trade. In the case of the US this was achieved some time ago.

Canadian firms lagged behind the rest of the world in imple-menting such rationalisation strategies because of the country's continuing high levels of protection for its small markets. The result has been declining competitiveness and a cost premium that persists in spite of the availability from the rest of the world of the latest management and technical knowledge, relatively similar factor stocks and similarity of wage rates with those in the US. This suggests Canada still has much to gain from improvements to production systems through increased scale, specialisation and cross-trade.

The significant economic benefits that would come from such rationalisation have been known for some time and were con-firmed again recently by research which showed there would be significant improvements in productivity and real incomes from a policy designed to reduce trade barriers through a policy of multilateral free trade. This would impose increased scale and specialisation on manufacturers, resulting in a doubling of the volume of trade for manufactured goods and a significant increase in cross-trade as manufacturers increased their scale and degree of specialisation through exports and contracting-out production to more efficient suppliers at home and abroad. There would also be considerable growth in employment within the manufacturing sector.[12] Another research study shows increased scale and specialisation would reduce the unit costs of Canadian manufacturers by about 20 per cent on average. This is approximately equal to the average unit-cost disadvantage currently existing between Canadian and US manufacturers as shown in Table 2.1.[13]

The high unit costs of production in Canada, relative to countries with firms that are larger in scale and more specialised, has unfavourably affected the nation's relative trade performance over the last decade or so. There have been major shifts in trade patterns worldwide as a result both of different rates of rationalisation between countries and of different rates of growth in factor stocks critical to export success. These changes have not been advantageous to Canada as shown by Canada's large net trade deficit on manufactured goods that increased over the 1970s as well as a decline in its share of world trade. The decline in market share has been masked, however, by an increase in the volume of world trade which caused total Canadian exports to increase even as market share declined. The impact of high costs and declining market share show up in the data in Table 2.2.

The decline in the Canadian share of world trade is also noticeable in Table 2.3 which shows the source, by country, of imports for the US. While this table is for US imports only, that market absorbs almost 80 per cent of Canadian exports. Also, while other countries may be increasing their imports at the same time as they increase their exports to the US and reduce Canadian market share there, they have not increased their imports from Canada sufficiently to offset the loss of Canadian market share in the US. Hence, the widening trade deficit for Canada on manufactured goods. Canada's lack of competitiveness in the markets of the EEC and the developing and Pacific-Rim countries largely explains why its share of the world market

Table 2.2: Increase in Volume of Exports, Manufactured Goods 1970−9, Selected Countries

Country	Per cent	Ratio (US = 1.00)
Japan	122	1.54
Italy	110	1.39
France	103	1.30
Netherlands	89	1.13
United States	79	1.00
Canada	70	0.89
Germany	63	0.80
United Kingdom	55	0.70

Source: US Department of Labor, *Report of the President on US Competitiveness*, Table 111.8.

Table 2.3: US Import Shares, Manufactured Goods, 1967 and 1976

Source of supply	Percentage of imports 1967	1976	Change in percentage
Canada	26.5	24.6	(1.9)
EEC (9 countries)	28.4	20.5	(7.9)
	54.9	45.1	(9.8)
Japan	14.0	18.9	4.9
Taiwan, Mexico, Hong Kong	4.9	9.3	4.4
Developing countries	15.8	21.7	5.9
	34.7	49.9	15.2
Miscellaneous	10.4	5.0	(5.4)
Total	100.0	100.0	0

Source: Canada (ITC), *Canada's Trade Performance, 1960−77*, Table 7.9.

for manufactured goods has declined.

The changing pattern of international trade over the 1970s captured in the data of Table 2.3 partly results from the improved cost performance of producers in other countries. Some of the improvements have come from their increasing specialisation and growing size as well as improvements in the quality of management. It also comes from increases in the relative availability of key factor inputs such as knowledge, labour skills and net investment in capital goods for some of these countries. The rates of growth in net capital stock as well as in knowledge and skilled labour through increased education and training, have exceeded those for Canada in many cases, as is shown by Table 2.4.

Table 2.4: Factor Endowment Ratios, Selected Countries

Country	Capital per Worker Constant 1966 US $		Skilled Labour per Worker	
	1975	1975/1963	1975	1975/1963
Japan	8,242	3.35	7.79	1.50
Korea	1,003	4.16	3.06	1.52
Mexico	2,969	2.02	6.53	1.52
Germany	9,422	1.66	12.07	1.44
France	11,353	2.01	14.43	1.46
Italy	6,560	1.70	8.03	1.52
US	11,270	1.22	14.35	1.16
Canada	12,463	1.38	13.73	1.20
UK	6,010	1.64	12.79	1.48
Netherlands	8,984	1.64	14.77	1.44
Sweden	12,438	1.61	19.15	1.31

Note: Skilled labour is the number of professional, technical and kindred employees.
Source: Adapted from US Department of Labor, *Report of the President*, Tables V-1 and V-2.

The inter-country comparisons in Table 2.4 should be interpreted with caution since many of the countries are in different stages of economic development which would influence the ratio of capital per worker. Other non-comparabilities also exist. However, the highest rates of growth in capital per worker were for the Pacific-Rim and EEC countries. The relatively low rate of growth for Canada reflects in part the initially high level from which it started in 1963 because of the large, capital-intensive resources sector.

The rate of growth in skilled labour per worker in most countries was over twice as great as for Canada with the only exception being the US. This reflects in part the higher levels from which Canada and the US started relative to the developing and Pacific-Rim countries. But, this does not explain the lower growth rates relative to the other industrial nations. It is

23

consistent with the US and Canada having the largest fall-off in productivity and international market share of all the industrial countries over the 1970s. The growth in the stocks of factors has continued in these developing countries into the 1980s, so that it would be reasonable to conclude that their ability to be competitive has increased even further.

Table 2.5: Capital and Skilled Labour per Worker Embodied in Manufactured Exports, Selected Countries

Country	K/L Ratio		S/L Ratio	
	1975	1975 / 1965	1975	1975 / 1965
Japan	10,493	1.17	9.1	1.28
Korea	5,229	0.47	4.5	1.37
Mexico	13,463	0.81	8.8	1.28
Germany	10,326	1.00	9.6	1.00
France	10,147	0.92	9.1	1.11
Italy	8,339	1.09	7.3	1.01
US	9,206	0.99	12.4	1.08
Canada	14,224	0.75	9.8	1.04
UK	9,350	0.96	10.6	1.09

Source: Adapted from US Department of Labor, *Report of the President*, Table V-5.

Table 2.5 shows that Canadian manufactured exports contained high levels of capital per worker because the products of the resources sector, which dominate total exports, utilise capital-intensive production techniques. However, the content of capital per worker in Canadian exports declined between 1965 and 1975, as it did for most countries.

The skilled labour per worker in Canadian exports was not much different by 1975 than for Japan, Mexico and the EEC countries. These countries, and the Pacific-Rim countries in particular, concentrate key factor inputs in their export-producing sector. Consequently, they are competitive with Canada and the other industrial nations in terms of access to knowledge and technical skills. The US had the highest skilled labour ratio in its exports, but the Pacific-Rim countries and Mexico were closing the gap between them and the other industrial nations. Korea, one of the lesser-developed Pacific-Rim countries was exporting goods with low capital and skilled labour per worker, but the skilled labour content was increasing quickly. Because of the relatively low wages in Korea and similar countries, their exports of unskilled-labour intensive goods would be extremely cost-competitive relative to similar Canadian-made goods.

The clear message from all this is that Canada will remain heavily dependent on its primary materials and resources sectors for exports, growth and employment unless it can improve the knowledge and skills of its work force. But continuing dependency on these sectors, which are slow-growing with declining prices, means high unemployment and a declining standard of living for Canadians. Improved growth in employment and incomes will depend to a large extent upon the degree to which manufacturers can improve their costs and lower prices.

PRIOR DEVELOPMENTS AFFECTING COSTS AND PRODUCTIVITY

A major reason for the high cost of Canadian manufacturers is their relatively small size and high levels of diversity which lower productivity and increase unit costs.[14] The quality of management also appears to be a contributing factor as is the tardiness of managers in adopting the latest state-of-the-art technologies and management practices.[15] All these factors reflect the impact on corporate decision-making in the past of high Canadian tariff levels in conjunction with small domestic markets.

The size of the domestic market in Canada is small compared to those accessible to producers elsewhere in their home countries (e.g. the US, Japan and the EEC). In addition, the Canadian market is dispersed over more than four thousand miles so that it is fragmented further into several smaller local and regional markets. Yet, for the larger firms, manufacturing plants tend to be about three-quarters the size of their counterparts in the US (see Chapter 1, note 7). These large plants, in relation to the available market in Canada, historically led manufacturers to increase their rate of capacity utilisation by producing a wider variety of products (horizontal diversification) and engaging in a relatively larger number of production activities (vertical diversification) than counterpart plants in the US.[16] Firms increased their diversity in order to benefit from economies of scope (i.e. lower unit fixed costs) associated with amortising fixed costs over a larger volume.

25

But there are costs associated with diversity. They are due to several influences which can only be briefly summarised here. Horizontal diversification, in which many products are produced in job lots and by small run sizes, raises costs because of: increased changeover time; reduced opportunity to garner the benefits of learning-by-doing; the improper matching of small-scale, labour-intensive production methods with equipment that is often highly automated and designed for continuous runs at high rates of output; increased investment in inventories; and increased complexity which adds to the costs of administration in both the factory and office organisations. These influences, collectively called product-specific diseconomies of scale, increase unit variable costs of production.

Vertical diversification, in which a wide variety of in-house production activities are undertaken to produce services, components and primary materials for a firm, has the same cost-increasing effect as horizontal diversification. In addition, there are opportunity costs associated with such contracting-in. Firms lose contact with technical changes that would otherwise be available from suppliers and which would improve productivity and the quality of their own products. And in-house production may become inefficient because of the lack of an external market test to ensure that internal transfer prices are based on the minimum, long-run average cost of efficient producers. These influences add to the product-specific diseconomies of scale and increase unit-variable costs.

The relatively high degree of horizontal and vertical diversification of Canadian manufacturers did increase rates of plant utilisation and reduce the per-unit fixed costs of capacity. But the benefit on fixed costs was more than offset on variable costs by the increased costs of diversity from increased complexity and product-specific diseconomies of scale.[17]

Instead of building large plants and packing them with products, owners could build smaller, specialised plants. However, this would increase unit fixed costs because of unexhausted plant-level economies of scale. Or, if the owners tried to avoid the fixed costs of plant by doing without key indivisible inputs, such as some management functions or R&D, productivity would be lower and unit-variable costs higher.

In any case, the signals from the economic environment led Canadian manufacturers to incur cost disadvantages compared to larger and more specialised foreign producers. Trade barriers

26

were relied upon for protection from imports. However, reliance on such protection is no longer possible because of the freer international trade environment which has developed over the past two decades and which will continue into the foreseeable future. Yet, despite this outlook, many Canadian producers continue in their traditional mission of being diversified import-competers serving the small domestic market with high-cost tariff factories.

The protective tariff structure also affected management attitudes and practices. High unit costs domestically along with high international barriers to trade prevented manufacturers from exporting and forced managers to turn inward, concentrating on just the small Canadian market. This viewpoint influenced the style and quality of management in Canada. Managers could get by without having fully to take into account international developments in such areas as competition and technical change. Consequently, they became less innovative and responsive to change than would otherwise have been necessary in a more competitive environment.

The profile of the average Canadian manager reflects these influences. Canadian managers tend to be older, to have moved through the ranks more slowly, to be less well-educated and generally less experienced than counterparts elsewhere in the world. This has made them less flexible and less open to change, although this is improving as the number of graduates from management programmes has grown in recent years.[18] The lack of flexibility and poor receptiveness to change shows up in the tardiness, relative to foreign-based competitors, of Canadian managers to adopt new technologies.[19] These attitudes have carried over into the present trade environment even though they are no longer appropriate. For instance, there is a managerial gap between Japanese managers and their Canadian counterparts, as measured by the slower adoption of quality circles, significantly less use of 'on-time' delivery and other inventory control techniques, a far lower proportionate use of robotics and CAD/CAM methods, and a much lower use of permanent employment practices with its attendant poorer employee relations and lower productivity.

FOREIGN MNEs, PRODUCTIVITY AND TRADE

In addition to creating inefficient resource allocation, Canada's protectionist policies significantly influenced the structure of Canadian industry by attracting large inflows of foreign direct investment. Foreign manufacturers, in order to gain access to Canadian markets, built plants behind the tariff wall since this was cheaper than exporting from a home country and paying the tariff. Also, tariffs were higher on finished goods than on intermediate ones, which increased the degree of effective protection for value-added in Canada and made import-competing tariff factories worth while (both foreign and Canadian-controlled). Foreign-controlled subsidiaries (mostly US) now account for over 50 per cent of total assets in the manufacturing sector, although it varies considerably by industry within the sector.

It is unlikely, however, that trade barriers alone are sufficient to explain the high levels of foreign direct investment, since it is not always associated with industries that have high tariffs. The textiles industry is a case in point. While tariffs are important, it is clear that MNEs are also associated with industries for which knowledge is a significant input, especially when it is required in indivisible units that are large in relation to domestic market sizes.

Knowledge is an important part of total cost in industries where technologically advanced production methods, advanced management practices and large inputs of research and development are significant factors. Also, the stock of intellectual capital needed by firms in these industries to produce their knowledge requirements can represent a large proportion of total assets. For instance, it has been estimated that in the pharmaceutical industry the stocks of intellectual capital account for about 30 per cent of total assets.[20]

The stock of intellectual capital that some firms have about production processes, products and management practices takes the form of intangible assets embedded in employees through experience and education.[21] Firms can increase their rent on this capital by selling the products in which it is embedded into new export markets. The marginal cost of the intellectual capital used often is close to zero because of its sunk-cost nature and because the knowledge it produces has the characteristic of a public good in the sense that its consumption in the production of goods does not diminish the amount available to the firm.[22]

However, when barriers to trade make exporting impractical, then setting up a subsidiary in a foreign country can be a profitable alternative for capturing rent on intellectual capital.

Canada's high barriers to trade caused MNEs to prefer using direct investment over exports as a means of achieving access to Canadian markets. Since direct investment allows knowledge to flow relatively unhindered between the parent and the subsidiary it was also preferred to the use of licensing knowledge to third parties. Licensing is less desirable than internal transfer to a subsidiary because of the uncertainty and risk associated with allowing third parties access to knowledge which may be proprietary in nature and because the parent could lose control over its use. The intra-firm transfer of knowledge has been called internalisation because it uses the internal markets of the MNE, rather than external ones, to transfer knowledge and exploit any rent advantage associated with it.[23] It is clear that setting up subsidiaries by foreign firms was a rational response by them to the presence of Canadian tariffs and other trade barriers in industries where intellectual capital is an important cost of production.

The subsidiaries have ready access to the knowledge and management practices of parents and affiliates, often at little or no cost to the subsidiaries.[24] This has proved beneficial to Canada. It not only improves productivity and profits in the subsidiaries, but also tends to spill over and improve the performance of Canadian-controlled manufacturers as well.[25] Furthermore, the tendency for subsidiaries to be in industries that require substantial inputs of knowledge means they provide above-average transfers of it, thereby improving the rate of technical progress and economic performance of the Canadian economy. In periods of large inflows of foreign direct investment from the US there has been faster growth in total factor productivity than in periods during which the flows declined. A major part of the productivity growth came about through technological improvement rather than through other influences such as economies of scale.[26] Also, access to state-of-the-art knowledge and the ease with which intra-firm transfers of it take place helps to explain why subsidiaries adopt technical changes sooner and why they have higher productivity than their Canadian-owned counterparts.[27]

Improved economic performance comes from access to new knowledge about more efficient techniques of production, better management practices, and new products, as has already been discussed. But firms also need access on a continuing basis to existing knowledge in these areas if they are to maintain productivity at prevailing standards for an industry.[28] But, while access to both new and continuing knowledge is key to improving and maintaining the productivity of a firm, it is not uniformly available to all and especially not to the smaller Canadian-controlled firms.

Quality knowledge is efficiently and relatively easily transferred to subsidiaries, even the small ones, by their large foreign parents and affiliates and it is usually available in divisible units at minimum marginal cost of production. Large Canadian-controlled firms also have access to quality knowledge, either by being able to purchase it in world markets or by producing it internally at minimum cost, because of their size and ability to attract qualified personnel from international markets. But smaller Canadian-controlled firms have a disadvantage in the acquisition and use of knowledge. They can try to produce the complete range required in such areas as marketing, production, accounting and finance and thereby incur a cost penalty because of unexhausted economies of scale. Or they can try to get along without some knowledge in order to avoid the cost of the indivisible inputs needed to produce it. However, this would lower productivity and raise production costs for final output. Moreover, smaller firms producing knowledge for in-house use tend to be restricted to the Canadian market for the personnel needed to do so. Canada has a relatively small supply of highly trained and educated managers compared to countries such as the US. Consequently, smaller firms would have lower productivity and higher unit costs compared to the large firms and the foreign-owned subsidiaries of all sizes. No matter how the smaller Canadian-owned firms proceed to acquire their knowledge requirements, their reduced access to quality knowledge will lower their productivity and raise their unit costs of production for final output.

The impact of trade barriers and small domestic markets has differentially influenced productivity between small, large and foreign-owned plants in Canada as is shown by Table 2.6. This table presents comparisons between the sectors of control for value-added per production worker (with the value for the Canadian sector of control expressed as a ratio of that for the subsidiaries) by different plant sizes. Plant size is expressed in terms of number of employees. The proportion that plants in each size category, and the sales of these plants, represent of total plants and sales in the manufacturing sector is also shown in the table.

Table 2.6: Selected Comparisons between Sectors of Control, Plant-level Data for 1974 (Manufacturing Sector)

Plant size measured in employees	Value-added/production worker (ratio Cdn to foreign)	Percentage of plants: Cdn foreign		Percentage of sales: Cdn foreign	
Fewer than 50	0.50				
		88	6	19	5
50 to 200	0.67				
200 to 400	0.75				
		2	4	23	53
Greater than 400	1.00				

Source: Daly & MacCharles, *Canadian Manufactured Exports*.

For the smaller plants, there clearly is a performance difference between the subsidiaries and the Canadian-controlled enterprises, with the subsidiaries being about 50 per cent more productive. It is only when the plants in the Canadian sector become larger that the difference disappears. The lack of a significant difference in productivity between the sectors of control for the larger establishments is attributed to the Canadian-controlled ones being able to garner the benefits of size and be as effective as the subsidiaries in terms of the quality of their management, their access to knowledge and their ability to produce in adequate volumes.

The significant variation in productivity between the sectors for the smaller plants is attributed to two major influences. First, the subsidiaries are able to import minor product lines as well as components from large, specialised foreign affiliates that are efficient. The affiliates are able to produce these products using high-volume production methods and at lower cost than could the subsidiaries who would have to do so in small run sizes by product-packing in their plants. Alternatively, the subsidiaries could acquire their minor product lines and components from domestic suppliers. But this would also entail higher costs than intra-company purchase because such suppliers

31

would tend to have cost disadvantages arising from their small scale and diverse production methods. Since the Canadian-controlled plants do not have access to large and efficient affiliates, they are mainly constrained to choosing between internal production or purchases from domestic suppliers, both of which raise their costs and lower productivity in comparison with the subsidiaries.

The second influence which gives the smaller subsidiaries improved productivity is their access to the management expertise and knowledge of parents and affiliates. The smaller Canadian-controlled manufacturers cannot readily acquire this knowledge because of their small size and reduced access to foreign sources of supply. If internally produced, the knowledge would be higher in cost and of lower quality than for the subsidiaries, as has already been discussed, because of Canada's comparative disadvantage in making it.[29] The net result is that the smaller Canadian-controlled manufacturers have lower productivity and higher costs than do their counterparts in the foreign sector of control.

Table 2.6 also shows a large number of small plants in the Canadian sector that represent a significant amount of production and sales for this sector. Note that while the larger plants in both sectors of control are equally productive, they are often high-cost in comparison to counterpart producers in the rest of the world because of their diversity. This disadvantage was discussed in relation to Table 2.1.[30] In summary, small-scale, high levels of diversity and differences in the quality of management are significant cost problems for Canadian manufacturers, especially for those in the Canadian sector of control.

COST REDUCTION AND INTRA-INDUSTRY TRADE

Import-competing firms, given their propensity to be high-cost, should respond to the changing trade environment with its increased competition by reducing unit costs through increased specialisation and scale. This response would influence the domestic and international trade flows for Canada.

An increase in specialisation would result in more contracting-out of minor product lines, intermediate goods and services to efficient suppliers at home and abroad, thereby increasing imports of manufactured goods.

An increase in scale, given the small size of the domestic market, can only be accomplished by increasing exports. Domestic markets have low price elasticities so that marginal revenue would fall faster than marginal cost if sales into the domestic market were increased. This is what historically inhibited domestic firms from specialising and increasing their scale of output based on domestic sales alone.[31] However, the freer trade environment has created an opportunity for Canadian manufacturers to gain improved access to international markets. Canadian manufacturers would be price-takers in them, facing much higher price elasticities than at home. Thus, it is possible to profitably engage in increased scale and specialisation through exporting. And increased export volume is the key means available for bringing costs and prices down to competitive levels. Prices would probably have to fall first so firms can acquire the market share and volume needed to increase their scale and specialisation. Costs would then fall in line with the earlier price reductions needed to be competitive.

Increased scale and specialisation by manufacturers would increase the international cross-trade in similar goods that is called intra-industry trade (IIT). Both imports and exports would simultaneously increase for these industries undergoing rationalisation. There also would be an increase in the ratio of purchased material to value-added for such industries. This is because there would be an increased level of trade in intermediate and final goods between producers as firms contract-out internally made goods. This increases the double count on trade in intermediate goods, raising the value of purchases relative to value-added, even though net economic activity may be unchanged.

The process by which intra-industry trade is created has two distinct aspects. One is related to firms engaging in product specialisation. When a firm concentrates on the production of just its major product line and exports that line, it may purchase the dropped minor lines from other specialised producers in the industry at home or abroad in order to continue offering a complete product range to its customers. Such actions, as already noted, would increase both imports and exports of similar goods produced within the industry and increase intra-industry trade.

Instead of purchasing the minor lines itself, the specialised producer could let firms in the wholesale sector purchase them for inclusion with the major line purchased from the specialised producer. In this case, unless imports by wholesalers are consolidated with those of manufacturers, specialisation would not result in intra-industry trade being recorded in the international trade data for the manufacturing sector alone. This is because the imported goods would be recorded in the wholesale sector's activities rather than in the manufacturing sector's so that imports would not appear to be increasing as manufactured exports increased.

Foreign-controlled manufacturers in Canada would be more prone to act as their own wholesalers, compared to Canadian-controlled firms, because of the availability of minor products and components at low cost from foreign affiliates. The subsidiaries act as both manufacturer and wholesaler in this circumstance.[32] Since both these activities would be caught in the measurement of trade by manufacturing industries, specialisation by the subsidiaries would show in the manufacturing sector's trade data as an increase in intra-industry trade. Canadian-controlled firms would be more apt to let wholesalers perform this task since they lack the necessary international affiliations to engage in it. Also, because of their access to international affiliates, the subsidiaries should also be able to use them as wholesalers and thereby gain access to international markets. This would tend to raise the export propensities for major product lines by the subsidiaries, even as their import propensities with affiliates for minor product lines would also be raised, relative to their Canadian-controlled counterparts. Therefore, it would be expected that the higher the level of foreign investment in an industry, the higher would be the industry's level of international intra-industry trade. This point will be pursued later in Chapter 4 when inter-sector comparisons are made of trade activity.

The second component causing intra-industry trade is related to the process of production specialisation. Manufacturers attempting to improve their unit costs would contract-out the manufacture of semi-finished materials, components and services to more efficient domestic and foreign suppliers (as well as switching purchases between domestic and foreign sources of supply as relative prices changed between countries and producers). This would cause imports to increase for the supplying industries, particularly since Canadian suppliers tend to be high-cost producers because of their small scale and their diversity.

At the same time, manufacturers in the supplying industries that were attempting to reduce their unit costs to internationally competitive levels by engaging in product specialisation and increased scale through exports would increase the exports of these same supplying industries. The combination of, on the one hand, increased imports through foreign sourcing by manufacturers outside the supplying industry along with increased scale and, on the other, specialisation through exports by manufacturers within the supplying industry (both in response to freer trade and increased competition) would result in an increased international cross-trade for industries producing such intermediate goods.

SUMMARY

Canadian manufacturers are trying to cope with an increasingly competitive environment. World trade patterns are undergoing realignment as factor endowment ratios in many countries, especially those of the developing and Pacific-Rim countries, approach those of Canada and the other industrial nations. Most of the other industrial nations have more efficient production systems with which to manufacture goods or are further along in the process of reallocating resources to achieve this. Their improved resource reallocation came about as manufacturers were pressed by competition to increase their levels of scale and specialisation.

But Canadian markets continued to be protected, so the incentive to rationalise was less pronounced with the consequence that Canadian manufacturers have been slower to respond to the changing international economic environment. The result is that they are now high-cost producers because of their small scale, the diverse nature of their production systems and the quality of their managers. The foreign MNEs in Canada have been able to circumvent some of these cost problems because of their access to the knowledge and products of efficient parents and affiliates.

It is no longer possible for Canadian manufacturers to ignore the increasing level of competition. Not only have Canadian barriers to imports been falling, but foreign producers have such a cost advantage that they can successfully sell over them and still compete against goods produced by Canadian manufacturers.

35

Consequently, the share of world markets held by Canadian manufacturers has declined. It is important that domestic manufacturers identify their strengths and areas of comparative advantage in order to know in which products and production activities they should specialise. They should also develop firm-specific strengths internally through increased training and education of workers and management. The specialised firms will then be in a better position to gain access to international market niches with quality products. The opportunity to specialise and grow that is provided by export markets allows firms to reduce costs and become more competitive. Many manufacturers have made such changes over the past few years in order to reduce costs and survive as competition increased and this has led to an increase in intra-industry trade. The MNEs are in a particularly good position to take advantage of rationalisation strategies and they should be leading in these developments.

Chapter 4 will explore Canadian data for evidence of this rationalisation by both Canadian and foreign-controlled manufacturers and its impact on the trade data. But before doing so, Chapter 3 will provide an overview of the developments in the international trade literature related to the intra-industry trade paradigm and its application to trade in manufactured goods for Canada and other nations.

NOTES

1. Daly, D. J. and D. C. MacCharles, *Focus on Real Wage Unemployment* (The Fraser Institute, Vancouver, 1986), Table 3-2 and Appendix A.
2. Daly and MacCharles, Table B-4.
3. Daly, D. J., MacCharles and W. Altwasser, 'Corporate Profit Drop Worse Since 1930's', *The Canadian Business Review* (Autumn 1982), pp. 6–12.
4. Statistics Canada, *Survey of Intentions on Business Investment Spending* (Minister of Supply and Services, Ottawa, 1985).
5. Astwood, D. M., 'Canada's Merchandise Trade Record and International Competitiveness in Manufacturing, 1960 to 1979' in K. C. Dwhan, H. Etemad and R. W. Wright (eds), *International Business: A Canadian Perspective* (Addison Wesley Publishers, Ontario, 1981), pp. 48–73. This data is updated in Canada, Department of External Affairs, 'Background Paper on International Trade' (National Economic Conference, Ottawa, 1985), Table 3. This information shows Canada's world market share at 5.7 per cent in 1970 which fell to an all-time low of 3.2 per cent in 1980. It has recovered somewhat since then and is now just above 4.0 per cent.

6. Britton, J. M. H. and J. M. Gilmour, *The Weakest Link, A Technological Perspective on Canadian Industrial Underdevelopment* (Minister of Supply and Services, Ottawa, 1978).

7. Canada, Department of External Affairs, 'Effect of Enhanced Trade on Investment: Survey Evidence' (Ottawa), mimeograph, Table 9; and Safarian, A. E., *Governments and Multinationals: Policies in the Developed Countries* (British-North American Committee, Toronto, 1983), Appendix 1, Tables 6 and 7.

8. Daly, D. J., *Canada's Comparative Advantage* (Economic Council of Canada, Ottawa, 1979).

9. It may be that even a devaluation would not provide any relief for the structural cost problems in Canada's manufacturing sector. This point is discussed in Daly and MacCharles, *Focus*, pp. 46–8. Two points are relevant. One is that the manufacturing sector has an import propensity higher than its export propensity so that a devaluation would result in an increase in cost pressures, rather than a reduction. Another is Canada's cost pressures arise from domestic wages growing faster than productivity (contrary to developments in its major trade partners) which is a problem of high real wages to be solved at the micro level rather than a macro problem of balance of payments disequilibrium requiring exchange rate adjustment, especially since there does not appear to be a fundamental disequilibrium in Canada's overall balance of international payments and receipts. Moreover, for a small country like Canada that is a price-taker in import and export markets, a devaluation does not change the terms of trade. A devaluation is useful to compensate for differences between the domestic rate of cost and price escalation and the rate of inflation in its major trade partners, and this is Canada's situation. This would not lead to resource reallocation, however, only the preservation of market share held by domestic import competers and the profits of exporters. Furthermore, in order to correct for high real wages by increasing the price level in a situation where domestically produced services and goods account for over 60 per cent of consumption, a devaluation would have to be about four times greater than that needed to compensate for just the high rate of inflation in the export and import competing sectors.

10. Astwood, 'Canada's Merchandise Trade'; and Canada, *Manufacturing Trade and Measures 1966–82: Tabulations of Trade, Output, Canadian Market, Total Demand and Related Measures for Manufacturing Industrial Sectors* (Department of Industry, Trade and Commerce/Regional Economic Expansion, Ottawa, August 1983).

11. Statistics, Canada, *Manufacturing Industries of Canada* (Minister of Supply and Services, Ottawa, various years).

12. Harris with Cox, *Trade, Industrial Policy*.

13. Daly and MacCharles, *Canadian Manufactured Exports*, Ch. 3.

14. See Ch. 1, note 9.

15. See Ch. 1, note 12.

16. Caves, *Diversification, Foreign Investment*; and Baldwin, J. R. and P. K. Gorecki with J. McVey, *Trade, Tariffs, Product Diversity and Length of Production Run in Canadian Manufacturing Industries:*

1970–1979 (Economic Council of Canada, Ottawa, 1983), Discussion Paper no. 247.

17. Daly, Keyes and Spence, *Scale and Specialization*.
18. See Ch. 1, note 12.
19. Daly and Globerman, *Tariff and Science Policies*; and Daly, 'Natural Science'.
20. Palda, K. S., *Industrial Innovation* (The Fraser Institute, Vancouver, 1984).
21. Machlup, F., *The Production and Distribution of Knowledge in the United States* (Princeton University Press, 1962).
22. Johnson, H. G., 'The Efficiency and Welfare Implications of the International Corporation', in C. P. Kindleberger, *The International Corporation* (MIT Press, Cambridge, Mass., 1976).
23. See Ch. 1, note 8, and also Dunning, J., 'Explaining the International Direct Investment Position of Countries: Towards a Dynamic or Developmental Approach' in *International Production and the Multinational Enterprise* (George Allen & Unwin, London, 1981).
24. Safarian, A. E., *Foreign Ownership of Canadian Industry* (McGraw Hill, Toronto, 1966).
25. Globerman, S., 'Foreign Direct Investment and "Spillover" Efficiency Benefits in Candian Manufacturing Industries', *Canadian Journal of Economics*, no. 12 (1979), pp. 42–56.
26. Cacnis, D. G., 'The Sources of Total Factor Productivity Growth in Canada, 1950–1976' (Adelphi University, New York, 1985), mimeograph.
27. MacCharles, D. C., *The Performance of Direct Investment in the Manufacturing Sector* (University of New Brunswick, Saint John, 1981), mimeograph.
28. MacCharles, *The Cost of Administrative Organizations*.
29. See Ch. 1, note 12.
30. See Ch. 1, note 13.
31. Daly, Keyes and Spence, *Scale and Specialization*; Daly, *Canada's Comparative Advantage*; and Daly, D. J., *Rationalization and Specialization in Canadian Manufacturing* (York University, Toronto, 1984), a survey paper for the Royal Commission on the Economic Union and Development Prospects for Canada, mimeograph.
32. There is substantial evidence for Canada of this behaviour as will be presented in Chapter 4. There is also evidence for Australia that foreign MNEs combine manufacturing and wholesale activities; see Williamson, Peter J., 'Multinational Enterprise Behaviour and Domestic Industry Adjustment Under Import Threat', *The Review of Economics and Statistics*, vol. LXVIII, no. 3 (1986), pp. 359–68.

3

Conceptual Issues and Prior Studies

INTRODUCTION

This chapter will review conceptual developments and prior studies in the international trade literature. The discussion will also touch on the two trade-related issues of intra-firm trade by foreign-controlled subsidiaries in Canada and the transfer prices used by them.

IIT THEMES IN THE LITERATURE

Grubel and Lloyd (G&L) presented the first theoretical description of IIT along with an empirical analysis of it in 1960s trade data for Canada and other industrial nations.[1] They explicitly stated the relationships between increased competition from freer trade, the response by manufacturers to this change with increased scale and specialisation and the consequent increase in IIT. They also developed an index for measuring the extent of IIT in total trade data for a country that is still extensively used by researchers.

The G&L index measures the extent of IIT in total trade. The index ranges between zero and one. It has been widely used either as developed here in its original formulation or with some variation to allow for disequilibrium in the trade data and to handle the problems of overlapped trade and categorical aggregation (which are discussed more fully later). The index is derived as follows:

$$\text{G\&L index of IIT} = \frac{[(X + M) - /X - M/]}{(X + M)}$$

where: $(X + M)$ is the sum of exports and imports for an industry (i.e. total trade); and $/X - M/$ is the net trade balance for an industry in absolute terms.

The net trade balance measures the net import or net export position of an industry. If it is relatively large, total trade for the industry is attributed to inter-industry trade. For instance, in the case of an industry with either imports or exports (but not both), the value of the IIT index would approach zero. If an industry has both imports and exports and they are equal, the value of the IIT index would approach one with total trade being attributed to IIT.

Grubel and Lloyd's work drew on prior developments in the literature on industrial organisation and micro-economic theory. Their major contribution was in identifying and relating them to emerging themes in the international trade literature. Interestingly, the developments in the industrial organisation literature were partly Canadian in origin and resulted from Canadian economists working on the reasons for the long-standing lack of competitiveness by Canadian manufacturers. This work resulted in establishing the importance of product-specific diseconomies of scale.[2] In turn, the Canadian research was based on earlier developments in the US on modern cost theory by Alchian and Hirschleifer which was organised around the concept of learning curves.[3]

Modern cost theory has come to be widely applied in the US by the Boston Consulting Group and other consultants. It integrates neo-classical production and cost theory with the theory of learning curves. Earlier research has shown that, for a given plant size, manufacturing productivity and costs are influenced by the number of products made and their cumulative, continuously produced output. In cases where there is product-packing in a plant, the loss in productivity can be a more important influence on unit costs than changes in plant scale which had traditionally been emphasised. The reason for this is that as product-packing increases, more line changeovers are required with labour having to move back up its learning curve each time as it relearns the production methods. Thus, as product-packing increases in a plant, the higher is the level of diversity, the lower is productivity and the higher are variable costs. This effect of diversity on unit costs is called product-specific diseconomies of scale. Even a relatively large plant, if it is highly diversified, can be high-cost despite its large scale of operation. Modern cost theory does recognise the traditional plant-specific diseconomies of scale in that, given a level of diversity, a small plant would have higher total unit costs than a large one.

The concept of product-specific diseconomies of scale was combined by Grubel and Lloyd with the then emerging idea of differentiated products from the micro-economic literature. Demand theory has been revised to allow for non-homogeneous goods by allowing for non-substitutability by consumers between basically similar goods because of their different characteristics which could be created by advertising and other forms of product differentiation.[4]

Product differentiation and the capability to achieve cost reductions through reductions in diversity within a plant, or increased specialisation, form the two basic postulates of the IIT Model. It is closer in emphasis to the older classical Ricardian model which used differences in labour productivity to explain trade flows than it is to the currently dominant HOS model which relies on differences in the availability of factors of production between countries to do so. The development of the IIT paradigm was in response to the need of the time and the growth in economic thought to accommodate that need since new constructs were required after the Second World War to explain such cross-trade phenomena as the export of Volvos from Sweden to Germany and the return flow of Volkswagens from Germany to Sweden. The prevailing Ricardian and HOS models were not particularly appropriate. Tests of the HOS model had found it wanting in terms of power to explain trade flows. For instance, the work of Leontieff showed the US exported relatively labour-intensive goods when the HOS model predicted it should export capital-intensive goods. This disparity between the model and reality cast some doubt on its efficacy. The Ricardian model, however, did stand up reasonably well to empirical testing. It is based on the concept of relative labour productivity differences between countries. A test of its efficacy showed a significant correlation between the productivity advantages of a country and the share of export markets held by its products.[5] However, the model did not explain why the countries exported some of all goods, including those in which they appeared to have labour productivity disadvantages. Also, like the HOS model, it only explains one-way flows with a country exporting those goods in which it has productivity and cost advantages while importing those goods in which other countries have advantages. It is possible some of the trade in the test of the Ricardian that was left unexplained was of the IIT type. While the Ricardian model, based on labour productivity differences, has some applicability it clearly did not fully explain international cross-trade in similar goods.

A DISSENTING VIEW ON IIT

There are critics of the IIT paradigm who insist it is not a phenomenon that requires discarding the HOS model. The basic criticism is that the data on trade are incorrectly recorded, which results in the anomaly of cross-trade in similar goods, or IIT. Two types of recording problems could exist. One problem is categorical aggregation and the other is overlapped trade.

Categorical aggregation exists when the allocation of imports and exports is to the same industry when they should be allocated to different ones. Consequently, what is actually inter-industry trade appears as cross-trade, or IIT, in the trade data. This could happen if industries are not disaggregated finely enough so that different types of goods are captured in the data and classed to one industry rather than to their several different ones.[6]

Overlapped trade occurs when the definition of an industry is incorrect so that goods produced by different factor-endowment ratios are classified to one industry. For instance, an industry that is internationally competitive because its products use a factor intensively that is in relatively abundant supply could be improperly defined to include products that are not competitive because they do not use that factor intensively or use another that is in relatively short supply. The competitive products would be exported while the non-competitive ones would be imported. Combining the industries and their trade data would result in the appearance of IIT, when in fact the trade is inter-industry.[7]

Both of these recording errors would influence the Grubel and Lloyd index which measures the ratio of IIT to total trade for an industry. Empirically, the errors are indistinguishable from one another in their influence on trade data even though they are conceptually different. The critics hold that it is these errors, rather than the existence of IIT, that the index is picking up. Therefore, IIT is not a phenomenon that requires a new trade paradigm to explain it, but only an anomaly in the data that would disappear if they were correctly recorded.

Finger is a leading critic of the IIT paradigm and represents a considerable body of opinion which exists in the US on this issue. In particular, Finger has dismissed IIT as a statistical aberration of no consequence to US trade policy. His position is that the definition used to classify imports to industries is based on the SITC concordance which allocates imports to those industries that would have produced the products had they been manufactured domestically. The SITC industries are defined on the basis of the complementarity of the characteristics of the products in their final use, which is a demand-oriented definition. For instance, production and imports of both plastic and china cups would be allocated to the cup industry.

However, for purposes of economic analysis, the definition of an industry follows that of the SIC concordance in which an industry is determined by the comparability, or homogeneity, of the factors used in production as well as the similarity in the proportions with which they are combined. By this definition, plastic cups would be allocated to the plastic extrusion industry and china cups would be allocated to the separate pottery industry. The SIC definition is used for purposes of the Census of Manufactures rather than for trade purposes. If plastic cups are imported and china cups produced domestically and exported, then by the SIC definition there would be no cross-trade recorded for either industry. However, trade data collected on the SITC definition of an industry would show cross-trade since both imports and exports would be allocated to the cup industry.

Finger's position is that it is not possible *per se* to have intra-industry trade and this would be evident if the trade data were allocated to industries as defined by the economic criterion. In this view factor-endowment ratios *must* vary between nations. Therefore, there *must* be a difference in unit costs between countries for a given product. Thus, using the economic definition of an industry, a nation must either export or import but cannot do both for the products produced in any given industry.

Finger tested to establish whether factor proportions varied

43

more within an industry than between industries, using the SITC definition. The test showed that approximately 40 per cent of the total variation in factor-input ratios was within industry groups at the three-digit level of disaggregation. This assessment was based on the use of two input ratios: physical capital intensity (defined as non-wage, value-added per employee) and human capital intensity.

The three-digit level of disaggregation is the one normally used in tests for IIT. Finger disaggregation reduces the problem of categorical aggregation, but increases the possibility of defining IIT out of existence. The measurement of IIT depends upon the product groups being broad enough to capture trade in similar but differentiated products but not so narrow that only one product or variation in it exists for a given industry. The three-digit level is usually assumed to balance adequately these two conflicting objectives.

Finger concluded on the basis of his test that the IIT index used by Grubel and Lloyd was inappropriate. Grubel and Lloyd had concluded that after a 'careful study of the SITC classification . . . the 3-digit SITC statistics separate commodities into groups most closely corresponding to the concept of an "industry" conventionally used in economic analysis'. Finger disagreed on the grounds the index was only recording a statistical aberration and dismissed the validity of the IIT paradigm.

It is important to understand that those holding to this viewpoint are often in an economic environment in which the need is not pressing for an IIT paradigm to explain trade flows. The IIT paradigm is relevant to economies with small, protected markets and high levels of direct foreign investment that are being subjected to increased competition. Markets are larger in the US than in Canada and individual European nations, and the US historically had high levels of domestic competition with low levels of direct foreign investment. Hence, there is much less need for US researchers to have a model which explains the cross-trade that arises when small, diverse and high-cost firms (often foreign-owned) are subject to increased competition. Because of the particular industrial structure in the US, IIT would be a much smaller part of total US trade and the IIT paradigm would be less important for conducting research there and for developing theoretical and policy issues.

It is also worth noting that Finger's criticism of the IIT paradigm is based on measurement problems and not on its theoretical value or its implications for policy. The IIT model is a paradigm about resource reallocation that focuses on firm-level decision making and behaviour at the level of the firm and how this impacts on trade flows. If the behaviour is theoretically possible then its implications for resource reallocation stand. The question of how important it is quantitatively is another issue. What is important is whether resources can be reallocated from the production of one product to another within a firm as specialisation takes place even if they are produced by different proportions of factor inputs. It is recognised that the shift in resources may notionally be inter-industry, but it is still within the firm and from a practical standpoint this is the major issue for purposes of setting public policy related to employee relocation and retraining in an era of increasing competition. To use the example developed earlier, if increased specialisation led a firm to produce only china rather than both china and plastic cups, it should make no difference to the employees as long as the production of china cups increased enough to offset the loss of employment in plastic cups and the employees were retrained in pottery from plastics production in order to remain employed in the firm. In such a case, major shifts of labour from one industry and region to others would not be necessary.

In this present study the problem of overlapped trade was partially resolved by collecting trade data at the level of the firm before it was aggregated up to the level of an industry. The problem of categorical aggregation was partially resolved by using a four-digit level of disaggregation of industries, as opposed to the usual three-digit level used in other studies. This reduces the possibility of collecting in one industry the trade of dissimilar goods, yet still allows for the capture of trade in similar but differentiated products at the industry level. Also, the import data which were allocated to industries on the basis of the SITC concordance were converted to the SIC concordance by use of an algorithm so that the industries more closely conformed to the economic definition of an industry. It is also possible partially to overcome the aggregation and trade overlap problems by using a corrected formula for the Grubel and Lloyd index. But this would have made the analysis more expensive and difficult to carry out within the given time and resource constraints.

The critics of the IIT paradigm are themselves open to criticism. Their position is rather narrow since the HOS model is not inclusive enough to explain all trade flows. For instance, it does not explain why china cups made in different countries with the same factor proportions are cross-traded internationally. Limoges china is produced in France and shipped to the UK, while Wedgwood products are made in the UK and shipped to France. Also, the emphasis in the HOS model is on the supply side which overlooks that trade flows are influenced also by demand-side considerations. Customer tastes are important in determining the success of products and they lead to product differentiation by manufacturers to meet these varying tastes. And as has already been discussed, such differentiation leads to cross-trade in the products of an industry even though the factor proportions used in production are almost identical for the various types of product.[8]

In summary, the IIT paradigm is a useful addition to the analytical tool kit of economists interested in empirically oriented research. It allows them to address policy issues based on analyses that can account for what is actually transpiring in the trade data. It is appropriate for small economies (with consequently small and diverse manufacturers) that were formerly protected and now subject to freer trade and increased price competition. It adds to, rather than replaces, the traditional models based on national labour productivity differences and national differences in relative factor endowment ratios so that it is more adept at explaining increases in trade among nations even when they have similar endowment ratios. The traditional HOS and Richardian models are oversimplifications of reality and in themselves do not provide a broad enough understanding of trade developments since the Second World War. The basic assumptions in the IIT model of product-specific economies of scale and product differentiation are the counterpart additions to trade theory and the development of commercial and industrial policy since the Second World War that the concepts of oligopoly and market power were to the theory of perfect competition. It also has been updated since the Second World War, making micro-economics a more meaningful tool of analysis in the areas of industrial organisation and anti-combines policy.

ANTECEDENT STUDIES ON CANADIAN IIT

Grubel and Lloyd's pioneering study of IIT was published in

1975. However, there was a more limited but earlier study by Lermer assessing Canadian IIT in twenty narrowly defined commodity groups for the years 1961 to 1971. It was published in 1973.[9] The study was partly in response to an observation by another researcher that lower tariffs appeared to stimulate product rationalisation and export activity by Canadian firms.[10] In part, it repsonded too to an earlier study which showed that Canadian manufacturers were high-cost because of their small scale and diversity.[11] In other words, it was an early identification of the relationships between increased scale, specialisation and cross-trade and is the logical starting point for an analysis of Canadian IIT.

Lermer tested for the effect of increased scale and specialisation on Canada's international trade by regressing exports and GNP on imports. The model was based on the assumptions that if imports and exports went up simultaneously (and significantly), after allowing for the influence of growth in GNP on the increase in imports, then this was evidence for cross-trade in similar goods. If imports and exports were negatively related (after allowing for the influence of change in GNP) then this would be evidence in support of inter-industry trade.

Lermer preselected four commodity groups within the automobile sector as a control group for the analysis. They were selected because, during the latter half of the 1960s, the Auto Pact had led to a significant increase in the scale and specialisation of the automobile producers in Canada and a subsequent growth in cross-trade. As expected, these results were confirmed in the regressions. Other commodity groups were also preselected (e.g. live animals and meats) with the foreknowledge that they were not subject to the forces of specialisation and increased IIT. Indeed, trade was expected to be inter-industry in nature for the food and other groups selected because of different comparative advantages between countries in these products and the existence of trade barriers.

Of the twenty commodity groups analysed, eleven showed a tendency for IIT (i.e. the four automobile groups, textiles, chemicals, machinery, farm machinery and miscellaneous products). The other nine groups did not show such a tendency (namely, live animals, meats, paper and board, plastics, primary iron and steel, steel plate, general purpose machinery, communications equipment, and miscellaneous equipment).

Lermer's work was updated for this present study to assess

whether its conclusions still held.[12] The update was based on data for the same twenty commodity groups but the time period was extended to cover 1963–81, with comparability in the data over the two decades.

For the period 1972–81, three of the four commodity groups in the auto sector showed a lessening in the movement toward IIT. This might be accounted for by diminishing returns to scale and specialisation in these groups after the initial period of rationalisation in the late-1960s and early-1970s. It could also reflect increased import penetration over the 1970s as the North American auto industry suffered a deterioration in its comparative advantage. The Japanese auto producers benefited from large productivity improvements (relative to wage gains) and a shift in the nation's factor endowment ratios, both of which improved their competitiveness relative to North American producers. Six of the seven non-auto groups indentified by Lermer as moving towards increased IIT also showed, subsequent to 1971, increased import penetration and a diminishing pace of increase in cross-trade.

Of the nine groups Lermer identified as not being involved in IIT, two of them (i.e. live animals, and primary iron and steel) stabilised their import penetration after 1971. This might have been due to improved unit costs or increased trade barriers. Another six commodity groups moved towards increased IIT (the exceptions being live animals, meat, and paper and board) and three of them did so very strongly — general purpose machinery, communications equipment, and miscellaneous equipment and tools. These results indicate that all engaged in increased specialisation while the three with the largest movement towards specialisation would now be recategorised into the IIT group.

The data were combined for the complete two-decade period of 1963 to 1981. Four of the original nine commodity groups that by Lermer's criteria were in the non-IIT (or inter-industry) category could still be so allocated (i.e. live animals, meat, paper and board, and steel plate). The balance of the groups indicate both increasing inter and intra-industry trade since the correlations between imports and GNP as well as between imports and exports were both positive and significant (i.e. plastics, primary iron and steel, general machinery, communications equipment, and miscellaneous equipment and tools).

For the eleven commodity groups which Lermer's data

indicated firms were engaging in specialisation and IIT, only one could now be unequivocably allocated to that category (farm machinery) while three appear to have slowed their specialisation and were being subjected to increased import penetration (textiles, material handling equipment, and mining machinery). The balance of the product groups appear to have been subjected to increased import penetration while at the same time having increased IIT (i.e. chemicals, road vehicles, auto parts, auto engines, and miscellaneous products).

The tests on the Lermer commodity groups for the decade following 1971 show the effects since then that were already discussed earlier which have influenced trade performamce generally. That is, the influences of freer trade and increased competition from new, offshore producers and the consequent decline in Canada's share of world markets. The import propensities increased in a number of cases. For some industries, the export propensities also increased, which is suggestive of greater specialisation and IIT. In others, only the import propensities increased, which meant they could no longer classified as having IIT to any great extent. This suggests that increased scale, specialisation and IIT are the results of a dynamic process. The pace of the rationalisation changes over time and different products are affected in different time periods. There appear to be decreasing returns at some point to increased rationalisation. Technical change and the speed of its adoption can influence the trade performance of an industry. So also can differential changes between nations in relative unit costs because of changes in inflation, productivity and factor-endowment ratios. In addition, barriers to trade also change and influence trade performance. All of these influences appear to have some influence on the results of the analysis.

CANADIAN IIT IN AN INTERNATIONAL CONTEXT

The topic of IIT has received more attention in Europe than in Canada, although several of the studies include research on Canadian data and the pioneering study by Grubel and Lloyd was influenced by the work of Canadian economists. G&L's work spawned much interest in Europe and has been followed up more fully there with additional research. For instance, the European Institute for Advanced Studies in Management has had several seminars on this subject and a book of readings on IIT has been published in Germany. Many articles have also appeared in European journals, relative to the US and Canada.[13] The reasons for the lack of interest in IIT in the US is attributed to the less pressing need there for such a paradigm. The relative lack of interest in Canada appears to be related partly to US academics and researchers overwhelming Canadian thinking on trade theory and issues. It may also be due in part to Canada being slower in adapting to the changing trade environment than European countries so that interest in it developed later and more slowly.

The Grubel and Lloyd study used SITC data at the three-digit level of disaggregation for ten industrial nations, including Canada. The analysis was done on the data for the three years 1959, 1964 and 1967. They estimated that Canadian IIT increased from 29 per cent of total trade in 1959 to 48 per cent by 1967. In 1959, the level of IIT for Canada was well below the international average of 38 per cent, with Canada ranking eighth of the total of ten countries. This could be interpreted as being due to the continuing protection of manufacturers here relative to those in Europe who were entering into more competitive common market arrangements and had to adapt to the increased competition sooner with consequent increases in IIT. The other two countries with lower levels of cross-trade than Canada were the highly protected economies of Australia and Japan. Canada was less involved in IIT than the European countries and the US. By 1967, the mean level of IIT for the ten countries was 48 per cent, Canada's level was now equal to the average, moving it into sixth position. Its level of IIT was closer to that for the US (49 per cent), Germany (46 per cent), and Italy (42 per cent). Canada still lagged behind the UK (69 per cent), France (65 per cent) and Belgium/Luxembourg (63 per cent).

In the opinion of Grubel and Lloyd, IIT was not the result of overlapped trade or categorical aggregation in the data since they believed the SITC definition of industries used by them conformed very closely to the SIC definition. A similar conclusion was also reached by the authors of a recent study on UK trade data. They used indices of IIT, both unadjusted and adjusted for categorical aggregation, and made a comparison of the results from the two methods of calculation. They concluded that while there was 'some variation in third-digit indices [that] is accounted for by categorical aggregation, it is far from being a complete explanation of the pattern of intra-industry trade'.[14]

A more recent study of IIT by Bergstrand used OECD data covering the years 1965 to 1976 for 18 commodity groups within the machinery and transport equipment sectors.[15] Seven countries, Canada amongst them, were included in the study. The IIT index in this study was adjusted through an iterative process to eliminate disequilibrium values from the net trade balances. The results showed the Grubel and Lloyd index to be a conservative measure of IIT because any disequilibrium value results in an overstatement of the net trade balance which is attributed to inter-industry trade.

Bergstrand's study showed IIT to be a significant portion of the total trade activity for Canada and that it had grown substantially over the time period of his analysis which extended a decade beyond the data in the G&L study. Bergstrand concluded, as did Grubel and Lloyd, that overlapped trade and categorical aggregation were not the reasons for IIT in the data. He further held that IIT increased between countries as manufacturers specialised to exploit economies of scale and that if specialisation is carried out as a result of trade liberalisation, then inter-industry trade declines in relative importance.

Aquino also did a study of disequilibrium-adjusted trade balances using the G&L index.[16] This work, too, showed the index to be a conservatively biased measure of IIT. Aquino's analysis covered 26 countries using 1972 trade data from the OECD and UN. The G&L index, unadjusted for trade balance disequilibrium, was 66 per cent while the adjusted index was slightly over 73 per cent. Canada's ranking was similar to Grubel and Lloyd's for 1967, placed fifth out of ten countries. This was well ahead of the US, Japan and Australia (approximately 57, 54 and 59 per cent respectively). Canada was close to Italy, West Germany and Belgium (72, 76 and 70 per cent respectively) but lagged behind France, the UK and the Netherlands (87, 82 and 79 per cent respectively).

Aquino developed a measure of the elasticity of exports with respect to imports. It was extremely high for Canada in comparison to the other nine industrial nations at 1.15. That is, exports increase relatively more than imports as imports increase. Only the Netherlands was higher, at 1.43. The UK and the US were very low at 0.02 with the rest of the countries ranging between 0.13 and 0.34. This indicates the adjustment process to freer trade for Canada would be easier than for most other nations, especially the US, and would result in export growth being greater than import growth. US manufacturers would derive little additional benefit from further increases in scale and specialisation, unlike Canadian manufacturers who would have significant gains as they achieved access to larger US and world markets.

The high elasticity noted for Canada in 1972 could reflect, to some extent, that Canada was later in adjusting to the changing trade environment relative to Europe and the US. Consequently, it started from a lower level of specialisation and moved more quickly towards it in the early-1970s than other nations. It also reflects the relatively high level of direct foreign investment. Subsidiaries can more easily implement rationalisation programmes than domestically controlled firms because of their international affiliations.[17]

CANADIAN IIT IN A DOMESTIC CONTEXT

There is also evidence of IIT in manufactured goods that comes from a study of just Canadian trade data for the period 1965–79, aggregated to the two-digit level of industry identification as well as for the manufacturing sector as a whole.[18] For the manufacturing sector as a whole, the export propensity increased from 16.6 per cent in 1965 to 31.4 per cent in 1982 while the import propensity went from 20.0 per cent to 32.6 per cent in 1979 but declined to 29.8 per cent by 1982 due to the influence of the severe recession in 1981–2. It has since recovered. These results are similar to those reported in a related study, covering the period 1965 to 1977, in which the value of manufactured exports grew by 14.4 per cent while imports grew by 14.7 per cent per annum.[19] At the same time gross output in the manufacturing sector grew by 10.1 per cent per annum. It is worth noting that in spite of the large changes in imports, exports and the level of competition, the self-sufficiency ratio for Canada has remained remarkably stable at the overall level for the manufacturing sector for these time periods.[20] The ratio is defined as shipments to domestic consumption, and its stability suggests that as imports rise so also do exports. This further supports Aquino's findings noted above on the elasticity of Canadian exports with respect to imports. As has already been discussed, these changes in trade and manufactured output are part of a worldwide trend and reflect the increase in cross-trade of similar goods as firms increased their specialisation and scale through exports.

A disaggregation of the manufacturing sector to the two-digit level (i.e. twenty industry groups) provides evidence for increased IIT generally across many industries (Table 3.1). It should be noted that at the two-digit level, the data suffer from both the problems of categorical aggregation and overlapped trade. Therefore, the conclusions drawn must be taken with some caution until the more detailed analysis in the next chapter provides supportive or contradictory evidence.

There is only one industry group for each ratio in Table 3.1 that has not had a simultaneous increase in both ratios between 1965 and 1979. And many have large IIT flows, based on the similar values for the two propensities with some industries

Table 3.1: Measures of Trade Performance (Manufacturing Sector, 1965 and 1979)

Industry	Import propensity		Export propensity		Dominant type of trade
	1979	$\dfrac{1979}{1965}$	1979	$\dfrac{1979}{1965}$	
Food & beverage	10.2	1.6	12.3	1.3	IIT (weak)
Tobacco products	1.7	1.4	0.7	3.5	IIT (weak)
Rubber & plastics	23.2	1.6	11.1	2.5	Imports
Leather	33.9	2.5	8.0	1.9	Imports
Textiles	28.9	1.2	7.1	1.9	IIT (weak)
Knitting mills	30.8	3.4	1.6	0.6	Imports
Clothing	12.7	2.7	5.2	3.1	Imports
Wood products	13.5	1.7	56.5	1.4	Exports
Furniture & fixtures	13.3	2.6	9.2	5.4	IIT (strong)
Paper & allied industries	9.7	1.6	57.2	1.2	Exports
Printing & publishing	15.5	1.3	3.1	3.1	IIT (weak)
Primary metals	34.9	1.4	44.5	1.1	Imports
Metal fabricating	15.0	1.3	7.5	3.4	IIT (strong)
Machinery	75.2	1.2	53.2	1.9	IIT (strong)
Transportation equipment	72.3	2.4	67.9	4.5	IIT (strong)
Electrical	40.2	2.0	20.5	2.6	Imports
Non-metallic minerals	18.5	1.2	12.5	2.3	Exports
Petroleum & coal	3.2	0.3	10.7	13.4	Exports
Chemicals	35.0	1.4	28.9	2.0	IIT (strong)
Miscellaneous	54.6	1.3	21.7	1.4	Imports

Sources: Canada (ITC), *Canada's Trade*; Astwood, *Canada's Merchandise*, Table 4.

having high values. This is consistent with increased cross-trade. However, there also was significant inter-industry trade for many industries based on the large differences between the import and export propensities and the dominance of one or the other of them.

The allocation of the industries to their dominant trade pattern was based on the difference between the change in the export propensity less the change in the import propensity between 1965 and 1979. If the difference was large and positive then the industry's dominant trade pattern was presumed to be in exports. If it was large and negative it was presumed to be in imports. Both of these allocations would normally represent inter-industry trade. A small difference in the change to the propensities indicated IIT was the dominant form of trade, with large simultaneous increases in the propensities indicating strong IIT trade activity, while a small increase indicated weak IIT trade activity.

There has been considerable change between 1965 and 1979 in the share of the domestic market held by domestic manufacturers. Many industries became more dependent upon imports while others became more export-oriented, reflecting changes of the inter-industry type. Industries such as knitting mills and clothing operate at a cost disadvantage because of the relatively large supply of low-wage but productive labour elsewhere. This resulted in the import-penetration ratio increasing more than the export-orientation ratio. Industries such as pulp and paper benefit from Canada's relative abundance of the primary materials and resources that are used intensively in producing the products of these industries which gives the manufacturers a comparative cost advantage in world markets. The result has been that the export-orientation ratio has increased more than the import-penetration ratio for these industries. At the same time, almost all industries had an increase in both their import- and export-orientation ratios which suggests they had some IIT as well as inter-industry trade (i.e. the electrical industry group).

The decline in the import-penetration ratio for the petroleum and coal industries reflects, in part, government regulation as much as it does market forces. The government has imposed programmes of import substitution and conservation in order to reduce imports of petroleum. At the same time there has been a significant increase in the export of coal to Japan.

DOMESTIC IIT

An increase in specialisation by manufacturers through increased contracting-out of minor product lines and components to more efficient suppliers at home and abroad would increase the value of purchased items relative to the value of costs added in production within plants (i.e. value-added). This would cause an increase in their ratio of purchased material to value-added. The improvements in productivity as a result of increased scale and specialisation would also increase the ratio since value-added would be reduced relative to purchased material, especially if a significant part of any increase in profit from the productivity improvements is passed on to customers as lower prices in order to achieve improved competitiveness.

A good indication of the total value of intra-industry trade can be obtained from the cost of purchased materials collected as part of the Census of Manufactures (as also is the data on value-added). The total cost of purchased materials records the value of finished goods that are purchased for resale as part of a firm's wholesale activities as well as the value of material and components purchased for use as inputs into the manufacturing process. The cost would include purchases from domestic and foreign suppliers that are both within the industry of the purchaser and in other industries. This is a comprehensive measure of total trade and, in the case of the Census data, it is separable into the trade in goods purchased just for resale and the trade in semi-finished materials and finished components used as inputs into the manufacturing system.

One of the disadvantages of this comprehensive measure is that it includes the cost of imported items as well as domestic purchases. As a result, it reflects increases in both international and domestic intra-industry trade. There is no readily available way to exclude the value of the imported goods from the statistic so that it would record just domestic intra-industry trade, although the domestic portion would normally dominate the statistic. Therefore, the cost of purchased material is used here as a proxy for the value of domestic intra-industry trade and changes in it even though this is not strictly correct.

The input-output tables also provide information on the cost of purchased materials (as well as value-added). These tables are useful because they separate out the type of materials purchased into: primary materials produced by the resources sector and used in the manufacturing sector; and components produced by firms in the manufacturing sector and used as inputs into the production systems of other firms in this sector. This split makes it possible to evaluate the extent of any bias in the cost of purchased materials arising from increases in the prices of resources (especially energy) over the past decade or so.

CENSUS DATA MEASURES

The ratio of purchased material to value-added was calculated from the Census data and is presented here as a time series. An increase in the ratio over time would be consistent with firms increasing their degree of specialisation as they sought to improve unit costs and become more competitive. Initially, the ratio should have been low in the early-1960s, since firms were more vertically and horizontally diversified then because of tariff and other barriers to trade. Since the early-1960s, the ratio should have increased because of the greater specialisation and increased contracting-out to more efficient suppliers at home and abroad that has taken place as a result of freer trade and competition. It should have increased more quickly over the 1970s as the movement to freer trade became stronger and its effects cumulative.

Table 3.2 shows the ratio for the Canadian manufacturing sector separately for production activity and for total activity. Total activity includes purchases of goods for resale (i.e. wholesale activity) as well as items purchased as intermediate goods for use as inputs in manufacturing activities. The table also shows the total activity ratio for the US.

The ratio, which is an aggregate for all the firms and industries in the manufacturing sector, could change over time due to influences other than just increased specialisation. For instance, it would vary with the business cycle because profits and purchased materials would be expected to decline more quickly than value-added in the downturn of the cycle and to rise more quickly in the upturn. Also, it would change over time if the weight of the shipments of some industries in the total shipments of the manufacturing sector changed and their production requirements for value-added differed from the average. Some industries, by their nature, require relatively more value-added to complete a product than others (i.e. transportation equipment *versus* clothing). It would also vary with any technical change which altered over time the proportion of value-added needed in production by an industry.

Table 3.2: Ratio of Purchased Material to Value-added (Manufacturing Sector, Selected Years 1960–79)

Year	Ratio for production activity	Ratio for total activity	
	Canada	Canada	US
1960	1.20	1.13	1.26 (1961)
1965	1.25	1.18	1.18
1970	1.28	1.20	1.12
1975	1.42	1.32	1.35
1979	1.49	1.40	1.34 (1977)

Sources: Statistics Canada, *Manufacturing Industries of Canada*; and US Dept. of Commerce, *Census Manufactures*.

The movement in the ratio is broadly consistent with that expected due to the business cycle and increases in specialisation by manufacturers since 1960. It shows some change that is coincident with the business cycle and it has steadily increased since 1960 with the rate of increase quickening after 1970.

The ratio for the US was initially higher than for Canada. This would be expected since US manufacturers were substantially more specialised than Canadian manufacturers in the early-1960s. The ratio for the US dropped significantly, however, between 1960 and 1965 and into 1970. No apparent explanation is available for this, although the US did have the largest decline in its share of world trade over this time period of any of the industrialised nations (including Canada) when it fell from 20.1 per cent to 14.9 per cent.[21] This may have led US manufacturers to contract-in more of their production requirements for components in order to increase plant loads as export sales fell off, or they may not have moved towards increased contracting-out to foreign suppliers as quickly as they should have and as quickly as did Canadian firms during this time period. However, this is conjectural and it is unknown to what extent the deteriorating export performance influenced the ratio except to note that the changes in the two statistics are consistent with one another. In spite of this, the long-term trend for the

US ratio has been to increase, as it has been for Canada as well.

Table 3.3 presents the ratio of purchased material to value-added for the manufacturing sector, disaggregated to the twenty-industry level for selected years from 1960 to 1979. This is the same industry breakdown as was used in Table 3.1 so that comparisons can be made for these industries of their performance on both international and domestic intra-industry trade. Some speculative inferences are then made about the specialisation activity of firms in these industries based on this picture of trade performance.

Table 3.3: Ratio of Purchased Material to Value-added, Production Activity (Manufacturing Sector, Selected Years 1960–1979)

Industry	Ratio			Change
	1960	1970	1979	1960–79
Food & beverage	1.83	1.92	2.29	(0.09)
Tobacco products	1.84	1.67	1.33	(0.55)
Rubber & plastics	0.90	0.90	1.12	0.36
Leather	1.03	0.98	1.24	(0.15)
Textiles	1.17	1.25	1.29	(0.02)
Knitting mills	1.12	1.31	1.12	0.21
Clothing	1.09	1.09	1.03	(0.04)
Wood products	1.32	1.44	1.24	0.14
Furniture & fixtures	0.93	0.89	0.94	0.06
Paper & allied industries	0.95	1.10	0.99	0.14
Printing & publishing	0.47	0.50	0.58	0.09
Primary metals	1.53	1.15	1.33	0.52
Metal fabricating	0.88	0.95	1.16	0.28
Machinery	0.91	1.02	1.14	0.23
Transport equipment	1.26	1.96	2.03	0.81
Electrical	0.87	1.06	0.96	0.13
Non-metallic minerals	0.62	0.66	0.76	0.22
Petroleum & coal	3.12	4.07	7.50	3.44
Chemicals	0.91	0.84	1.12	0.15
Miscellaneous	0.79	0.70	1.49	0.81

Source: Statistics Canada, *Manufacturing Industries of Canada*.

Except for printing and publishing, the four industries in Table 3.1 categorised as having weak IIT had a decline in the ratio of purchased material to value-added. There are also seven industries in Table 3.1 that are dominated by imports, even after allowing for their export propensity. Two of these industries had a decline in the ratio of purchased material to value-added. The

58

decrease in the ratio is consistent with firms increasing their degree of diversification in an attempt to maintain plant loads in the face of declining market share, which in the longer run would likely prove to be cost-increasing rather than improving their competitiveness. The other five industries suffering from the loss of domestic market share had an increase in the ratio of purchased material to value-added (which was very large for the rubber and plastics, primary metals, and miscellaneous industries). This suggests that the firms in these industries may have captured productivity improvements by specialising and contracting-out their less efficient production activities. However, the productivity improvements were apparently insufficient to overcome some other problems in their cost structures, thus allowing them to become competitive with foreign producers.

Four industries in Table 3.1 are strongly export-oriented, even after allowance is made for their import propensities. These industries also had an increase in the ratio of purchased material to value-added. So also did five other industries that had extensive intra-industry trade. It appears the natural comparative advantages held by firms in the export-oriented industries have been buttressed by achieving productivity increases through increased specialisation. Firms in the other industries with no apparent resource-based advantage maintained their market share at least partly through increased specialisation.

The influence of the Auto Pact on all the ratios (import-penetration, export-orientation and purchased material to value-added) for the transportation equipment industry is most noticeable. It had the second largest increase in the ratio of purchased material to value-added of all the industries (with the petroleum and coal industry having the greatest increase). During the period 1960 to 1970, the transportation equipment industry undertook significant increases in specialisation in Canada which would cause the ratios to rise. The quick increase in them indicates the speed with which specialisation was carried out and the low level initially of specialisation. This was a highly protected industry with small-scale plants and considerable diversity within them for both final products and components which made them inefficient by world standards. These subsidiaries are now highly specialised, larger in size and extensively involved with intra-industry on a North American basis.

The significant increase in the ratios since 1960 confirms that these statistics do pick up the influence of changes in scale and specialisation on domestic and international intra-industry trade. Further, the increases in the ratios demonstrate the beneficial effect that subsidiaries can have on Canadian income and employment, as well as IIT. They have access to international markets and products through their foreign affiliates which enhances their ability to adapt in a changing trade environment, provided the domestic and head office management groups correctly intercept the changes needed to respond to the changing environments and rationalise their Canadian subsidiaries to cope appropriately with the change.

INPUT-OUTPUT DATA MEASURES

Additional evidence for an increase in domestic intra-industry trade as a result of specialisation was sought through the data provided by the input-output tables. These data are also useful for sorting out primary materials produced in the resources sector from intermediate goods produced in the manufacturing sector. Table 3.4 provides evidence on these topics.

Table 3.4 shows the unit cost structure of the manufacturing sector as a whole by various types of inputs. In 1961, the costs of energy to the manufacturing sector, as represented by the cost of mineral fuels, represented 3 per cent of total unit cost. By 1978, it represented 8 per cent. Most of this increase would be due to price rather than volume changes since it did not start until after 1975. This was after the major increases in the world price of petroleum in 1974 and the later introduction of the national programme to raise domestic petroleum prices in Canada closer to the international price level.

The proportion of unit cost devoted to energy costs increased over the 1970s. However, the proportion spent on other primary material inputs declined by an almost equal amount. Consequently, in total, the impact of energy price increases on the total value of purchased primary inputs was offset so that the ratio of purchased material to value-added was not significantly influenced by price changes for primary inputs, including energy. It should also be noted that the proportion of total unit cost represented by energy costs, even after they doubled over the 1970s, was still relatively small, at 8 per cent, in comparison to the costs of labour and intermediate inputs.

The value of intermediate goods (i.e. items produced by firms

Table 3.4: Composition of Relative Unit Cost (Manufacturing Sector, Selected Years 1961–78)

Cost Categories	1961	1970	1978
Percentage primary material			
Mineral fuels	3	3	8
Agriculture	7	5	5
Other	7	6	5
Sub-total	17	14	18
Percentage components			
Intermediate goods	30	33	34
Total percentage purchased material	47	47	52
Percentage value-added			
Labour income	24	25	22
Return to capital	12	10	11
Services & miscellaneous	17	18	15
Total (percentages)	100	100	100
Ratio of intermediate goods to value-added[a]	0.57	0.62	0.69

Note: a. Value-added is the sum of labour income return to capital, and services and miscellaneous.

Source: Statistics Canada, *The Input-Output Structures of the Canadian Economy*, various years.

in the manufacturing sector for use by other firms in this sector) is a truer measure of intra-industry trade in finished and semi-finished items than is total purchased material because it excludes the purchases of primary materials from the resources sector. The proportion of total unit cost represented by inter-mediate goods increased by 13 per cent between 1961 and 1978. At the same time, value-added declined by 10 per cent from its 1961 level, whether value-added is defined as just labour income or labour income plus the returns to capital, services and the miscellaneous category of costs.

The combined effect of the increase in the proportion of unit cost represented by purchased materials with the decline in value-added, was an overall increase in the ratio of purchased material to value-added of about 25 per cent between the early-1960s and the late-1970s. This increase, based on the input-output data presented in Table 3.4, is similar to that for the Census data as shown in Table 3.2, in which there is an increase in the ratio of 24 per cent between 1960 and 1979.

In summary, the various studies on Canadian IIT, when compared and viewed over an extended period of time, show that there has been an increase in cross-trade relative to inter-industry trade and this change took place later in Canada than among most other industrial nations. This is consistent with Canada originally maintaining its protective barriers to trade as other nations moved towards freer trade in terms of having tariff-free access to larger common markets. Subsequently, with freer trade and increased competition domestically, Canadian manufacturers in the 1970s started to increase their scale and specialisation which increased the level of IIT in the trade data. The high levels of DFI in Canada would also help to explain the high elasticity of exports to imports and increased IIT since the 1960s. Most of the researchers of IIT conclude that it is not a phenomenon related to categorical aggregation or overlapped trade, but a real force at work in the trade data.

IIT AND INTRA-FIRM TRADE

It has already been noted that there is a close association between direct foreign investment (DFI) and trade levels. This issue has been explored in several studies and is reviewed here because of its impact on the results of the trade analysis in the next chapter. In a review of a study by the US Tariff Commission on the exports of MNEs from the US, Lall pointed out that MNEs in 1970 accounted for about 70 per cent of total exports.[22] Almost one-half of these exports (or about one-third of total US exports) went to majority-owned foreign subsidiaries. One of the implications of this is that subsidiaries in countries such as Canada would be importing about one-third of their goods on an intra-firm, or tied, basis and two-thirds from independent suppliers. Lall also drew on a study by Bradshaw using 1965 data which showed one-third of intra-firm exports went to Canada.[23] This reflects the high proportion of US DFI that went to Canada prior to the time period covered in Bradshaw's study.

There also is a significant reverse flow of exports by the subsidiaries to US affiliates.[24] The imports of finished and unfinished goods by US firms from foreign affiliates (defined as having 5 per cent or more control by the US firm) in OECD countries on a related-party transaction basis, accounted for more than 60 per cent of all imports of manufactured goods by the US in 1977. However, the identity of the US firms receiving exports from Canadian firms was significantly different than for the firms in the other OECD countries. The Canadian subsidiaries shipped about 80 per cent of their exports to affiliates that were US-owned. But the subsidiaries in the EEC countries shipped about 70 per cent to non-US-owned affiliates, while the Japanese shipped almost 100 per cent to non-US-owned affiliates. That is, the high level of US DFI in Canada along with the low level of Canadian DFI in the US meant that the majority of exports by Canadian firms were by subsidiaries to affiliates of US parents, while in the case of the other countries they were by resident-owned firms to their own US subsidiaries.

A study by the Economic Council of Canada, using more recent data, indicates there has been an increase in the intra-firm trade between Canadian subsidiaries and their foreign affiliates.[25] The council estimates that almost 90 per cent of imports from the US are by subsidiaries of US enterprises. However, all of these imports may not be on an intra-firm basis. A portion could be from third-party suppliers and they may or may not be suppliers to US affiliates. But, based on a special survey by the Council of selected Canadian industries, it was estimated that intra-firm trade rose from about two-thirds of imports in 1965 to almost four-fifths in 1979, which implies that about 70 per cent of total Canadian imports are on an intra-firm basis by subsidiaries. This ratio appears to be high in light of the information from Lall's work (as noted above) in which it was estimated that on average for all countries including Canada, intra-firm trade on imports from the US would be about 30 per cent of total imports. It is possible that the propensity is higher for Canadian subsidiaries than the average for all subsidiaries of US MNEs. The study by the Economic Council also estimated that exports by the subsidiaries to US affiliates rose from about two-thirds of total Canadian exports in 1965 to about four-fifths throughout the 1970s.[26] There was considerable variation in intra-firm trade from industry to industry and the total value of it was strongly influenced by the large value of imports and exports on an intra-firm basis since 1965 arising from the Auto Pact.

The disaggregation of the data by type of good is also of

interest. Over one-half of intra-firm exports by US firms to foreign affiliates, according to Lall's interpretation of Bradshaw's results, were finished goods meant for resale without further processing. About one-third was materials and components meant for further processing by the foreign subsidiaries. Less than 10 per cent represented capital equipment and miscellaneous types of transactions. A later study than Bradshaw's found similar percentages by type of good.[27] Moreover, it was found that in the case of exports by Canadian subsidiaries to US affiliates, less than 15 per cent represented finished goods for resale with most of the balance representing material and components meant for further processing.[28]

Comparisons with the ratios used in the next chapter are made easier if the imports and exports are stated in terms of the total shipments of the subsidiaries. It has been estimated by Lall that in 1970, as an average for all manufacturing, intra-firm exports from the US to foreign affiliates represented about 10 per cent of the affiliates' domestic shipments.[29] Combining this result with those in the preceding paragraph leads to the conclusion that imports by foreign subsidiaries in Canada of finished goods for resale from US affiliates represent about 6 per cent of their shipments. Imports of materials and components would represent about 4 per cent of their domestic shipments. Again, Lall found that there was considerable variation in the ratio from industry to industry. For instance, in the machinery and equipment industries purchased more than 15 per cent of their shipments from US affiliates, while the proportion in the beverage industry was less than 1 per cent.

The trade data collected especially for this study were used to calculate the import propensities of the subsidiaries in Canada in as close a manner as possible to those of Lall. On this basis, the foreign-controlled subsidiaries have an average ratio of imports from all sources to domestic shipments of about 30 per cent, excluding the auto sector data (this is about double the ratio for the domestically controlled firms in the manufacturing sector). If Lall's estimate is correct that intra-firm trade represents about one-third of total imports by subsidiaries, then the imports by the subsidiaries in this study from affiliates would be 10 per cent of their shipments, which is also consistent with Lall's estimates. These results suggest the estimates by the Economic Council are somewhat high. However, some of the difference could be due to an increase over the 1970s in imports by subsidiaries in the auto sector from foreign affiliates. It could also be due in part to the Council including purchases from third parties that are tied in some manner to purchases by affiliates from the same suppliers. The Canadian subsidiaries could be required to purchase from specified independent suppliers for such reasons as the need to fill volume-related purchase commitments by the foreign affiliates with these suppliers.

In summary, there is evidence that foreign subsidiaries in Canada have a large cross-trade in finished and intermediate goods and a significant part of this trade is intra-firm with US affiliates (i.e. from about one-third according to Lall to over three-quarters according to the Economic Council). This, of course, should be expected given the network of affiliates and the potential it provides for the subsidiaries to act as wholesalers as well as giving them access to low-cost components produced by affiliates. The exports by the subsidiaries to US affiliates are mainly of unfinished goods meant for further processing in the US while over one-half of imports by the subsidiaries are finished goods purchased for resale in a wholesale capacity. This latter point is important for the analysis in the next chapter.

THE TRANSFER PRICE ISSUE

In a study done for the IMF, Goldsbrough found that price elasticities were significantly lower for intra-firm trade than for conventional trade between third parties.[30] Another study found that foreign-controlled subsidiaries were slower than their Canadian-controlled counterparts in responding to exchange rate changes through increased exports.[31] This suggests that the intra-firm trade between subsidiaries and foreign affiliates has a high propensity to be tied by fiat rather than determined by market forces, so that it is less responsive to being switched to lower-cost sources and potential new markets as exchange rates and prices change. There is a greater propensity to switch purchases to more competitive sources of supply at home and abroad if the transactions are between independent purchasers and suppliers. More research is needed on two related issues arising from this information. One is whether transfer prices between subsidiaries and their affiliates are efficient and competitive. The other is whether purchasing agents in the Canadian subsidiaries are free to engage in global searches for the most

65

competitive sources of supply or are tied by fiat to corporate purchasing decisions.

It is not meant to infer that intra-firm trade is non-competitive *per se*. It is possible that affiliates are the most competitive sources of supply because of benefits from bulk-buying practices when purchasing is centralised in a corporation. Also, foreign affiliates may be more specialised and generally more efficient in producing some finished goods and components than third parties (especially compared to smaller Canadian suppliers). Furthermore, external markets can be used by managers to provide a check on internal transfer prices and the income tax and customs departments regularly monitor transfer prices. And search and transaction costs would probably be lower on intra-firm purchases. In addition, foreign affiliates may be the only source of supply for certain finished goods and specialised components.

The internal dynamics of the MNE also help to ensure that transfer prices are kept in tandem with market prices. The managers of the Canadian subsidiaries are judged, in part, on the profitability of their enterprises. This creates an incentive to purchase from the most competitive source of supply and countervail against any corporate decision to force the subsidiaries to do otherwise. It should be remembered, too, that price is only one dimension of the purchasing decision. Other important ones are the ability to supply items on time, security of supply and product quality. It may be that, in many cases, third-party suppliers are less able to meet these criteria than are the affiliates.

In a recent study, Owen presented evidence that subsidiaries purchase finished goods from US industries that have above-normal profits and their purchases of intermediate goods are sourced from US industries that are not highly concentrated.[32] If high profits are indicative of efficient costs and prices, Owen's information suggests that foreign subsidiaries do purchase from competitive sources of supply, although admittedly the evidence is weak.

It is not intended here to present an apology for the subsidiaries' high levels of intra-firm purchases or their relative lack of responsiveness to price changes. Rather it is to present arguments in defence of these practices that are based on efficient use of resources and to provide an offset to a prevalent attitude that the purchasing practices of the subsidiaries are, *per se*, detrimental to employment and income of the host country. It would seem to be more rational to assume that there are good grounds, based on a desire to maximise profits and to create efficient use of resources, for such behaviour.

Alternatively, it may be that domestically owned manufacturers are not searching widely enough for competitive suppliers and consequently rely too heavily on high-cost domestic sources of supply. In the longer run this, too, would unfavourably affect exports, domestic market share, employment and incomes. A tendency by domestically controlled firms to use domestic suppliers almost exclusively, even if they are high-cost sources, is also a form of tied purchasing if it arises from the use of inadequate search procedures. However, no matter which side of the question one takes, it is apparent that further research is needed on the purchasing practices and behaviour of Canadian manufacturers, whether domestically or foreign-controlled.

SUMMARY

This chapter has shown that the concept of IIT is a useful addition to the tools of analysis of value to those interested in the empirical aspects of international trade. It extends and enriches the understanding and analysis of trade flows provided by traditional concepts in a world where both product differentiation and productivity differences exist on an international basis between firms producing similar goods. It is particularly appropriate for countries such as Canada that have serious productivity and cost problems relative to producers in other parts of the world and that are moving from being small, protected economies to more open ones in a world of increasing competition.

All the major studies show IIT to be a significant proportion of the total international trade flows for Canada. It also appears to influence some industries more than others and to exert its influence at different times for the various industries. But almost all industries appear to have had some degree of IIT over the past twenty years. This is reflected in the simultaneous increase in both the import and export propensities for many industries at the two-digit level of disaggregation. It is also reflected in the pervasive increase in the ratio of purchased material to value-added. The major exceptions are for those industries suffering from severe cost problems which would inhibit their ability to engage in two-way trade. A good example of the relationship between increased scale and specialisation and the level of IIT is provided by the data for the auto sector on the late-1960s and into the 1970s. This suggests that a movement towards freer trade by Canada, particularly with the US, would result in most of the gains accruing to Canadians since our major trading partners have already realised their gains (to a greater or lesser extent) through earlier increases in competition, scale and specialisation.

IIT is related to some extent to the level of DFI in an industry because of the increased opportunity provided to subsidiaries by the network of foreign affiliates. This gives the subsidiaries access to international export markets as well as the opportunity to import low-cost finished and intermediate goods. This creates significant levels of intra-firm trade, which may have some transfer price problems associated with it. It also allows the subsidiaries to carry on extensive wholesale operations relative to their Canadian-controlled counterparts. The high level of intra-firm transactions has a significant impact on the total imports and exports of manufactured goods for Canada. It also contributes to the high elasticity of exports with respect to imports. This is beneficial to Canada and, by extension, to other countries as they move towards freer trade. While imports may rise, so also will exports. In fact, this is demonstrated by the self-sufficiency ratio for Canada, which has remained stable in spite of the large increase in both competition and total trade activity.

In general, while Canada may have been slower in making improvements to production conditions than other industrial nations, there is evidence it is now doing so with consequent increases in the level of IIT. The next chapter will assess the extent of IIT, at a more detailed level than has been done so far, on a cross-section basis for 1979 along with some related analyses of exports and other variables related to increased scale and specialisation on a time-series basis.

NOTES

1. Grubel, H. and P. Lloyd, *Intra-Industry Trade: The Theory and Measurement of International Trade in Differentiated Products* (John Wiley & Sons, New York, 1975).

2. Daly, Keys and Spence, *Scale and Specialization*; and Wonnacott, P. and R. Wonnacott, *US-Canadian Free Trade: The Potential Impact on the Canadian Economy* (The Private Planning Association of Canada, Montreal, 1967). This early work has since been confirmed on an international basis for several products in Scherer, F. *et al.*, *The Economics of Multi-Plant Operation: An International Comparisons Study* (Harvard University Press, Cambridge, Mass., 1975).

3. Alchian, A., 'Costs and Output' in M. Abramovitz (ed.), *The Allocation of Economic Resources* (Stanford University Press, Stanford, 1959); Hirshleifer, J., 'The Firm's Cost Function: A Successful Reconstruction?', *Journal of Business*, vol. XXV, no. 3 (July 1962), pp. 235–54; Keachie, E., *Manufacturing Cost Reduction Through the Curve of Natural Productivity Increase* (University of California, Institute of Business and Economic Research, Berkeley, 1964); Keachie, E. and L. Preston, 'Cost Functions and Progress Functions: An Integration', *American Economic Review* (March 1964), pp. 100–7. For a more recent theoretical integration of these ideas see Alchian, A. and W. Allen, *University Economics* (Wadsworth Publishing Company, Belmont, Calif., 1972), Ch. 15; and Scherer, F., 'Economies of Scale and Industrial Concentration' in H. Goldschmid *et al.*, *Industrial Concentration: The New Learning* (Little, Brown & Co., Boston, 1974) along with other articles in this book. A summary of these themes and their importance for Canadian researchers is contained in Daly, D., 'The Empirical Applicability of the Alchian-Hirshleifer Modern Cost Theory' (York University, undated), mimeograph.

4. Lancaster, K., 'A New Approach to Consumer Theory', *Journal of Political Economy*, vol. 74, no. 2 (April 1966), pp. 123–57.

5. MacDougall, G., 'British and American Exports: A Study Suggested by the Theory of Comparative Costs', *Economic Journal* (December 1951).

6. Greenaway and Milner, 'On the Measurement'.

7. Finger, J., 'Trade Overlap and Intra-Industry Trade', *Economic Inquiry* (December 1975), pp. 581–9. See also US Department of Labor, *Report of the President*. Finger was a major contributor to, and had a significant influence on, this document.

8. Wolf, B., *Canada-US Free Trade: Lessons from the European Experience* (York University, May 1981), mimeograph. This study of the European bearing industry shows that production rationalisation through increased scale and specialisation does result in IIT. Prior to the development of the EEC, SKF had plants in many of the countries that eventually entered into this common market arrangement. The plants in each country produced every variety and size of ball bearing at a high cost for sale mainly into just the domestic market of the county in which a plant was located. After free trade was established between the countries in the common market arrangement, the plants in each country were specialised (partly in response to increased competition from the Japanese) to produce a much smaller range of bearing types that were sold into the much larger total common market. This allowed the plants to capture volume and product-specific economies of scale. The plants imported from foreign affiliates the bearings not produced

69

locally while exporting their major product lines to them. All the different types of bearing were produced by essentially the same factor inputs using much the same factor proportions. The increased scale and specialisation resulted in similar but differentiated bearings being produced and traded on a cross-trade basis within the bearings industry, even by Finger's definition of an industry.

9. Lermer, G., 'Evidence from Trade Data Regarding the Rationalizing of Canadian Industry', *The Canadian Journal of Economics*, vol. 1, no. 2 (May 1973), pp. 248–56.

10. Wilkinson, B., *Canada's International Trade: An Analysis of Recent Trends and Patterns* (The Private Planning Association of Canada, Montreal, 1968).

11. Daly, Keyes and Spence, *Scale and Specialization*.

12. MacCharles, D., *Note on the Updating of Lermer Data* (York University, 1982), mimeograph.

13. Giersch, H., *On the Economics of Intra-Industry Trade* (J. B. Mohr, Tübingen, 1979). The relatively large number of European versus US journal articles and other papers on IIT can be assessed from the references in a recent article by Greenaway and Milner, 'On the Measurement'. In addition, there has been a Canadian book on world product mandating, which is a theme directly related to IIT, by Rugman, A. (ed.), *Multinationals and Technology Transfer: The Canadian Experience* (Praeger, New York, 1983).

14. Greenaway and Milner, 'On the Measurement'.

15. Bergstrand, J., 'The Scope, Growth, and Causes of Intra-Industry International Trade', *New England Economic Review* (September/October 1982), pp. 45–61.

16. Aquino, A., 'Intra-Industry Trade and Inter-Industry Specialization as Concurrent Sources of International Trade in Manufactures', *Weltwirtschaftliches Archiv.*, vol. CXIV (1978), pp. 90–100.

17. Daly and MacCharles, *Canadian Manufatured Exports*; and Baldwin, J. and P. Gorecki, *Entry and Exit to the Canadian Manufacturing Sector* (Economic Council of Canada, Ottowa, 1983). In the Daly and MacCharles study, about 40 percent of the subsidiaries in their small sample of firms were import competers only and their original rationale for staying in Canada as tariffs were reduced was no longer appropriate. Yet, they were staying and attempting to work out adaptive strategies through world product mandates and plant specialisation agreements with affiliates. In the Baldwin and Gorecki study, the subsidiaries did not change their pattern of entering and leaving industries as much as did Canadian-controlled firms when tariffs, growth and profits were declining. This is interpreted here to mean that the subsidiaries were adapting to the new trade environment in Canada, as did the firms in the Daly and MacCharles study, rather than reallocating their resources to new locations and industries. The result, under these circumstances, would be an increase in both exports and imports.

18. Astwood, 'Canada's Merchandise Trade'.

19. The propensities are from Canada, *Manufacturing Trade* and the other data from Canada, *Canada's Trade Performance, 1960–1977*,

Volume 1, General Developments (Industry, Trade and Commerce, Economic Intelligence Group, Ottawa, 1978).

20. Canada, *Manufacturing Trade*.

21. McCulla, D., *Evaluating Measures of Canada's Industry Trade Performance: Comparative Advantage and Competitiveness* (Department of Industry, Trade and Commerce, Ottawa, December 1980), mimeograph, Table 3.19.

22. Lall, S., 'The Pattern of Intra-Firm Exports by U.S. Multinationals', *Oxford Bulletin of Economics and Statistics*, vol. 40, no. 3 (August 1978), pp. 209–22.

23. Bradshaw, M., 'U.S. Exports to Foreign Affiliates of U.S. Firms', *Survey of Current Business* (May 1969), pp. 34–51.

24. Helleiner, G., and R. Lavergne, 'Intra-Firm Trade and Industrial Exports to the United States', *Oxford Bulletin of Economic and Statistics*, vol. XLI, no. 4 (November 1979), pp. 297–311.

25. Economic Council of Canada, *The Bottom Line* (Minister of Supply and Services, Ottawa, 1983). See also Economic Council of Canada, *Au courant*, vol. 4, no. 2 (1983), p. 7.

26. Ibid.

27. Helleiner, G., 'Transnational Corporations and Trade Structure: The Role of Intra-Firm Trade' in H. Giersch (ed.), *On the Economics of Intra-Industry Trade* (J. B. Mohr, Tübingen, 1979), pp. 159–81.

28. Helleiner and Lavergne, 'Intra-Firm Trade'.

29. Lall, 'Pattern of Intra-Firm Exports'.

30. Goldsbrough, D., 'International Trade of Multinational Corporations and Its Responsiveness to Changes in Aggregate and Relative Prices', *IMF Staff Papers*, vol. 28, no. 3 (September 1981), pp. 573–99.

31. Daly and MacCharles, *Canadian Manufactured Exports*.

32. Owen, R., *Trade and Investment: A Disaggregate Study for Canadian Manufacturing* (University of Wisconsin, Madison, 1982), mimeograph.

4

Analysis of Data

INTRODUCTION

This chapter presents an analysis of the data assembled especially for this study. The main data are from the Canadian Census of Manufactures and the international trade statistics for 1979, the latest year for which complete data are available on both import and exports. The emphasis here will be on the trade information, especially as it relates to IIT and the adjustment by Canadian manufacturers to increased competition during the 1970s.

This study provides a major break in several respects with prior ones on Canada's trade, manufacturing and IIT. Firstly, data were collected at the level of the plant (i.e. establishment) and firm (i.e. unconsolidated and consolidated enterprises) before being aggregated up to the level of an industry, rather than being collected initially at the industry level only, as has been past practice. Detailed definitions of the different economic units (i.e. establishment, unconsolidated enterprise and consolidated enterprise) are available elsewhere for the interested reader.[1] Secondly, the trade data have been linked directly to other data on production activities which allows for a much richer analysis. Thirdly, and perhaps most importantly, the data on imports and exports have been matched using plants as the connecting link. This related the data to the micro-economic unit responsible for trade activity as well as ensuring imports and exports were collected using a common nomenclature. It also allowed for the calculation of net trade balances at the level of the firm. Fourthly, data on imports, exports, shipments and other measures of manufacturing activity could be aggregated up to the level of the consolidated enterprise. Fifthly, within an industry, unconsolidated enterprises were allocated to four categories representing different types of trade activity. The four categories are: importer only; exporter only; both importer and exporter; and neither importer nor exporter. This is the first time such a categorisation has been possible.

The matching of trade data at the level of the unconsolidated enterprise was done because, as has already been discussed, IIT is viewed here as resulting from the responses by firms to increased competition. Therefore, it seemed appropriate to assemble the data initially on that economic unit before aggregating up to the level of an industry. This is in distinction to prior studies that used the industry as the economic unit on which to assemble data. One of the problems associated with these other studies, as a result of using this procedure, is that the import nomenclature is different from that for exports. Consequently, the relationship between imports and exports of similar products is not as tightly matched as might be desired. By using common nomenclature and the firm as the link between sources of data, the information used in this analysis is more accurate than has so far been available, as well as being theoretically defensible.

DESCRIPTION OF DATA SOURCES

The Census of Manufactures was the source of information on exports.[2] This information is collected at the level of the plant, or establishment. The source of information for imports was a special study on 1979 trade data by Statistics Canada using the documents prepared at the port of entry.[3] This information is collected at the level of the unconsolidated enterprise. Each establishment is assigned a unique number (BRID code) that connects it to the consolidated enterprise to which it belongs.[4] The BRID identifier allowed the export data collected at the establishment level to be aggregated up to the level of the unconsolidated enterprise where it could be related to the import data collected at this level. Both the import and export data could then be further aggregated to the level of the consolidated enterprise through the use of the BRID identifier.

It was also possible to gather other data from the Census of

Manufactures on shipments, purchased materials and value-added for each establishment and enterprise and relate it to the trade data. The Census data were also useful for calculating other variables of interest to the study, such as indices of product diversity, ratios of imports, exports and shipments of an enterprise's primary group to the total value of its imports, exports and shipments, and the net trade balance for each consolidated enterprise.

In the case of establishments, their shipments and exports were allocated to the commodity categories as reported on the Census form which are based on definitions in the Industrial Classification Code (ICC). The commodity groups were then converted to the appropriate industry codes using the Standard Industrial Classification (SIC) concordance. This information was then matched with other data, such as imports, collected by unconsolidated enterprise and aggregated into 159 industry groups, representing the four-digit SIC industries. Data for consolidated enterprises were allocated to the industry associated with their major product lines, even though some of the shipment and other data were not related to that industry.

The data for each industry were partitioned into several cells. There are two cells for sector of control: Canadian; and foreign-controlled. In the case of unconsolidated enterprises there are two cells for size classes: less than $10 million in shipments; and shipments equal to or greater than $10 million. The consolidated enterprises were allocated to three cells for size classes: less than $10 million in sales; sales equal to or greater than $10 million but less than $50 million; and sales equal to or greater than $50 million. Sales were defined as shipments plus imports (i.e. production value of domestically manufactured output plus goods imported for resale), even though technically inventory change should be taken into account. Most of the data are for 1979, although data were also available on some items such as exports, shipments, purchased materials and value-added (total activity) for 1974. The 1979 Census of Manufactures data covered the universe of establishments since it included those reporting on both the short and long Census forms.

The data for 1979 on shipments, exports and imports for the unconsolidated enterprises were further partitioned into four categories, depending upon the type of trade activity an enterprise was involved in. Since, within a size class, an enterprise could be in either the Canadian or foreign sector of control, eight categories were needed. They were given identifying numbers for purposes of presentation in this analysis. The classification scheme is presented below to aid the reader in relating the identifying numbers to the type of trade activity of the enterprises. Also, throughout the balance of this chapter, imports and exports will be identified with their traditional acronyms of M and X, respectively.

International trade activity of enterprise	Foreign sector	Canadian sector
M only	1	5
X only	2	6
Both X & M	3	7
No X or M	4	8

While there are some mainly minor problems from disaggregating the enterprises into trade-relegated groups (see the section on Import Propensities and Double-count of Enterprises in the Appendix), there are also some advantages. Enterprise groups 3 and 7 ('Both X and M') would tend to be those enterprises engaging in cross-trade of similar products. That is, they are the ones more clearly associated with IIT arising from product specialisation and are the ones of major interest to this study. Enterprise groups 2 and 6 ('X only') would tend to be those enterprises associated with one-way trade normally identified with the HOS model. Enterprise groups 4 and 8 ('No X or M') would tend to be tariff factory enterprises supplying just domestic markets, as would enterprise groups 1 and 5 ('M only'). However, this latter group would also include those enterprises engaging in increased contracting-out as they specialised production activities. Thus, the identification of different types of enterprises within an industry based on their international trade activities provides some insight into trade activity (by size of firm and domicile of its ownership) that has not been possible until now.

OVERVIEW OF THE STATISTICS

This section presents a basic outline of the data by reviewing averages on the major variables for the manufacturing sector as a whole before the detailed analysis is presented. Some preliminary conclusions will be drawn from this overview which will be more formally tested later.

In the following series of tables data are presented in two ways relating to the larger enterprises in the foreign sector of control that are in the 'Both X and M' group of enterprises. One shows the values for a cell, including the automobile and auto parts industries, and is described with the notation 'incl.' to reflect that these industries are included in the data for the relevant variables. The other shows the values excluding the data for these industries and is labelled 'excl.' The reason for presenting both results is that the auto and auto parts industries are significant in terms of shipments, exports and imports, ranging from one-third to one-half of their reported values. In addition, the auto industries are mostly foreign-controlled and no significant counterpart exists in the Canadian sector of control. Consequently it would be misleading to present information on variables that includes these industries when comparisons are being made between the sectors of control.

Table 4.1 presents information on the number of unconsolidated enterprises, by size class and sector of control.

Table 4.1: Number of Unconsolidated Enterprises, by Sector of Control and Size based on Shipments (Manufacturing Sector, 1979)

| Enterprise group | Sector of control | | | | Total |
| | Foreign | | Canadian | | |
	<$10M	>$10M	<$10M	>$10M	
1 and 5	26,093	381	17,141	205	43,820
2 and 6	335	95	2,137	194	2,761
3 and 7 'incl.'	798	718	1,114	443	3,073
3 and 7 'excl.'	798	660	1,114	443	3,015
4 and 8	553	59	25,074	207	25,893
Total 'incl.'	27,779	1,253	45,466	1,049	75,547
Total 'excl.'	27,779	1,195	45,466	1,049	75,489

Source: See text.

Three major points need to be made about the information in Table 4.1. First, the number of unconsolidated enterprises that ship over $10 million is relatively small. Further, by international standards, even shipments of $10 million do not represent a very large manufacturing operation. This reinforces the point made in an earlier chapter that the manufacturing sector is dominated by a relatively large number of small plants by international standards, although a significant proportion of them do not have some type of involvement with international trade (i.e. all but groups 4 and 8). Also, the enterprises in the Canadian sector of control are clustered in group 6 ('X only'), relative to those in the foreign sector of control. This group is associated with one-way trade of the inter-industry type that conforms to the HOS model of trade. The enterprises in the foreign sector of control, however, are clustered more in group 3 ('Both X and M') which is associated with cross-trade conforming to the IIT model of trade.

Second, there is a relatively large number of Canadian-controlled enterprises in group 8 ('No X or M'). These enterprises have no involvement with international trade, except perhaps as minor importers of unfinished and finished goods distantly related to their major product lines. There is no significant counterpart group in the foreign sector of control. This is surprising since one of the expected results, based on the earlier discussion of why subsidiaries are in Canada, was that they would be mainly tariff factories serving just the Canadian market. In fact, by far the larger portion of them are exporters, presumably because of their access to export markets through foreign affiliates. It is the smaller firms in the Canadian sector of control that are insular and not trading in international markets. Also, because they are small, it is likely they are the ones that are high-cost and most vulnerable to increased competition unless they have some natural advantage, such as high freight costs associated with competitors reaching the regional and local markets that many of them serve almost exclusively. In fact, as Table 2.1 showed, in comparison to their larger counterparts, these firms have low productivity and high costs, accounting to a large extent for Canada's cost disadvantage relative to the US, Japan and some other industrial nations.

The third point, which is more of a caveat, is discussed at greater length in the Appendix. It is that there is a relatively large number of enterprises in groups 1 and 5 ('M only'). Much of this is due to the duplicate count of establishments importing components and minor product lines distantly related to their major product lines. As a result they are counted as separate entities in the importing industry and also in the industry of their major product lines. The duplicate count should be relatively higher for the subsidiaries because they have access to low-cost products of foreign affiliates which increases their propensity to import components and minor product lines. In fact, the smaller subsidiaries are heavily represented in this group.

Some understanding of the extent of the duplicate count on the number of enterprises can be obtained by comparing the results in Table 4.1 with those in Table 4.2. The latter shows the count for consolidated enterprises whose imports have been aggregated across the various enterprises and industries into the one firm and industry to which each total firm has been allocated. This eliminates the extra count in distantly related industries that influenced the results shown in Table 4.1.

Table 4.2: Number of Consolidated Enterprises by Sector of Control and Size based on Sales (Manufacturing Sector, 1979)

	Sector of control						Total
	Foreign			Canadian			
	<$10M	$10–50M	>$50M	<$10M	$10–50M	>$50M	
1	842	400	285	26,036	633	157	28,403
2	842	400	261	26,036	633	157	28,379

Note: 1 = 'Incl.'; 2 = 'Excl.'
Source: See text.

The count of small subsidiaries falls from the 27,779 shown in Table 4.1 to 842 in Table 4.2 as a result of eliminating the duplicate count. This decrease is far larger in both relative and absolute terms for the subsidiaries than for the Canadian-controlled firms. This reflects the much more extensive involvement of the subsidiaries in the use of foreign suppliers, both third-party and affiliated, for the sourcing of components and minor product lines.

Table 4.2 also shows the subsidiaries to be concentrated relatively more in the large size class as compared to the Canadian-controlled firms that are more in the intermediate size class. This is so even after adjusting for the greater relative representation of the Canadian-controlled firms in the small size class. It is also worth noting that the large enterprises across both sectors of control would most likely be the ones that are competitive at home and internationally. But they represent less than one-fifth of the total number of enterprises, although they represent a larger proportion of manufactured output, as will be shown below.

Tables 4.3, 4.4, 4.5 and 4.6 present information on the major variables of sales, exports, imports and shipments, respectively, by sector of control and size of enterprise that are a major focus of this study.

Tables 4.3 and 4.6 are very similar because they both have shipments as their dominant subject and their base data. The major point to be taken from these tables is that over one-half of sales and shipments are by the larger unconsolidated enterprises in groups 3 and 7 (i.e. those enterprises engaged in cross-trade). Moreover the subsidiaries account for over twice the value of sales and shipments as do the Canadian-controlled firms

Table 4.3: Sales of Unconsolidated Enterprises (in $ millions), by Sector of Control and Size based on Shipments (Manufacturing Sector, 1979)

Enterprise group	Sector of control				Total
	Foreign		Canadian		
	<$10M	>$10M	<$10M	>$10M	
1 and 5	6,546	12,301	6,454	6,128	31,429
2 and 6	728	3,785	3,762	8,418	16,693
3 and 7 'incl.'	2,663	74,095	3,046	36,894	116,698
3 and 7 'excl.'	2,663	46,339	3,046	36,894	88,942
4 and 8	851	2,402	14,520	4,420	22,193
Total 'incl.'	10,788	92,583	27,782	55,860	187,013
Total 'excl.'	10,788	64,827	27,782	55,860	159,257

Source: See text.

Table 4.4: Exports of Unconsolidated Enterprises (in $ millions), by Sector of Control and Size based on Shipments (Manufacturing Sector, 1979)

Enterprise group	Sector of control				Total
	Foreign		Canadian		
	<$10M	>$10M	<$10M	>$10M	
2 and 6	252	1,860	1,179	2,316	5,607
3 and 7 'incl.'	488	18,819	728	10,549	30,584
3 and 7 'excl.'	488	9,746	728	10,549	21,511
Total 'incl.'	740	20,679	1,907	12,865	36,191
Total 'excl.'	740	11,606	1,907	12,865	27,118

Source: See text.

Table 4.5: Imports of Unconsolidated Enterprises (in $ millions), by Sector of Control and Size based on Shipments (Manufacturing Sector, 1979)

Enterprise group	Sector of control				Total
	Foreign		Canadian		
	<$10M	>$10M	<$10M	>$10M	
1 and 5	4,334	4,183	2,263	1,428	12,208
3 and 7 'incl.'	540	19,919	322	2,436	23,217
3 and 7 'excl.'	540	6,586	322	2,436	9,884
Total 'incl.'	4,874	24,102	2,585	3,864	35,425
Total 'excl.'	4,874	10,769	2,585	3,864	22,092

Source: See text.

Table 4.6: Shipments of Unconsolidated Enterprises (in $ millions), by Sector of Control and Size based on Shipments (Manufacturing Sector, 1979)

Enterprise group	Sector of control				Total
	Foreign		Canadian		
	<$10M	>$10M	<$10M	>$10M	
1 and 5	2,212	8,118	4,191	4,700	19,221
2 and 6	728	3,785	3,762	8,418	16,713
3 and 7 'incl.'	2,122	54,175	2,724	34,458	93,479
3 and 7 'excl.'	2,122	39,753	2,724	34,458	79,057
4 and 8	851	2,402	14,520	4,420	22,193
Total 'incl.'	5,913	68,480	25,197	51,996	151,606
Total 'excl.'	5,913	54,058	25,197	51,996	137,184

Source: See text.

(including the auto industries). To some extent this is because there are relatively more subsidiaries in the larger size class that tend to have larger shipments and sales per enterprise than in the Canadian sector. But, clearly, the major reason for the dominance of the subsidiaries is the enterprises in the auto industries that are mainly foreign-controlled.

The subsidiaries, however, account for a relatively smaller portion of the sales and shipments by enterprise groups 1 and 5 ('M only') in light of the large number of them that are in this group relative to the Canadian sector of control. The Canadian-controlled enterprises represent a relatively large proportion of sales and shipments in groups 2 and 6 ('X only') as well as groups 4 and 8 ('No X or M'), which is consistent with the relatively large number of them in this group, as was noted in Tables 4.1 and 4.2.

Table 4.4 shows that it is mainly the larger firms in both sectors of control that account for the bulk of exports, while at the same time being involved in cross-trade (i.e. groups 3 and 7). Also, although the subsidiaries dominate exports in total, this is not the case after the auto industries are removed from the data. In terms of those enterprises just exporting only (groups 2 and 6), Canadian-controlled firms account for over one-half of the total, although the total amount involved in this group is relatively small compared to total exports. The smaller subsidiaries are virtually not involved in export activity.

Imports, as shown by Table 4.5, are dominated by the subsidiaries across all the groups of enterprises, even after allowing for the influence on the data of the automotive industries. The enterprises in groups 1 and 5 that import only have very sizeable imports, accounting for over one-half of total imports (excluding the auto industries). The subsidiaries are particularly involved with these imports, which would mainly comprise components and minor product lines removed from their major product lines. The reasons for this were discussed when the information in Tables 4.1 and 4.2 was presented, showing a relatively large number of unconsolidated and consolidated subsidiaries in group 1. But, the subsidiaries in trade group 3 also extensively import finished goods related to their major product lines, compared to their counterpart Canadian-controlled enterprises in trade group 7.

In summary of the overall data on trade activity, it is the larger firms that are involved in it and especially the subsidiaries. This appears to reflect the subsidiaries' ability to trade on an intra-firm basis with foreign affiliates in order to acquire components, as well as minor and major product lines at low cost. This access provides an avenue to lower costs that is not available to domestically controlled firms. It also appears to reflect a greater involvement generally with independent foreign suppliers who are also likely to be lower cost than internal production or purchase from domestic suppliers. The use of independent foreign suppliers is an avenue to lower costs open to Canadian-controlled firms, but it appears to have been relatively underutilised. The impact of the import and export trade in

81

autos, trucks and their parts is very large and is dominated by
large foreign MNEs. Domestically controlled firms have very
little involvement in this international trade among the MNEs.

Table 4.7 for unconsolidated enterprises and Table 4.8 for
consolidated enterprises present, on a per-enterprise basis,
average imports, exports and shipments.

The information in Table 4.7 on average shipments for enterprises in groups 1 and 5 ('M only') should be interpreted with
some caution because of the effect that the duplicate count of
unconsolidated enterprises has on the average for the small

Table 4.7: Average Shipments per Unconsolidated Enterprise (in
$ thousands) by Sector of Control and Size based on Shipments
(Manufacturing Sector, 1979)

| Enterprise group | Sector of control | | | |
| | Foreign | | Canadian | |
	<$10M	>$10M	<$10M	>$10M
1 and 5	85	21,307	245	22,927
2 and 6	2,173	39,842	1,760	43,391
3 and 7 'incl.'	2,659	75,452	2,445	77,783
3 and 7 'excl.'	2,659	60,230	2,445	77,783
4 and 8	1,539	40,712	579	21,353
Total 'incl.'	213	54,653	554	45,567
Total 'excl.'	213	45,230	554	49,567

Source: See text.

Table 4.8: Average Shipments per Consolidated Enterprise (in $
thousands) and Total Shipments (in $ millions) by Sector of Control and
Size based on Sales (Manufacturing Sector, 1979)

| | Sector of control | | | | | |
| | Foreign | | | Canadian | | |
	<$10M	$10–50M	>$50M	<$10M	$10–50M	>$50M
Average						
1	2,659	17,100	229,200	818	19,200	278,800
2	2,659	17,100	190,919	818	19,200	278,800
Total						
1	2,239	6,857	65,310	21,298	12,144	43,767
2	2,239	6,857	49,830	21,298	12,144	43,767

Note: 1 = 'Incl.'; 2 = 'Excl.'
Source: See text.

size class. This effect is noticeable particularly for the subsidiaries. Table 4.7 shows their average shipments in total, across all the small enterprise groups, as $213,000, compared to the counterpart average shipments in Table 4.8 of $2,659,000. Also, the average value of shipments for a small, consolidated subsidiary is about thirteen times that for a small, unconsolidated subsidiary. In the Canadian sector of control, the ratio is almost one to one between Tables 4.7 and 4.8 (i.e. $554,000 versus $818,000). Because the subsidiaries are active importers of components and minor product lines across a wide range of industries, the consequent double-count of unconsolidated enterprises reduces their average shipments in comparison with Canadian-controlled enterprises. This difference in average shipments is an indication of the much greater extent to which the subsidiaries are involved in the international sourcing of products and parts.

The comparison of average shipments between the sectors of control shown in Table 4.8 indicates that the smaller foreign-controlled firms in Canada have more plants per consolidated enterprise than do Canadian-controlled firms. Because of this, the smaller subsidiaries would benefit from firm-level economies of scale — more so than their Canadian-controlled counterparts. In conjunction with the access subsidiaries have to their large foreign parents and affiliates, this would give them a considerable management advantage over the small Canadian-controlled plants. This explains part of the productivity difference between the sectors for the smaller plants that was noted in Table 2.6. The small enterprises in the Canadian sector of control appear to be mainly one-plant operations which would put them at a considerable disadvantage in acquiring access to the management expertise, technology and products that are normally associated with larger, firm-level operations. Almost one-third of shipments by Canadian-controlled enterprises are by these small firms, compared to less than 5 per cent for the subsidiaries, which means that a significant portion of output by the Canadian sector is produced under such disadvantages.

Table 4.8 also shows a difference in size between the sectors of control for the biggest consolidated enterprises, with the larger ones being in the Canadian sector. However, because the foreign sector has relatively more large, consolidated enterprises, almost 90 per cent of that sector's shipments are by large enterprises, compared to 60 per cent for the Canadian-controlled enterprises.

Table 4.7 presents a comparison between the sectors of control for the average shipments of unconsolidated enterprises, by trade group. The small, unconsolidated enterprises (or plants) in the foreign sector tend to be smaller than their Canadian-controlled counterparts for groups 1 and 5, but this comparison is misleading because of the duplicate count of firms in the foreign sector, as has already been discussed. There is no appreciable difference between the sectors for the small and large enterprises in groups 2 and 6 ('X only') and groups 3 and 7 ('Both X and M'). Nor is there any significant difference between the sectors for the large enterprises in groups 1 and 3 ('M only'). However, both the small and large subsidiaries that are just serving domestic markets (groups 4 and 8) do appear to be larger than their Canadian-controlled counterparts. Enterprises in this trade category are the most vulnerable to increased competition from imports because of their insularity, with the Canadian-controlled firms being the more vulnerable because of their small size and lack of access to firm-level advantages of scale.

T-tests were performed on the data presented in Table 4.7 to assess the significance of the noted differences. The results are presented in the Appendix, under the heading 'T-tests on Statistics'. Generally, the tests support the statements made above.

Tables 4.9 and 4.10 present information on exports and imports for the consolidated enterprises. The statistics shown are for: total exports and imports; average exports and imports per enterprise; and the ratio of exports and of imports to shipments.

There is no appreciable difference in average exports between the sectors of control in Table 4.9 except for the small enterprises. The small subsidiaries have a propensity to export that is about double that for the Canadian-controlled enterprises. However, the subsidiaries do account for the largest proportion of total exports because of their greater number in the large size class, compared to the Canadian sector. But, if the auto industries are excluded, the export propensity is higher for the Canadian sector of control. Also, the large enterprises in both sectors of control account for over three-quarters of total exports. Their export propensities, at about one-quarter of shipments, are significantly higher than for the small and intermediate size firms. The export performance of the large enterprises indicates they are more competitive internationally than

Table 4.9: Average Exports (in $ thousands), Total Exports (in $ millions) and Exports as a Percentage of Shipments for Consolidated Enterprises, by Sector of Control and Size based on Sales (Manufacturing Sector, 1979)

		Sector of control				
		Foreign			Canadian	
	<$10M	$10−50M	>$50M	<$10M	$10−50M	>$50M
Average						
1	310	2,980	70,050	50	3,050	72,060
2	310	2,980	37,510	50	3,050	72.060
Total						
1	262	1,191	19,966	1,371	2,088	11,314
2	262	1,191	9,970	1,371	2,088	11,314
Per cent						
1	12	17	31	6	17	26
2	12	17	20	6	17	26

Note: 1 = 'Incl.'; 2 = 'Excl.'

Source: See text.

Table 4.10: Average Imports (in $ thousands), Total Imports (in $ millions) and Imports as a Percentage of Shipments for Consolidated Enterprises, by Sector of Control and Size based on Sales (Manufacturing Sector, 1979)

		Sector of control				
		Foreign			Canadian	
	<$10M	$10−50M	>$50M	<$10M	$10−50M	>$50M
Average						
1	710	6,010	91,160	26	1,850	29,350
2	710	6,010	41,965	26	1,850	29,350
Total						
1	598	2,407	25,982	678	1,176	4,607
2	598	2,407	10,953	678	1,176	4,607
Per cent						
1	26	35	40	3	10	11
2	26	35	22	3	10	11

Note: 1 = 'Incl.'; 2 = 'Excl.'

Source: See text.

the smaller firms. This contrast in export performance is particularly noticeable in relation to the small firms in the Canadian sector of control. The small Canadian-controlled firms have the weakest performance on export activity, with an export propensity about one-quarter that of the large firms, and they are outperformed by even the small subsidiaries who have a propensity double that of their Canadian-controlled counterparts. This indicates that the small Canadian-controlled firms are the ones having the greatest difficulty in being internationally competitive and the difference in export performance with even the small subsidiaries that have access to foreign affiliates suggests part of their problem concerns marketing and is related to their lack of access to international marketing channels.

Table 4.10 shows the subsidiaries import more in total and per consolidated enterprise than firms in the Canadian sector of control. Also, in distinction to the Canadian-controlled firms, the subsidiaries import more than they export on a per enterprise basis and in total across all the size classes. Almost three-quarters of imports are by the large enterprises in both sectors of control even after removing auto industry imports by the subsidiaries. The consolidated enterprises in the foreign sector of control import far more than their Canadian-controlled counterparts on a per enterprise basis and in total. Consequently, all the import propensitites of the subsidiaries are higher than for their counterparts in the Canadian sector of control. This reflects, in part, the access the subsidiaries have to the unfinished and finished products of their foreign affiliates as well as their greater use of independent foreign suppliers. Presumably, the extensive use by the subsidiaries of imported items in place of domestically produced ones sourced either from domestic third-party suppliers or from internal production in Canada, is because it is efficient to do so. However, it is worth noting here (because this point will be picked up later in this chapter) that as the subsidiaries become larger their relative dependence on foreign sources of supply declines (excluding the auto industries), whereas it increases for the Canadian-controlled firms. The evidence for this is in the declining import propensity between the small and the large subsidiaries and the increasing propensity between the small and large firms in the Canadian sector of control. It should also be noted that these propensities are for consolidated enterprises, using total shipments of the enterprise rather than just those of the industry to which the imported goods belong.

Table 4.11 shows net trade balances (i.e. exports minus imports) for the consolidated enterprises. They are presented as an unweighted average of the 159 industry propensities, disaggregated by sector of control and size of enterprise.

Table 4.11: Unweighted Average of Net Trade Balances as a Percentage of Sales; Consolidated Enterprises for 159 Industries, by Sector of Control and Size based on Sales (Manufacturing Sector, 1979)

	Sector of control				
	Foreign			Canadian	
<$10M	$10–50M	>$50M	<$10M	$10–50M	>$50M
(10)	(18)	(9)	3	7	15

Source: See text.

The net trade balances for the subsidiaries are negative (i.e. imports exceed exports), while those for the domestically controlled firms are positive. This is because of the high import propensities of the subsidiaries. However, the relatively low import propensities for the Canadian-controlled enterprises may not necessarily be desirable. They could be the result of inefficient purchasing practices if the Canadian-controlled firms are limiting their search for suppliers to just Canadian firms or their own internal production. Since these sources would tend to be at higher cost than foreign ones, such a practice could be harmful to the longer-run competitiveness of Canadian-controlled firms. The low export propensities of the small Canadian-controlled enterprises, coupled with their low import propensities, suggest they are inward-looking and perhaps not using the lowest-cost sources of supply. T-tests were performed on the data presented in Table 4.11 to assess the significance of the noted differences. The results are presented in the Appendix, under the heading 'T-tests on Statistics'. The tests support the statements made above.

Tables 4.12 and 4.13 present information on average exports and imports, per unconsolidated enterprise, that have been disaggregated by trade category, size and sector of control of the enterprises. The export and import propensities are calculated using shipments as the denominator. These propensities are not directly comparable to those in Tables 4.9 and 4.10 because of their further disaggregation by trade category. Also, the propensities in Tables 4.9 and 4.10 are for consolidated enterprises, while those in Tables 4.12 and 4.13 are for unconsolidated enterprises. Import and export propensities of the consolidated enterprises are calculated using their total shipments across all the industries in which they operate, whereas those for the unconsolidated enterprises are calculated using just their shipments in the individual industries of their plants.

Table 4.12: Average Exports (in $ thousands) per Unconsolidated Enterprise and Exports as Percentage of Shipments by Trade Category, Sector of Control and Size based on Shipments (Manufacturing Sector, 1979)

Enterprise group	Sector of control			
	Foreign		Canadian	
	<$10M	>$10M	<$10M	>$10M
Average				
2 and 6	750	19,578	600	11,938
3 and 7 'incl.'	611	26,210	653	23,813
3 and 7 'excl.'	611	14,766	653	23,813
Per cent				
2 and 6	35	49	31	28
3 and 7 'incl.'	23	35	27	31
3 and 7 'excl.'	23	25	27	31

Source: See text.

Several new points of information in relation to the smaller enterprises are provided by Table 4.12, compared to those already noted in relation to Table 4.9. First, the difference in average exports per enterprise between the sectors of control is considerably narrower. Second, the export propensity for the small Canadian-controlled enterprises that are in group 2 ('X only') is higher and declines for the large enterprises. However, in the case of the subsidiaries, it increases from the small to the large ones. Third, the increase in the propensity from the small to the large subsidiaries in group 3 ('Both X and M') is largely a result of the influence of the large, export-oriented subsidiaries in the auto industries. These differences were masked in the data presented in Table 4.9 because of the dominance of groups 3 and 7 on total exports.

Table 4.13: Average Imports (in $ thousands) per Unconsolidated Enterprise and Imports as Percentage of Shipments by Trade Category, Sector of Control and Size based on Shipments (Manufacturing Sector, 1979)

Enterprise group	Sector of control			
	Foreign		Canadian	
	<$10M	>$10M	<$10M	>$10M
Average				
1 and 5	166	10,979	132	6,966
3 and 7 'incl.'	677	27,742	289	5,499
3 and 7 'excl.'	677	9,970	289	5,499
Per cent				
1 and 5	86	6	21	3
3 and 7 'incl.'	25	37	12	7
3 and 7 'excl.'	25	17	12	7

Source: See text.

It is not immediately apparent why the export performance of the specialised exporters in the Canadian sector of control declines as they become larger while the performance of the subsidiaries improves. It may be a result of a lower ability to gain access to foreign markets, relative to the subsidiaries who can utilise foreign affiliates. This does not appear to be the case for the Canadian-controlled enterprises in groups 3 and 7, however. The substantial increase in the export propensity of the subsidiaries in group 3 when the automotive industries are added to the data suggests that free trade arrangements result in subsidiaries specialising on an intra-firm basis, improving their competitiveness and export performance.

In the case of the import propensities for enterprise groups 1 and 5 ('M only') shown in Table 4.13, the narrow market definition was used (see the Appendix for details) which excludes shipments by trade groups 4 and 8 (no 'X' or 'M') from the denominator of the calculation. This improves the degree of comparability in the data between the sectors of control. However, two anomalies still remain in the data that distort the inter-sector comparisons. One is the greater propensity of the subsidiaries to import components and minor product lines distantly related to their major product lines, which results in a double-count of them in group 1 relative to the Canadian-controlled enterprises in group 5. The other bias (extent unknown)

89

is due to shipments of major product lines by importing enterprises being put in an industry other than the one to which the
imports of minor products and components have been allocated.
This would have two effects. One is that the imports of minor
products and components would be allocated to enterprises in a
smaller size class than the one to which the overall corporation
belongs. The other is that the denominator of the import propensities for trade groups 1 and 5, which are calculated using
shipments, would be understated because the shipments of many
of the enterprises doing the importing have been allocated to
another industry representing their major product lines. Both
these measurement problems would be greater for the foreign
than for the Canadian sector of control because of its relatively
larger imports of minor products and components. These
anomalies in the data explain a large part of the difference in
import propensities between the sectors of control for trade
groups 1 and 5.

In order to make a partial assessment of the effects of these
biases between the sectors of control, the imports in groups 1
and 5 were summed across the two size classes within each sector
of control and taken as a ratio of the non-auto shipments using
the narrow market definition. The resulting import propensities
are 15 per cent for the subsidiaries and 6 per cent for the
Canadian-controlled enterprises. It is stressed again, however,
that a lower propensity does not necessarily imply efficient purchasing practices if the reason for it is inadequate search procedures for potential low-cost suppliers, including foreign ones.
It is clear, however, that no matter how the data are adjusted to
remove noncomparabilities between the sectors, the subsidiaries
have the higher import propensities and higher imports per
enterprise, relative to firms in the Canadian sector of control.
This is so even if the auto industries are removed from the comparisons, although doing so does considerably reduce the difference in the import propensity and the average imports per
enterprise between the sectors for groups 3 and 7.

Table 4.14 provides some information on the degree of
specialisation by consolidated enterprises in each of the sectors
of control, disaggregated by their size. The measures are: the
ratio of primary products shipped to total shipments; the ratio
of primary products exported to total exports; and the ratio of
imports of primary products to total products imported. The
values shown in Table 4.14 are the unweighted averages for the

Table 4.14: Unweighted Averages of Shipments, Exports and Imports of Major Product Lines as Percentage of Total Shipments, Exports and Imports; Consolidated Enterprises by 159 Industries, by Sector of Control and Size based on Sales (Manufacturing Sector, 1979)

| | Sector of control | | | | | |
| | Foreign | | | Canadian | | |
	<$10M	$10-50M	>$50M	<$10M	$10-50M	>$50M
Shipments						
Incl.	90	82	68	94	85	59
Excl.	90	82	65	94	85	59
Exports						
Incl.	94	88	75	94	90	58
Excl.	94	88	69	94	90	58
Imports						
Incl.	40	47	37	52	35	21
Excl.	40	47	37	52	35	21

Source: See text.

159 industries. The small subsidiaries are somewhat less specialised in the products they ship than are the Canadian-controlled enterprises. However, in this size class the consolidated enterprises in the foreign sector have more plants per firm than those in the Canadian sector of control. Consequently, the subsidiaries could be shipping a wider variety of products but their plants could be more specialised than those of their domestically controlled counterparts. In the case of the large subsidiaries, they are more specialised across all three variables than are the firms in the Canadian sector of control, even after removing the influence of the auto industries.

The small subsidiaries are also less specialised in imports. This reflects their higher propensity to import components and minor product lines distantly related to their major product lines. However, the subsidiaries increase their specialisation in imports as they become larger and for the large ones are more specialised than their Canadian-controlled counterparts. At the same time, the Canadian-controlled enterprises decrease their specialisation in imports as they become larger. It appears the Canadian-controlled enterprises increasingly contract-out to foreign suppliers their requirements for components and minor product lines as they become larger and have a more extensive degree of use of foreign suppliers than the large subsidiaries or the small

91

enterprises in the Canadian sector of control. This is consistent with their using more efficient search procedures for suppliers and increased contracting-out to them as they become larger. This point will be drawn on later in the chapter.

There is a significant increase in the diversity of products shipped, as well as of exports, by the enterprises in the Canadian sector of control as they become larger. Eventually, the products of the large firms are more diverse than those of the small firms and even of the large subsidiaries. This would contribute to these firms having product-specific diseconomies of scale unless their individual plants are specialised. But if the plants are specialised, then they could have diseconomies of scale because of their small size. It is known that relative to the subsidiaries, Canadian-controlled firms stress product development in their R&D rather than the development of cost-reducing technologies.[5] In the longer run this would tend to make them diverse in their output and exports as well as higher cost than more specialised producers because of the product-specific diseconomies of scale associated with diversity.

T-tests were performed on the data underlying the variables presented in Table 4.14 to assess the significance of the noted differences. The results are presented in the Appendix, under the heading 'T-tests on Statistics'. The tests support the statements made above in relation to Table 4.14.

Table 4.15 provides information on import and export propensities, but just for the major product lines of the consolidated enterprises. They can be compared to the propensities shown in Tables 4.9 and 4.10.

A major difference is apparent between the large enterprises in both sectors of control when the exports and export propensities of Table 4.9 are compared to those in Table 4.15 for major products. This is further evidence to that presented in relation to Table 4.14 in which the firms appeared to become more diverse in their exports as they became larger, rather than becoming more specialised. This is especially so for the large Canadian-controlled enterprises since the gap is largest for them, suggesting that the Canadian-controlled enterprises become more diversified than the subsidiaries in their exports as they become larger. It also appears, based on the lack of a difference between the two tables in the export propensities for the small firms in both sectors of control, that the small firms are highly specialised in their exports and do not export minor product

Table 4.15: Unweighted Averages of Exports and Imports of Major Product Lines as Percentage of Total Shipments; Consolidated Enterprises by 159 Industries, by Sector of Control and Size based on Sales (Manufacturing Sector, 1979)

| | Sector of control | | | | | |
| | Foreign | | | Canadian | | |
	<$10M	$10–50M	>$50M	<$10M	$10–50M	>$50M
Exports						
Incl.	11	15	23	6	15	15
Excl.	11	15	14	6	15	15
Imports						
Incl.	11	16	15	2	3	2
Excl.	11	16	8	2	3	2

Source: See text.

lines. But, for the large firms the difference increases to 6 per cent of shipments for the subsidiaries and 11 per cent for the Canadian-controlled firms, after adjusting for the influence of the auto industries on the statistics.

Adjusting for the exports of the auto industries has a large impact on the export propensity for the large subsidiaries as is shown by Table 4.15 where the propensity to export major product lines falls from 23 per cent of total exports to 14 per cent after the adjustment. This indicates that the proportion of major product lines exported by subsidiaries in the auto industries is higher than the average. That is, they are specialised in major product lines that are exported, rather than being like the other subsidiaries that export minor product lines to a greater extent. Other than this, the large subsidiaries are no different in terms of their degree of specialisation in major product lines exported than are the large firms in the Canadian sector of control (after adjusting for the auto industries). However, the small subsidiaries have a propensity to export major product lines that is almost twice as great as for their counterparts in the Canadian sector of control. This suggests the small subsidiaries benefit from their access to foreign affiliates by being able to use them to sell major product lines into international markets and can do so more readily than Canadian-controlled enterprises that do not have similar access to international marketing channels.

The difference in the import propensities of Table 4.10 and those of Table 4.5 for imports of just major product lines

93

increases significantly as the Canadian-controlled enterprises become larger. There is no such difference for the subsidiaries as they become larger (after adjusting for the auto industries). This indicates the subsidiaries start at and stay at a high level of imported components and minor product lines from foreign suppliers, while Canadian-controlled enterprises start at a lower level and increase it as they become larger. This interpretation is also consistent with the one for Table 4.14. That is, the Canadian-controlled firms increase the efficiency of their purchasing practices as they become larger and source more internationally relative to their use of domestic suppliers.

The influence of the auto industries on import propensities for the large subsidiaries is significant and increases the difference in them between Tables 4.10 and 4.15. In addition, the increase in the propensity between the 'incl.' and 'excl.' values is greater for total imports than for imports of just major product lines. That is, the diversity of minor products and components from foreign suppliers is significantly increased. This is attributed to the auto producers extensively importing parts and components from more efficient US suppliers. It appears the subsidiaries in the auto industries are highly diversified in their imports of components and minor product lines but highly specialised in the export of their major product lines (as was noted above in the results for Table 4.14), giving them the best of both worlds. That is, they enjoy the cost advantages of sourcing from the most efficient suppliers internationally along with the cost advantages of being specialised in their shipments and exports.

Table 4.15 shows that enterprises in the Canadian sector of control import a significantly lower proportion of their major product lines than do counterpart subsidiaries. Again, this reflects the enhanced ability of the subsidiaries to purchase for resale in Canada the finished goods of foreign affiliates. The difference is not great between Tables 4.10 and 4.15 on the import propensities of the small firms in the Canadian sector of control (i.e. one per cent). This suggests these small firms source very little of their components and minor products from abroad. The low value of the propensity in Table 4.15 also suggests they do not import very much in the way of major product lines either and this applies to all size classes. These results are in contrast to the small subsidiaries that have a large difference in the propensities between the tables (i.e. 15 per cent), apparently because they utilise foreign suppliers extensively for components and minor product lines. The higher value for the propensity in Table 4.15 also suggests they import major product lines more extensively than their Canadian-controlled counterparts, although the relative level of this activity decreases as the subsidiaries become larger (excluding the auto industries). This decrease could reflect the greater use of domestic suppliers and internal production to displace imports of finished goods as the subsidiaries become larger.

SUMMARY OF OVERVIEW OF TRADE DATA

One of the major points that emerges in the above discussion is that the bulk of exports and imports by Canadian manufacturers is by a relatively small number of large enterprises that simultaneously import and export their products. Their large size likely accounts, to some extent, for their success in international markets. But, by international standards, many of even the large firms are small-scale producers. In addition, there is a relatively large number of manufacturers that appear to be inward-looking, serving just domestic markets with their products and not engaging substantially in the international sourcing of purchased inputs. Their small size may have something to do with their lack of export success, since this would impose a cost penalty on them.

The subsidiaries are major importers of finished and unfinished goods, probably with a significant proportion on an intra-firm basis. They also have an extensive wholesale activity in finished goods for which there is no counterpart activity by firms in the Canadian sector of control. By being able to source internationally, the subsidiaries are likely to be acquiring inputs at a lower cost than if they were produced in Canada, either by themselves or by domestic suppliers. The small Canadian-controlled enterprises do not source very much from foreign suppliers in comparison to the subsidiaries. This could be undesirable if it prevents them from getting components and products at the lowest possible cost. Enterprises in the auto industries provide an insight into how firms attempting to be internationally cost-competitive through rationalisation would influence Canadian trade data. There would be an increased level of cross-trade in finished and unfinished goods that would increase both import and export propensities. Such producers, by becoming larger and more specialised, would import a greater variety of components and minor product lines while at the same time specialising in their major product lines for export.

Firms that just supply the domestic market as import competers are mainly Canadian-controlled rather than tariff-factory subsidiaries. Also, the subsidiaries in this group tend to be larger than their Canadian-controlled counterparts. The Canadian-controlled enterprises that do engage in international trade tend to be somewhat larger than the subsidiaries, but more diversified in the products they produce and export. The small subsidiaries also tend to be part of multi-plant firms whereas the Canadian-controlled firms tend to be one-plant enterprises. This would give the subsidiaries the benefits of firm-level economies of scale as well as the benefits of having access to the management expertise, technology and products of their parents and affiliates. The combination of these factors helps to explain why they are more productive and lower-cost (as was noted in Chapter 2) than their counterparts in the Canadian sector of control. The small subsidiaries also outperform the small Canadian-controlled firms in terms of exports, probably because of the easier access they have to international markets through their foreign affiliates, along with lower costs for components and minor product lines acquired from them. The impact of the transportation industries (mainly foreign-controlled) on international trade flows is very significant.

EXPORT ACTIVITY, 1974–9

Data on exports were available for both 1974 and 1979 so that, unlike the situation with respect to imports for which only 1979 data are available, it was possible to test for differences in the ratio of exports to shipments over this time period. The 1974 data on exports were not partitioned into size classes or enterprise groups for the exporting establishments. Therefore, in order to be consistent, the 1979 data were aggregated across the size and enterprise groups in arriving at the total ratio, by sector of control, for an industry. Note that in this case the ratio is based on the wide-market definition, which includes the shipments of all the enterprise groups including groups 4 and 8 ('No X or M'). It should also be noted that the data used here are from the Census of Manufactures which is based on the establishment as the reporting unit.

96

Each of the 159 industries in each year were allocated to one of two categories representing the type of international trade that dominated in an industry (i.e. IIT or non-IIT). The definition and basis for allocating industries to the IIT and non-IIT categories are described more fully in the Appendix under the section 'The IIT Indices', to which the reader is referred. But, for purposes of this present discussion, it is only necessary to note that one category represents those industries in which there is significant IIT (i.e. those industries with a two-way flow of similar goods) and the other in which non-IIT is significant (industries with one-way trade flows of the HOS type). A variant of the Grubel and Lloyd index was used to allocate the industries to one of these two categories. The T-tests were for significant differences in the ratio of exports to shipments between the sectors of control for both 1974 and 1979 (inter-sector tests) and between the years 1974 and 1979 for each sector (intra-sector tests). The results of the tests are presented in Table 4.16, for the 159 industries.

For the inter-sector tests on the IIT industries, both sectors of control show an increase in the export propensity between 1974 and 1979. It should be noted, however, that there is a different mix of industries in the trade categories between the two years so that some of the change in the propensity could be attributable to this factor. In 1974, the foreign sector shows an average propensity of 13.7 per cent versus 9.9 per cent for the Canadian sector of control. In 1979, the comparable values are 16.0 per cent and 16.3 per cent. In 1974, the difference in the propensity between the sectors was statistically significant (at the 0.05 level), but this was not so in 1979. This is attributed to a larger increase in export propensity by the Canadian sector between 1974 and 1979. The R^2 of the correlation of the ratio between the sectors of control is higher in 1979 than in 1974 as is also the slope of the correlation. That is, the variation in the export propensities between the sectors of control diminished between 1974 and 1979 while the correspondence between the industries active in exporting had increased for the two sectors. Both of these results are consistent with the Canadian sector of control having a larger increase in its export propensities than the foreign sector and in the same industries in which the subsidiaries initially had higher ratios. This result is important, at least for those industries in which IIT is a significant part of total trade since it shows enterprises in the Canadian sector of control had caught

Table 4.16: Results of T-tests on Ratio of Exports to Shipments per Unconsolidated Enterprise, based on Establishment-level Data between Sectors of Control and Years 1974 and 1979; by Trade Category for 159 Industries (Manufacturing Sector)

Description	IIT		non-IIT		IIT		non-IIT		IIT		non-IIT		IIT		non-IIT	
	Fgn.79	Fgn.74	Fgn.79	Fgn.74	Cdn.79	Cdn.74	Cdn.79	Cdn.74	Fgn.79	Fgn.74	Fgn.79	Fgn.74	Cdn.74	Cdn.74	Fgn.74	Cdn.74
Number of industries	79	79	80	80	44	44	115	115	44	44	115	115	70	70	89	89
Unweighted averages (per cent)	17.4	12.8	10.9	13.2	16.3	11.6	10.8	8.5	16.0	16.3	13.5	10.8	13.7	9.7	12.5	9.1
Significance of T-test	0		0.20		0.01		0		0.89		0.04		0.05		0.03	
R^2 of correlation	0.81		0.50		0.42		0.75		0.38		0.59		0.18		0.47	
Slope of correlation	1.03		0.64		0.72		0.96		0.91		0.88		0.69		0.89	

Note: IIT = all industries with a MINDF, MINDC or MINDT index >0.1; non-IIT = all industries with a MINDF, MINDC or MINDT index <0.1.
Source: See text and Appendix.

up to the export performance of the subsidiaries. Although it represents only one indication of a faster response over the 1970s by Canadian-controlled firms to the changing trade environment, it is consistent with other similar conclusions that will be noted later in this chapter.

On the intra-sector comparisons, both sectors of control had an increase in the ratio of exports to shipments between 1974 and 1979. The ratio for the subsidiaries went from 12.3 per cent to 17.4 per cent while that for the Canadian-controlled establishments went from 11.6 per cent to 16.3 per cent. The same IIT industries were used in each of the two years being compared, within a sector of control, for the intra-sector comparisons being discussed here. However, there is a different mix and number of industries in these tests than for the inter-sector comparisons discussed above. As a result, the intra-sector comparisons show a significant increase in the export propensity for *both* sectors of control between 1974 and 1979 and they are both statistically significant even though for the inter-sector comparisons only the Canadian sector had a significant increase in the ratio. The inter-sector comparison provides the more accurate result.[6] The increase in the export propensity between 1974 and 1979 for the non-IIT industries was not as great as it was for the IIT industries and while the export propensity did rise for the Canadian sector of control it declined for the foreign sector.

TESTS ON THE IMPORT AND EXPORT PROPENSITIES

T-tests on the import and export propensities used various combinations of partitions in the data to address the different questions of interest to this study. One set of questions is whether the propensities differ between size classes; sectors of control; and trade groups. Another set of questions is whether the export propensities within a sector of control increase commensurate with the import propensities across the industries, for the different trade groups and size classes. These questions will now be addressed.

The export and import propensities for trade groups 3 and 7 ('Both X and M') will receive particular emphasis. The enterprises in these trade groups are involved in IIT as indicated by their extensive involvement in cross-trade of similar goods. The results for the larger firms will also be emphasised since they account for a significant part of the total trade in manufactured exports and imports. The trade propensities for the enterprises in trade categories 3 and 7 are partitioned by size group and by sector of control within each industry and are identified by the acronyms EXSH3 and IMSH3 for the foreign sector, and EXSH7 and IMSH7 for the Canadian sector of control. The acronyms stand for *ex*port and *im*port *sh*ares of domestic production and consumption, respectively, for an industry. The numerical suffixes identify the major type of trade activity by the enterprises in the trade groups.

Import and export propensities by industry were calculated for the other trade groups as well, using the same partitions of industry, sector of control and size classes as for trade groups 3 and 7. The propensities for trade groups 2 and 6 ('X only') are identified by the acronyms EXSH2 for the foreign sector of control and EXSH6 for the Canadian sector of control. Similarly, the acronyms for the propensities of trade groups 1 and 5 ('M only') are IMSH1 for the foreign sector of control and IMSH5 for the Canadian sector of control.

In addition to the propensities partitioned by trade groups within an industry, total propensities for each industry were also calculated. These statistics are based on the total imports and exports for an industry, as determined by summing them over all the trade groups within a particular partition of sector of control and size class. The acronyms used to identify them are EXSH23 and IMSH13 for the foreign sector of control and EXSH67 and IMSH57 for the Canadian sector of control.

It is worth noting again, even though the issue is discussed more fully in the Appendix, that any of the import propensities using data from trade groups 1 and 5 can have two different values. This is because their denominators can take either of two values for the size of the domestic market, depending upon whether the narrow- or wide-market definition is used. The narrow-market definition excludes the shipments of enterprise groups 4 and 8 ('No X or M') in the denominators of the propensities, whereas the wide-market definition includes them. This means there are two variations on the import propensities that could be used in any particular T-test. Only the tests based on the narrow-market definition are presented here because of the similarity of the results no matter which definition is used.[7] The export propensities are invariant in their calculation and include in their denominators just the shipments of the enterprises in the trade group being analysed.

The particular G&L index and its critical value used in the following tests to allocate industries to the IIT and non-IIT categories is described in the Appendix under the headings 'The IIT Indices' and 'Critical Values for the Indices'.

T-tests on import propensities

The results of T-tests on the import propensities are discussed first. They are presented in Tables 4.17 and 4.18 for the small and large enterprises, respectively. The industries have been allocated to either an IIT or non-IIT category, using the critical value of 0.10 for the MINDT index to do so. As already noted, the propensities used in these tests are based on the narrow-market definition.

For the smaller firms, Table 4.17 shows an unweighted average import propensity of 26.0 per cent for the subsidiaries that are involved in the cross-trade of major product lines and that are in industries extensively involved in IIT (IMSH3). The counterpart propensity for the non-IIT industries is 17.4 per cent. The T-tests on the import propensities of enterprises in trade group 3 include 96 per cent of their imported goods, of which 89 per cent are associated with the IIT industries. The subsidiaries in IIT industries also have a significantly higher unweighted average import propensity than their counterparts in the Canadian sector of control (IMSH7). In the case of the Canadian-controlled enterprises in trade group 7, the T-tests include 99 per cent of their imports, with 85 per cent being associated with IIT industries.

These results for the IIT industries are consistent with those already noted before when the overview of the trade data was presented. In that discussion it was noted the subsidiaries would be expected to have higher import propensities for manufactured goods than Canadian-controlled firms because they have access to the products of their foreign affiliates and as a result have more opportunity to act as wholesalers of items purchased just for resale. In the case of the non-IIT industries, where there is no significant difference in the import propensities between the sectors of control for cross-traded goods (IMSH3 and IMSH7), it appears the subsidiaries do not have an extensive wholesale function and behave more like their counterparts in

101

Table 4.17: Results of T-tests on Import Propensities between Sectors of Control; for Unconsolidated Enterprises with Shipments <$10 million, by Trade Groups and Categories (Manufacturing Sector, 1979)

Description	IIT		non-IIT		IIT		non-IIT		IIT		non-IIT	
	IMSH3	IMSH7	IMSH3	IMSH7	IMSH1	IMSH5	IMSH1	IMSH5	IMSH13	IMSH57	IMSH13	IMSH57
Number of industries	61	61	41	41	77	77	69	69	77	77	69	69
Per cent of imports in trade group in T-test	89	85	7	14	81	76	19	23	82	77	18	22
Unweighted averages (per cent)	26.02	15.8	17.4	17.8	51.8	33.1	42.2	17.2	57.1	36.1	44.4	18.0
Significance of T-test	0		0.94	0	0		0		0		0	
R^2 of correlation	0.15		0		0.27		0.21		0.34		0.21	
Slope of correlation	0.46		0.06		0.45		0.67		0.50		0.68	

Note: IIT = MINDT >0.10; non-IIT = MINDT <0.10.

Source: See text and Appendix.

the Canadian sector. However, the enterprises in trade groups 3 and 7 that are in non-IIT industries account for only a small portion of the total imports of major product lines by enterprises in these trade groups.

The small subsidiaries in trade group 1 ('M only'), whether in IIT or non-IIT industries, have significantly higher import propensities than their Canadian-controlled counterparts (IMSH1 and IMSH5). The T-tests on these trade groups included virtually all of the imports by the small enterprises. The types of goods imported by firms in these trade groups tend to be components and minor product lines removed from a major product lines of the importing enterprises. The difference in propensities reflects a much greater tendency for the subsidiaries to use foreign sources of supply, presumably because they are lower cost than if the goods were produced in Canada by the subsidiaries or purchased from domestic suppliers. The tendency on the part of subsidiaries to use foreign suppliers also influences the total import propensities (IMSH13 versus IMSH57), because the value of components and minor product lines they import is large relative to the imports of both major products and to total imports. Consequently, the difference between the sectors of control for total imports remains significant and the subsidiaries have the higher propensities.

To summarise the information provided by Table 4.17, the major difference between the sectors of control for smaller firms appears to be the extensive wholesale role of these subsidiaries trading products internationally on a two-way basis. The counterpart wholesale activity by the Canadian sector of control is undertaken by firms in the distribution sectors, so that the comparisons between the sectors of control in just manufacturing is biased by understating imports for the Canadian-controlled firms. In addition, the subsidiaries do import relatively more minor products and components than the firms in the Canadian sector of control, presumably because they engage in more contracting-out of small-run products and components to foreign suppliers, including their affiliates. These activities are consistent with the subsidiaries being specialised in the products and production activities they undertake in Canada, at least until they become larger enterprises (as is discussed in relation to the next table).

Table 4.18 presents the same information as Table 4.17, except that it is for the larger enterprises. Since these larger firms are

103

Table 4.18: Results of T-tests on Import Propensities between Sectors of Control; for Unconsolidated Enterprises with Shipments >$10 million, by Trade Groups and Categories (Manufacturing Sector, 1979)

Description	IIT		non-IIT		IIT		non-IIT		IIT		non-IIT	
	IMSH3	IMSH7	IMSH3	IMSH7	IMSH1	IMSH5	IMSH1	IMSH5	IMSH13	IMSH57	IMSH13	IMSH57
Number of industries	57	57	23	23	42	42	22	22	64	64	36	36
Per cent of imports in trade group in T-test	70	88	1	9	65	79	5	14	74	86	2	13
Unweighted averages (per cent)	21.7	13.5	8.4	3.5	9.3	10.7	12.5	13.8	26.4	17.1	12.7	11.2
Significance of T-test	0		0.29		0.68		0.63			0		0.54
R^2 of correlation	0.36		0.02		0.01		0.87			0.21	0.68	
Slope of correlation	0.79		−0.82		0.04		0.69			0.53		0.79

Note: IIT = MINDT >0.10; non-IIT = MINDT <0.10.

Source: See text and Appendix.

responsible for the major part of Canadian imports of manufactured goods, the results presented in Table 4.18 and the relationships underlying the data are considerably more important.

Some of the results for the larger enterprises are similar to those for the smaller ones. For instance, the subsidiaries in industries that are categorised as being extensively involved in IIT have a higher average import propensity for major products at 21.7 per cent, compared to the 13.5 per cent for the Canadian sector of control (IMSH3 versus IMSH7).

However, the import propensities are different in some important ways for these larger enterprises than for the smaller ones. One difference is that the imports of components and minor product lines (IMSH1 and IMSH5) by the subsidiaries in both IIT and non-IIT industries are similar to those for firms in the Canadian sector of control, as a ratio of their shipments. This suggests the larger subsidiaries rely relatively more on domestic suppliers and internal production as they become larger, while the domestically controlled firms rely more on contracting-out to foreign suppliers. Another difference is that for larger enterprises in the non-IIT industries that import only (IMSH1 and IMSH5), there is a higher import propensity for both sectors of control.

The lower proportion of imports accounted for by subsidiaries in the T-tests presented in Table 4.18, compared to the proportion for Table 4.17, is due to the exclusion of the auto industry. It was excluded from Table 4.18 because of the lack of a Canadian sector of control with which to compare it.

T-tests on export propensities

The results on the T-tests on export propensities are presented next. Table 4.19 sets out the results for the smaller enterprises. The industries were again categorised as being either IIT or non-IIT in nature, using MINDT with a critical value of 0.10 for doing so. Table 4.20 presents the same information as for Table 4.19, but for the larger enterprises.

In these tests, the percentage of exports accounted for within a trade group is large, at 95 per cent of the exports by both the subsidiaries and the Canadian-controlled firms engaged in cross-trade (EXSH3 and EXSH7) and at 100 per cent and 92 per cent for firms in the foreign and Canadian sectors of control,

Table 4.19: Results of T-tests on Export Propensities between Sectors of Control; for Unconsolidated Enterprises with Shipments <$10 million, by Trade Groups and Categories (Manufacturing Sector, 1979)

Description	IIT		non-IIT		IIT		non-IIT		IIT		non-IIT	
	EXSH3	EXSH7	EXSH3	EXSH7	EXSH2	EXSH6	EXSH2	EXSH6	EXSH23	EXSH67	EXSH23	EXSH67
Number of industries	61	61	41	41	53	53	47	47	69	69	65	65
Per cent of exports in trade group in T-test	78	75	17	20	44	26	56	66	54	47	32	51
Unweighted averages (per cent)	20.0	21.9	19.3	21.8	30.1	21.5	22.7	23.3	22.4	32.8	20.8	21.5
Significance of T-test	0.51		0.54		0.02		0.86		0.37		0.84	
R^2 of correlation	0		0.03		0.12		0.25		0.01		0.11	
Slope of correlation	0.03		0.17		0.58		0.57		-0.02		0.38	

Note: IIT = MINDT >0.10; non-IIT = MINDT <0.10.

Source: See text and Appendix.

respectively, engaged in one-way trade as specialised exporters (EXSH2 and EXSH6). The percentage of total exports by firms engaged in cross-trade that is accounted for by the IIT industries is high, at 78 per cent and 75 per cent respectively for the foreign and Canadian sector of control (EXSH3 and EXSH7). However, in the case of the specialised exporters (EXSH2 and EXSH6), the percentage of exports accounted for by the non-IIT industries is larger than for the IIT industries, at 56 per cent and 66 per cent respectively for each sector of control. These results would be expected, given the tendency for firms involved in cross-trade to be associated with IIT industries and firms involved in one-way trade of exports to be associated with the non-IIT industries. These results provide some confirmation that the IIT indices do allocate the industries reasonably well to their correct category of trade orientation.

There is no significant difference between the sectors of control for the export propensities engaged in cross-trade, whether they are in IIT or non-IIT industries (EXSH3 and EXSH7). In fact, the only significant difference in the export propensities between the sectors of control is for the specialised exporters in the IIT industries (EXSH2 and EXSH6) and the *foreign* sector of control has the higher export propensity. The low values, across all the partitions, for the R^2 of the correlation between the export propensities in each sector of control, along with the low values of the slopes of correlations (except between EXSH2 and EXSH6), suggest the two sectors export substantially different products. In the case of the specialised exporters, who conform more to the HOS model of trade, there is a greater similarity between the sectors of control in the products exported than for the exporters engaged in cross-trade. This would be expected, since one-way trade in exports should be based on international comparative cost advantages which are country- and industry-specific. However, exports of products that are cross-traded would tend to be associated with advantages that are based on product differentiation and firm-specific factors not necessarily common to both sectors of control.

The total export propensities (EXSH23 and EXSH67) reflect the above influences and are not significantly different between either the sectors of control or the industry categories. However, the unweighted average export propensity for the Canadian sector of control in the IIT industries does appear to be somewhat

107

Table 4.20: Results of T-tests on Export Propensities between Sectors of Control; for Unconsolidated Enterprises with Shipments >$10 million, by Trade Groups and Categories (Manufacturing Sector, 1979)

Description	IIT		non-IIT		IIT		non-IIT		IIT		non-IIT	
	EXSH3	EXSH7	EXSH3	EXSH7	EXSH2	EXSH6	EXSH2	EXSH6	EXSH23	EXSH67	EXSH23	EXSH67
Number of industries	57	57	23	23	9	9	21	21	60	60	35	35
Per cent of exports in trade group in T-test	48	42	17	55	3	2	73	64	75	39	22	59
Unweighted averages (per cent)	21.9	21.0	24.9	25.8	27.3	12.9	31.5	28.7	21.1	21.8	23.6	24.8
Significance of T-test	0.74		0.78		0.26		0.59		0.90		0.71	
R^2 of correlation	0.33		0.64		0.03		0.50		0.3		0.55	
Slope of correlation	0.61		0.77		0		0.83		0.65		0.77	

Note: IIT = MINDT >0.10; non-IIT = MINDT <0.10.
Source: See text and Appendix.

higher than for the foreign sector (32.8 per cent versus 22.4 per cent), although the statistical tests do not show the difference as being significant.

Table 4.20 presents the results of tests on export propensities for the larger enterprises. These are the important results because of the large percentage of total exports accounted for by these firms. The percentage of exports accounted for by subsidiaries engaged in cross-trade, summed across both the IIT and non-IIT categories, is less than for firms in the Canadian sector of control (i.e. 65 per cent and 97 per cent, respectively). This is because the requirement of having to pair industries across the sectors necessitated removing the foreign-controlled auto industry from the T-test. This industry accounts for a large percentage of exports by the foreign sector.

One of the major points that can be drawn from the information in Table 4.20 is that there is no significant difference in the export propensities of the larger firms between the sectors of control across any of the partitions of the data. However, the non-IIT industries do tend to generally have higher export propensities than the IIT industries within each trade group, and this is especially so for the specialised exporters in the Canadian sector of control (EXSH2 and EXSH6). Note also that for the specialised exporters there are very few industries that are associated with IIT trade. These results are consistent because firms in the non-IIT industries should be specialised exporters, more involved with inter-industry trade on a one-way basis, which would also account for their higher export propensities because of their international comparative advantages. Also, exports by the Canadian sector of control tend to be associated more with the non-IIT industries while exports by the subsidiaries are associated more with IIT industries. This result was also noted for the smaller firms in Table 4.19 and reflects the tendency for subsidiaries to be more involved in two-way, intra-firm trade with affiliates.

It is interesting that, in contrast to the smaller firms, the larger enterprises have a greater correspondence between the sectors of control in the products exported. This is apparent from the higher R^2s and the higher values for the slopes of the correlations, especially for the non-IIT industries. The relatively lower correspondence, for the IIT industries, could be accounted for by the greater horizontal diversity of the subsidiaries engaged in two-way trade because of their greater involvement in wholesale activities.

109

The total export propensities reflect all the above influences (EXSH23 and EXSH67). The exports of the subsidiaries are primarily in IIT industries, while those of the Canadian-controlled firms are primarily in non-IIT industries. However, there are no significant differences in the export performances of the two sectors of control. These results reflect the influence of the different nature of the firms in the two sectors. The subsidiaries are actively involved in cross-trade with affiliates because of their wholesale activities and tend to be associated with IIT industries, while the domestically-controlled firms tend to be specialist exporters and are involved more with non-IIT industries that have one-way flows of goods. Once this difference is adjusted for, the propensities tend to be the same in each sector of control.

COMPARISONS OF IMPORT AND EXPORT PROPENSITIES

The next set of T-tests compare for significant differences between the import and export propensities within a sector of control, by trade group and size of enterprise. If the import and export propensities within a sector of control are approximately the same for an industry and change together by about the same amount across the industries, then this would be indicative of trade flows that are IIT in nature. If the import and export propensities are significantly different for an industry and change in opposite directions across the industries, then this would be indicative of trade flows that are inter-industry in nature. Tables 4.21 and 4.22 present the results of T-tests, for the small and larger enterprises respectively, that were undertaken to determine how the propensities do compare and change across industries. Some special data problems related to the data used for Tables 4.21 and 4.22 are explained in the Appendix under the heading 'Data Related to Tables 4.21 and 4.22'.

The results presented in Table 4.21 for the small subsidiaries do not show a significant difference between their import and export propensities for cross-trade in major products (IMSH3/EXSH3). This applies to both the IIT and non-IIT industry category. The non-IIT industries do, however, appear to have a larger difference between the import and export propensities than the IIT industries, with the net balance favouring imports. This suggests in the non-IIT industries the subsidiaries are

Table 4.21: Results of T-tests Comparing Import and Export Propensities within a Sector of Control; for Unconsolidated Enterprises with Shipments <$10 million, by Trade Groups and Industry Categories (Manufacturing Sector, 1979)

Description	IIT		non-IIT		IIT		non-IIT		IIT		non-IIT		IIT		non-IIT	
	IMSH3	EXSH3	IMSH3	EXSH3	IMSH7	EXSH7	IMSH7	EXSH7	IMSH13	EXSH13	IMSH23	EXSH23	IMSH57	EXSH67	IMSH57	EXSH67
Number of industries	72	72	43	43	67	67	54	54	78	78	52	52	52	52	92	92
Per cent of variable in trade group in T-test	E81	E84	E19	E16	E78	E76	E20	E21	84	71	15	28	63	37	37	56
Unweighted averages (per cent)	21.8	21.8	25.5	19.7	16.0	19.8	14.0	22.2	53.3	23.1	40.7	20.5	35.4	36.5	22.4	19.4
Significance of T-test	0.98		0.29		0.01		0.06		0		0		0.93		0.30	
R^2 of correlation	0.51		0.05		0.43		0		0.03		0.03		0.39		0	
Slope of correlation	0.72		0.28		0.55		0.03		0.21		0.20		0.16		0.03	

Note: IIT = GIND3 and GIND7 >0.30; non-IIT = GIND3 and GIND7 <0.30; MINDF and MINDC >0.10; non-IIT = GIND3 and GIND7 <0.30; MINDF and MINDC <0.10. Where: GIND3 applies to IMSH3/EXSH3; GIND7 applies to IMSH7/EXSH7; MINDF applies to IMSH13/EXSH23; and MINDC applies to IMSH57/EXSH67. E = estimate.

Source: See text and Appendix.

oriented more towards being involved in inter-industry trade with specialisation in imports, perhaps as tariff factories. However, the percentage of the total imports and exports of major product lines associated with the non-IIT industries is relatively small compared to the IIT industries. In the case of the Canadian-controlled firms there is a significant difference between the import and export propensities for both the IIT and non-IIT industries, with the export propensities being higher than the import propensities (IMSH6/EXSH7). Overall, in contrast to the subsidiaries, the Canadian-controlled enterprises in the non-IIT industries tend to be more involved in inter-industry trade as specialised exporters. These results are similar to those already discussed above for the import and export propensities separately and reflects the large wholesale role of the subsidiaries.

There is a significant difference for the foreign sector of control between the total import and the total export propensities. This applies to both the IIT and non-IIT industries (IMSH13/EXSH23). The total import propensities are about double the total export propensities (EXSH23) and also about double the import propensities for just major product lines (IMSH3). That is, the imports of components and minor product lines are about equal to the imports of major product lines resold on a wholesale basis. It was noted in the discussion in Chapter 3 on the literature review that, overall, about one-third of total imports by the subsidiaries are unfinished goods and two-thirds are finished goods. In order for the aggregated propensity IMSH13 to reflect this, the disaggregated results for the value of total imports of components and minor product lines (IMSH1) would have to be made up of about two-thirds components (i.e. unfinished goods) and one-third minor product lines (i.e. finished goods). The total import propensities for the smaller subsidiaries may be biased upwards somewhat, compared to those for the Canadian-controlled enterprises, because components and minor product lines imported by the larger firms (whose major products are in another industry) would be allocated to the small size class, as has already been discussed.

The inclusion of imported components and minor product lines with the imports of major products for the Canadian-controlled enterprises also results in a large increase in the total import propensities. Consequently, there is no significant difference between the total import and the total export propensities in either the IIT or the non-IIT categories (IMSH57/EXSH67) as there was for just enterprises in trade group 7 ('Both X and M'). However, the proportion of exports accounted for by the non-IIT industries is considerably higher than for the subsidiaries. That is, in contrast to the subsidiaries that extensively use affiliates and foreign suppliers generally for finished and unfinished goods resulting in an orientation towards cross-trade, the Canadian-controlled enterprises have a much stronger orientation towards one-way trade of an inter-industry type. In the case of the IIT industries this is biased in favour of specialisation in exports.

The R^2 of the correlation between the import and export propensities within the IIT industries for trade groups 3 and 7 ('Both X and M') is higher than for the non-IIT industries. The slopes of the correlations are also higher in the IIT than in the non-IIT industries. These conditions exist in both sectors of control, but are stronger for the foreign sector. This suggests there is a tendency in the IIT industries for export and import propensities of major products traded on a two-way basis to be similar and for export propensities to increase as import propensities increase across the industries. For trade groups 3 and 7, the association of higher export with higher import propensities across the industries and the similarity between the average values for the propensities are both consistent with the IIT paradigm. These relationships are not significant for the non-IIT industries in either sector for any of the trade groups. This indication here is that the non-IIT industries tend to be either import- or export-oriented in conformity with the HOS paradigm of inter-industry trade. Also, the relationships between the propensities for trade groups 3 and 7 do not exist for the total import and export propensities, which include imports of components and minor products imported by firms whose major products are associated with other industries. The lower significance of these relationships when components and minor products are included in the total import propensities suggests contracting-out for these types of goods may be related to inter- rather than intra-industry trade. This point will be discussed more fully in the next section in relation to the larger firms and the data presented in Table 4.22.

In summary of Table 4.21, the smaller subsidiaries are more involved in balanced cross-trade of their major product lines than are their counterparts in the Canadian sector of control.

113

This reflects their greater access to the products and markets of affiliates, largely on a wholesale basis. However, in terms of total trade, the foreign sector is more import-oriented than the Canadian sector because of both the large wholesale activity of the subsidiaries and their greater propensity to use foreign suppliers. The net result is that total trade is unbalanced in favour of imports for the smaller enterprises in the foreign sector of control compared to the Canadian sector. This would be likely to be the case even if the Canadian sector were adjusted by including the imports of manufactured goods by firms in the wholesale sector to make the manufacturing sector's wholesale activities comparable to those of the foreign sector. Nevertheless, for those firms in trade groups 3 and 7 primarily involved in cross-trade, the export and import propensities do tend to be similar and rise together across the industries and this holds for both sectors of control.

Table 4.22 shows the same information as Table 4.21, except that it is for the larger manufacturing enterprises which account for the bulk of shipments, imports and exports of manufactured goods.

One of the major differences between the small and larger enterprises is that the larger ones have a considerably lower propensity to import components and minor product lines relative to their total activities. This applies to both sectors of control.

Like the small subsidiaries, there is no significant difference for the larger ones between the import and export propensities for firms engaged in cross-trade of their major product lines (IMSH3/EXSH3) that are in IIT industries. But, the R^2 of the correlation (i.e. 0.76) between the import and export propensities, IMSH3 and EXSH3, for the IIT industries, as well as the slope of the correlation (i.e. 0.90) between the propensities, is considerably higher than for the smaller subsidiaries in the same trade groups and industry categories. The IIT industries account for over three-quarters of the imports of major product lines which is considerably larger than for the non-IIT industries. In general, the larger subsidiaries show a strong orientation to cross-trade in their major product lines which is IIT in nature.

However, in comparing the performance of the small and large enterprises in non-IIT industries, there is a difference in their import and export propensities and the difference is attributable to the much lower import propensity of the larger firms. Indeed, their import propensities are similar to those for

Table 4.22: Results of T-tests Comparing Import and Export Propensities within a Sector of Control; for Unconsolidated Enterprises with Shipments >$10 million, by Trade Groups and Industry Categories (Manufacturing Sector, 1979)

Description	IIT		non-IIT		IIT		non-IIT		IIT		non-IIT		IIT		non-IIT	
	IMSH3	EXSH3	IMSH3	EXSH3	IMSH7	EXSH7	IMSH7	EXSH7	IMSH13	EXSH23	IMSH13	EXSH23	IMSH57	EXSH67	IMSH57	EXSH67
Number of industries	67	67	34	34	51	51	43	43	80	80	24	24	51	51	47	47
Per cent of variable in trade group in T-test	E80	E77	E3	E14	E47	E28	E16	E8	98	79	2	19	81	32	17	41
Unweighted averages (per cent)	21.0	20.0	7.6	22.0	13.1	16.8	6.3	27.1	22.0	20.3	11.4	19.4	17.0	21.7	7.6	21.5
Significance of T-test	0.43		0.01		0.01		0		0.36		0.26		0.07		0	
R^2 of correlation	0.76		0.01		0.71		0.01		0.49		0		0.33		0	
Slope of correlation	0.90		−0.09		0.84		−0.04		0.76		−0.06		0.63		−0.03	

Note: IIT = GIND3 and GIND7 >0.30; non-IIT = GIND3 and GIND7 <0.30; MINDF and MINDC >0.10; MINDF and MINDC <0.10. Where: GIND3 applies to IMSH3/EXSH3; GIND7 applies to IMSH7/EXSH7; MINDF applies to IMSH13/EXSH23; and MINDC applies to IMSH57/EXSH67. Ė = estimate.

Source: See text and Appendix.

115

their counterparts in the Canadian sector of control. As a result, the larger enterprises in trade group 3 associated with non-IIT industries are export-oriented, unlike their small counterparts, but like their Canadian-controlled counterparts. Further, the enterprises in non-IIT industries engaged in cross-trade of their major products have no significant degree of correlation between their import and export propensities. To the extent that there is a correlation, it is negative. This suggests that high export propensities are associated with low import propensities (and vice versa) for these enterprises. This is consistent with these industries being dominated by inter-industry trade as opposed to the intra-industry type associated with the IIT industries.

The enterprises in the Canadian sector of control that are engaged in cross-trade of their major product lines (IMSH7/EXSH7) do have a significant difference between their import and export propensities, with the import propensities being lower. This applies to both the IIT and non-IIT industries. In the case of enterprises in the IIT industries, this significant difference between the propensities does not exist for their counterparts in the foreign sector of control because of the higher propensity of the subsidiaries to import major products from affiliates. But, like the foreign sector of control, the IIT industries in the Canadian sector have a high correlation between the propensities (i.e. 0.71) and increased import propensities across the IIT industries. The result is a relatively steep slope for the correlation (i.e. 0.84). For the non-IIT industries, the R^2 of the correlation is very low at 0.01 and the slope is negative. Thus, like their counterparts in the foreign sector of control, the non-IIT industries display characteristics consistent with inter-industry trade which is specialised in exports. Also, for the Canadian sector of control, non-IIT industries account for a larger proportion of trade in major products than it does in the foreign sector. While the foreign sector is more actively involved in the two-way exchange of similar major products, both sectors have a significant level of it.

The patterns noted above for just major products of the larger enterprises exist as well for their total trade propensities (IMSH13/EXSH23; IMSH57/EXSH67) that include minor products and components. In the case of the non-IIT industries, both sectors of control are export-oriented with the Canadian sector accounting for a larger proportion of its total trade in this category. The foreign sector of control displays a greater propensity towards cross-trade. The subsidiaries do have higher import propensities than their Canadian-controlled counterparts, but for the larger enterprises this appears to be accounted for more by their larger wholesale role than by their significantly greater use of foreign-produced components and minor products. Compared to the smaller enterprises, the larger ones have a smaller difference in their import propensities between the sectors of control, as has already been noted. This appears to be related to a combination of increased contracting-out to foreign suppliers by the Canadian-controlled enterprises along with import replacement by internally manufactured domestic production as they become larger, and greater use of domestic suppliers by the subsidiaries as they become larger.

EXTENT OF IIT

Table 4.22 shows that, for enterprises in trade groups 3 and 7 engaged in the cross-trade of their major product lines, there are 67 industries in the foreign sector of control and 51 in the Canadian sector that are in the IIT category (i.e. IMSH3, EXSH3 and IMSH7, EXSH7). These industries were reviewed in detail to assess the extent of IIT in them. The review disclosed that a significant number of the industries allocated to the IIT category based on the Grubel and Lloyd index, while having relatively high levels of IIT, were not involved in it in a major way. This arises because of the manner in which the Grubel and Lloyd index is calculated. It is a relative measure which expresses the level of cross-trade as a percentage of total trade. But, it does not take into account the level of cross-trade relative to the total production activity in an industry. Consequently, while the relative measure can be high, the importance of cross-trade in the total activity of an industry can be low. For instance, if exports are equal to imports then the IIT index would be at its maximum level of 1. However, if the imports and exports are only 1 per cent of shipments, then the amount of cross-trade is insignificant. One way to overcome this problem is to use not only the Grubel and Lloyd index, but also the import and export propensities in evaluating the significance of IIT in an industry. These propensities allow for the level of imports and exports (the numerators), as well as the level of shipments in an industry (the denominators).

The propensities, in conjunction with the G&L index, were used to sort the industries noted in Table 4.22 as belonging to the IIT category into two groups: those industries in which the level of IIT is significant in relation to shipments; and those industries in which IIT is not significant in relation to shipments. Allocation of an industry to either group was determined on the basis of whether the import or export propensity for an industry was less than 0.10. If so, then the industry was allocated to the group in which IIT was not significant in relation to the total activity in an industry. Otherwise, the industry was allocated to the group in which IIT was significant in relation to total activity. For the larger enterprises, the industries allocated to this latter group from those originally allocated to the IIT group of industries in Table 4.22 are listed in Table 4.23.

It has already been noted that firms in the foreign sector of control are extensively involved in cross-trade of their major products and have higher propensities (especially for imports) than do their counterparts in the Canadian sector of control. However, even for the subsidiaries, significant levels of IIT relative to the total activity in an industry are associated with a relatively low number of industries. Table 4.23 lists 32 such industries for the foreign sector of control and only 18 in the Canadian sector, out of the total of 159 industries. A perusal of the industries listed in Table 4.23 shows that they tend to be concentrated in particular types of goods. The products tend to be industrial goods used as intermediate products and capital inputs (e.g. steel, aluminum, wire, office furniture, machinery and equipment, transportation equipment, electrical products, non-metallic mineral products, chemicals and plastics).

What is clear from Table 4.23 is that IIT is not significant for many industries in comparison to shipments, nor is it widespread across the manufacturing sector. This result is not supportive of the impression conveyed by the studies discussed earlier in the literature review section of Chapter 3. These studies, using the Grubel and Lloyd index, did not allow for the absolute level of cross-trade in an industry and hence tended to overstate its significance. Nor did the studies disaggregate by sector of control to determine the important point that the domestic sector of control is not as highly involved in IIT as the foreign sector of control. The generally higher import propensities for the foreign sector of control reflect the greater involvement of the subsidiaries as wholesalers on behalf of their foreign

Table 4.23: Industries with Significant IIT in Major Product Lines, based on IIT Index > Critical Value of 0.10 and Import and Export Propensities > 0.10; for Unconsolidated Enterprises with Shipments > $10 million, by Sector of Control (Manufacturing Sector, 1979)

Industry	Foreign sector		Canadian sector	
	Import propen. (per cent)	Export propen. (per cent)	Import propen. (per cent)	Export propen. (per cent)
Sugar products	42	15	—	—
Rubber products	20	21	15	24
Man-made fibre mills	14	11	41	14
Fur products	—	—	12	46
Plywood mills	—	—	11	40
Office furniture	10	26	—	—
Publishing	—	—	14	12
Iron & steel mills	33	32	—	—
Steel pipe mills	26	43	—	—
Aluminum mills	14	13	21	26
Wire products	14	27	—	—
Hardware	18	28	—	—
Misc. metal fabrications	22	24	—	—
Agricultural implements	90	78	41	51
Misc. machinery & equipment	51	40	43	35
Refrigeration equipment	26	26	47	46
Office & store machinery	87	82	23	53
Aircraft	62	80	88	79
Autos	62	69	—	—
Auto parts	86	65	13	63
Railroad equipment	33	39	21	53
Television	73	64	35	20
Communications equipment	60	60	23	27
Misc. electrical	16	17	—	—
Batteries	16	19	11	12
Glass	19	15	—	—
Abrasives	23	57	—	—
Refractories	43	59	—	—
Plastics and resins	23	22	—	—
Industrial chemicals (inorganic)	14	25	—	—
Industrial chemicals (organic)	29	19	—	—
Misc. chemicals	28	12	16	13
Instruments	41	26	69	64
Sporting goods	40	13	—	—
Toys	31	14	—	—
Unweighted averages	36	36	26	38
Number of industries	32	32	18	18

Source: see text.

119

affiliates, relative to the Canadian-controlled manufacturers who rely more on independent importers in the wholesale sector to perform this function. That is, IIT is largely a phenomenon of cross-trade among MNEs which tends to be intra-firm. One implication of these results is that there is still considerable room for increased product specialisation in Canadian manufacturing industries as well as for increased contracting-out to foreign suppliers.

Table 4.23 presented information on those industries in which IIT is significant in relation to shipments, but it was only for the major products of firms engaged in cross-trade. In addition, firms import minor product lines and components which, if added to the trade in major products, could increase the level of IIT to a more significant level for many industries.

Table 4.24 presents the results after such imports are added to the cross-trade in major products.[8] The imports of enterprises in trade groups 1 and 5 ('M only') were combined with those for trade groups 3 and 7 ('Both X and M') to arrive at the total import propensity for each sector of control in an industry (IMSH13 and IMSH57). The MINDF index for the foreign sector and the MINDC index for the Canadian sector of control were used to determine the IIT industries for each sector of control by setting it at a critical value of 0.10. The industries so allocated to the IIT category were then reviewed and those with an import or export propensity of less than 0.10 were removed from the IIT category. The total import propensities, IMSH13 and IMSH57 for the foreign and Canadian sectors respectively, have shipments in their denominators for only trade groups 1 and 3 (foreign sector), and 5 and 7 (Canadian sector). The results presented in Table 4.24 are for the larger enterprises only, as was the case for Table 4.23. Table 4.24 summarises the results, rather than listing the industries individually as was done in Table 4.23. The important point is how the import propensities change and the number of industries extensively involved in IIT increase when total imports (IMSH13 and IMSH57) are used to determine IIT rather than just the imports of major products (IMSH3 and IMSH7).

The number of industries that can be classified as being extensively involved in IIT more than doubled for the foreign sector and tripled for the Canadian sector of control when import propensities included minor product lines and components. The volume of trade that can be classified as IIT in

Table 4.24: Industries with Significant IIT — Comparison between Major Products and Total Imports, based on IIT Index > Critical Value of 0.10 and Import and Export Propensities > 0.10; for Unconsolidated Enterprises with Shipments > $10 million, by Sector of Control (Manufacturing Sector, 1979)

Description	Foreign sector		Canadian sector	
	Major products	Total imports	Major products	Total imports
Unweighted averages per cent	34	58	33	41
Number of industries	26	54	13	39

Source: See text and Appendix.

nature is also considerably increased. The unweighted average of the import propensities also increases, with the increase being considerably greater for the subsidiaries because of their greater propensity to contract-out minor products and components to foreign suppliers (including affiliates) as compared to their Canadian-controlled counterparts. The industries added to the list of those presented in Table 4.23 include food (meat and feed), textiles (rugs), wood (plywood and doors), metal processors (boilers, heating equipment, metal coatings and metal stampings), electrical goods (small and major appliances, and lighting fixtures) and non-metallic minerals (clay). These products comprise both final goods imported as minor product lines (e.g. electrical appliances and textiles) and intermediate goods imported as components (e.g. metal stampings).

SUMMARY OF T-TESTS ON IMPORT AND EXPORT PROPENSITIES

The enterprises in the foreign sector of control have higher import propensities for both components and final products than do their Canadian-controlled counterparts. This reflects the greater access the subsidiaries have to affiliates. It may also reflect more efficient purchasing practices that result in subsidiaries extensively purchasing small-run products and components from low-cost foreign suppliers. The subsidiaries also tend to be more involved in IIT than do the Canadian-controlled firms, with the Canadian-controlled firms being more involved

121

in international trade as exporters only. One-half of the imports by the subsidiaries take the form of minor products and components, as opposed to major products. Generally speaking, widespread and significant levels of IIT were not observed and IIT was lower for the firms in the Canadian sector of control. This suggests there is still considerable room for increased scale and specialisation by Canadian manufacturers and especially for those in the Canadian sector of control.

One important change in import performance was observed as the Canadian-controlled enterprises became larger. They tended to import relatively more, resulting in a convergence in the import propensities between the sectors of control. Presumably, this reflects greater import replacement behaviour by the subsidiaries as they become larger, along with increased use of foreign suppliers by the Canadian-controlled firms. The latter behaviour appears to be the dominant type since the import propensities of the larger subsidiaries are not materially lower than for the smaller ones, but they are significantly higher for the larger Canadian-controlled firms than for the small ones.

For the export propensities, there generally is not a significant difference in them between the sectors of control. This was especially so for 1979, after the firms in the Canadian sector of control had a significant increase in their export propensities from 1974, which allowed them to catch up to the export performance of the subsidiaries.

A significant part of total trade, especially by the subsidiaries, is in the form of cross-trade in major products. There is a strong relationship between increased imports and increased exports for the industries involved in this type of trade, with the relationship being stronger for the subsidiaries. This is presumably because of their international affiliations. These results suggest that a movement to freer trade by Canada would result in largely offsetting increases by imports and exports.

SCALE AND SPECIALISATION

Emphasis so far has been on international trade flows. But the hypothesis developed earlier in which the relationships between increased competition and trade flows were outlined also included a discussion of the impact of increased competition on plant scale and the degree of product and production

122

specialisation. The following section analyses some new data for evidence of the extent to which changes in plant scale and product specialisation took place between 1974 and 1979. Following that, additional data will be searched for evidence of changes in production specialisation over the same time period.

Plant scale and product specialisation

A proxy measure for changes in plant scale was developed from information on the Census of Manufactures. It is the ratio of the 1979 value of shipments in an industry to the value in 1974, in constant 1974 dollars. It was necessary to adjust the data for the entry and exit of firms in an industry over the time period involved, otherwise the statistic would have been influenced by factors other than just the growth in shipments by existing producers. This would have affected the usefulness of the statistic as a proxy for increases in plant scale. This adjustment was made by using only the shipments of establishments common to both the opening and closing years of 1974 and 1979 and that had reported on the long Census of Manufactures form. Approximately 11,000 establishments constituted this group. They were partitioned by two sectors of control (foreign and Canadian) and by the two trade categories (IIT and non-IIT). In order to test for the sensitivity of the analysis to the index used to allocate industries to either the IIT or non-IIT categories, it was carried out twice. One analysis used the GIND index with a critical value of 0.30 to allocate the industries and the other used the MIND index with a critical value of 0.10 to allocate them. T-tests were carried out on the statistic to determine if there were significant differences between the sectors of control, by the IIT and non-IIT industry categories. The results of the analysis are presented in Table 4.25.

The results of the T-tests are similar for both the GIND index and the MIND index. Average plant shipments increased by about 25 per cent between 1974 and 1979 for the IIT industries and there was no significant difference in this growth between the sectors of control. However, for the non-IIT industries, the growth in shipments differed significantly between the sectors of control, with the Canadian sector having a rate of growth more than double that for the foreign sector and about equal to that for the IIT industries. The subsidiaries did not increase their

123

Table 4.25: Results of T-tests on Growth in Shipments between Sectors of Control for 159 Industries, based on Long-form Establishments Common to 1974 and 1979 (Manufacturing Sector)

Description	Based on GIND index				Based on MIND index			
	IIT		non-IIT		IIT		non-IIT	
	Foreign	Cdn	Foreign	Cdn	Foreign	Cdn	Foreign	Cdn
Number of industries	78	78	81	81	70	70	89	89
Unweighted averages	1.23	1.26	1.07	1.30	1.18	1.28	1.12	1.28
Significance of T-test	0.44		0		0.11		0.02	
R^2 of correlation	0.08		0		0.02		0	
Slope of correlation	0.27		− 0.05		0.13		− 0.01	

Note: IIT = Index > critical value; non-IIT = Index < critical value.
Source: See text and Appendix.

scale to the same extent as either the Canadian-controlled firms that are specialised exporters or the firms in both sectors of control that are engaging in increased specialisation and cross-trade. The implication of this is that tariff factory subsidiaries that are primarily in the non-IIT category are not achieving the growth of their Canadian-controlled counterparts.

Other studies have also noted a positive relationship between increased scale and the degree of specialisation of firms.[9] This information, along with the results noted here, would suggest that the subsidiaries which are achieving increases in scale may be doing so by moving from tariff-factory missions to ones with more specialised product mandates. Their increased specialisation would increase their ability to lower unit costs which in turn would make them more competitive and more able to increase their scale through exports. This would allow them to engage in cross-trade rather than being just importers on a one-trade basis and explains why the subsidiaries with the lowest growth in shipments are in the non-IIT category. These would tend to be high-cost tariff factories with extensive one-way import activities of the inter-industry type and unable to export and grow because of their high costs.

124

The issue of changes in specialisation was also addressed. It was not as easy to develop a statistic that would serve as a proxy for specialisation as it was for changes in scale. This is partly because of the wide variety of measures that exist for specialisation. But, more importantly, it is also because none of the measures can capture accurately the extent of specialisation. The degree of specialisation is dependent on the number of *variations* of a product needed to meet customer tastes. But, most measures of product diversity can only measure the number of products or *commodities* produced by a plant or firm, rather than the number of variations on them. For instance, a firm could be in the shoe business and the Census of Manufactures would be able to count the number of Industrial Commodity Classifications (ICC) in which the firm was manufacturing. However, within the commodity group of women's shoes, the firm could produce a number of different styles that were dependent upon colour, heels, strappings, materials used and other factors. No measure of diversity at this level is available from the Census data. But, given these limitations on the measures of specialisation, an attempt was made to assess the degree of product specialisation by sector of control and type of trade activity in the enterprises.

Several measures of product specialisation were developed for the years 1974 and 1979, by sector of control. One measure is the primary product specialisation ratio (PPSR), which is the ratio of the value of primary products to the value of total products produced by an establishment. This ratio, by establishment, was weighted by the shipments for each establishment in an industry and then averaged over the number of establishments to arrive at an industry-level measure of diversity. Another measure of specialisation is the average number of ICC products produced at the five-digit level of product disaggregation (AN5D). Note that unlike the other measures, AN5D would decrease as specialisation increased. This measure was calculated for each establishment and weighted by its shipments and then averaged over all the establishments in an industry to arrive at the industry-level index. A third measure is the percentage of output accounted for by the leading five-digit ICC products (APCQ). This statistic was also calculated by establishment, weighted by its shipments and averaged over all the establishments in an industry to arrive at the industry-level measure. The final measure of diversity is a Herfindahl index (HERF). It is a

125

measure of diversity at the five-digit ICC level of disaggregation. The index was weighted for each establishment to arrive at the industry-level measure. The HERF index can vary between zero and one, with the higher values associated with high levels of product specialisation. Table 4.26 presents the unweighted averages of the ratios, by sector of control, for both 1974 and 1979.

Table 4.26: Unweighted Averages of Various Measures of Specialisation by Sector of Control for 159 Industries based on Establishment-level Data, 1974 and 1979

Description	Unweighted averages			
	1979		1974	
	Foreign	Cdn	Foreign	Cdn
Primary products specialisation (PPSR)	0.82	0.85	0.81	0.85
Av. no. of 5-digit ICC products (AN5D)	4.1	4.1	4.7	4.2
Av. percentage of output by 5-digit ICC (APCQ)	0.69	0.74	0.67	0.73
5-digit ICC Herfindahl index (HERF)	0.61	0.66	0.59	0.65

Source: See text and Appendix.

The results presented in Table 4.26, for all measures of specialisation, show that the establishments in the Canadian sector of control were more specialised in the products they produced than were the subsidiaries for both 1974 and 1979. Also, there was an increase in the degree of product specialisation between 1974 and 1979 for both sectors of control.

In order to test formally for differences in the degree of specialisation between the sectors of control, T-tests were carried out on the 1979 statistics within each of the two trade categories of IIT and non-IIT industries. The GINDT index with a critical value of 0.10 was used to allocate the industries between the two trade categories. The results are presented in Table 4.27.

All of the significant differences in specialisation between the sectors of control are in the non-IIT industries, and the Canadian sector of control is equal to or more specialised than the subsidiaries for all the statistics associated with these

Table 4.27: Results of T-tests on Various Measures of Specialisation between Sectors of Control for 159 Industries by Industry Categories, based on Establishment-level Data (Manufacturing Sector, 1979)

Description	IIT industries								Non-IIT industries							
	PPSR		AN5D		APCQ		HERF		PPSR		AN5D		APCQ		HERF	
	Foreign	Cdn	Foreign	Cdn	Foreign	Cdn	Foreign	Cdn	Foreign	Cdn	Foreign	Cdn	Foreign	Cdn	Foreign	Cdn
Number of industries	78	78	78	78	78	78	78	78	81	81	81	81	81	81	81	81
Unweighted averages	0.86	0.86	4.6	4.5	0.70	0.72	0.61	0.63	0.77	0.84	3.6	3.6	0.69	0.75	0.62	0.68
Significance of T-test	0.92		0.74		0.52		0.35		0.07		0.96		0.03		0.04	
R^2 of correlation	0.02		0.24		0.04		0.06		0.13		0.35		0.09		0.13	
Slope of correlation	0.17		0.45		0.21		0.27		0.58		0.71		0.51		0.52	

Note: IIT = GINDT > 0.10; non-IIT = GINDT < 0.10.

Source: See text and Appendix.

127

industries. The subsidiaries are just as specialised as their Canadian-controlled counterparts in the IIT industries. This indicates that the subsidiaries engaging in cross-trade are specialising in products mandated to them by their parents for world distribution. But, in non-IIT industries, some of the subsidiaries appear to be continuing as diversified tariff-factory manufacturers with high levels of imports and serving just the domestic market while their Canadian-controlled counterparts (as well as some of the counterparts in the foreign sector) are specialised as exporters. This tariff-factory role for some subsidiaries would reduce the degree of specialisation by the foreign sector. The higher degree of specialisation in Canadian-controlled firms in the non-IIT industries is associated with their tendency to be specialised as exporters only. This tendency was discussed earlier when the export propensities were examined, at which time it was noted the Canadian-controlled firms are more extensively involved in inter-industry trade as exporters only. It now appears they are also more specialised in the products they export than are the firms in the foreign sector and than the firms in both sectors in the IIT industries.

The above information suggests the subsidiaries in the non-IIT industries are lagging in their response to freer trade by not specialising horizontally and increasing their scale as much as their counterparts in the IIT industries in both sectors of control and as much as their counterparts in the Canadian sector of control within the non-IIT industries. By continuing in their traditional role as tariff factories they would be high-cost and rely extensively upon imports from affiliates. This issue will be investigated further in the next section when vertical specialisation is analysed. But, from a policy standpoint, it is the subsidiaries in the non-IIT industries that appear to be the least adaptive to the changing environment.

Domestic IIT and product specialisation

The preceding section assessed changes in product, or horizontal, specialisation. This section will address the issue of changes in production, or vertical, specialisation due to increased contracting-out. The analysis so far has focused primarily on the issue of international intra-industry trade. However, the freer trade and increased competition that have led to international IIT through increased specialisation and contracting-out to foreign suppliers should also have led to increased contracting-out to efficient domestic suppliers as manufacturers attempted to lower unit costs. The result would be an increase in domestic intra-industry trade. Both increased domestic IIT and changes in vertical specialisation can be analysed through the use of the same statistic of purchased material to value-added. Some additional insight into horizontal specialisation can be gained by breaking down this statistic into that portion of it attributable to wholesale activity and horizontal specialisation by manufacturers and that portion attributable to just their manufacturing activity.

Chapter 3 discussed why the ratio of purchased material to value-added is useful for evaluating the extent of domestic IIT. Basically, as increased specialisation and contracting-out of products and components to suppliers take place, purchased materials for an industry would increase while value-added would decline. Thus, the ratio would tend to increase as competition, specialisation and contracting-out increased. The statistic does include imported as well as domestically purchased materials so that it is a measure of total, rather than just domestic, IIT. However, the domestic purchases would dominate in the statistic.

The ratio of purchased material to value-added was disaggregated to measure separately wholesale activity (i.e. total purchases of material and goods as well as total value-added in firms, less purchased material and value-added related to just manufacturing activities) and manufacturing activity. The value of materials included in the wholesale measure would be finished goods purchased for resale of both minor and major product lines while the value of materials included in the manufacturing measure would be components for further processing. It would be expected that the ratio measuring wholesale activity would increase over time with increased horizontal specialisation and contracting-out to suppliers and that it would be higher for the subsidiaries than for the Canadian-controlled firms because of their more extensive wholesale activities. Similarly, the ratio measuring manufacturing activity should also increase over time with increased vertical specialisation and contracting-out to suppliers.

The ratio, disaggregated by wholesale and manufacturing activities, was calculated for the 159 industries in the data bank

129

Table 4.28: Results of T-tests on Ratio of Purchased Material to Value-added Wholesale Activity between Sectors of Control and Years 1974 and 1979, for 159 Industries by Industry Categories (Manufacturing Sector)

Description	IIT		non-IIT		IIT		non-IIT		IIT		non-IIT		IIT		non-IIT	
	Fgn.9	Fgn.4	Fgn.9	Fgn.4	Cdn.9	Cdn.4	Cdn.9	Cdn.4	Fgn.9	Cdn.9	Fgn.9	Cdn.9	Fgn.4	Cdn.4	Fgn.4	Cdn.4
Number of industries	79	79	80	80	44	44	115	115	70	70	89	89	70	70	89	89
Unweighted averages (per cent)	23	9	10	11	7	9	13	14	24	9	11	13	7	12	13	14
Significance of T-test	0.14		0.53		0.60		0.63		0.08		0.51		0.63		0.65	
R^2 of correlation	0.01		0.28		0.15		0.46		0		0.11		0		0.10	
Slope of correlation	0.06		0.87		-1.86		0.69		-0.02		0.48		-0.02		0.28	

Note: IIT = MINDF, MINDC and MINDT >0.10; non-IIT = MINDF, MINDC and MINDT <0.10. Where: MINDF, MINDC and MINDT apply to the appropriate intra-sector comparisons of the statistic and MINDT applies to the inter-sector comparisons.

Source: See text and Appendix.

for the two years 1974 and 1979, by sector of control. These statistics were tested, within sector of control, for significant differences between the two years 1974 and 1979, for both the IIT and non-IIT industry categories. They were also tested for significant differences within a year between the sectors of control for both the IIT and non-IIT industry categories. The acronyms used to identify the statistic for the foreign sector of control are Fgn.9 and Fgn.4 for the years 1979 and 1974 respectively. The counterpart acronyms for the Canadian sector are Cdn.9 and Cdn.4 for these years. Table 4.28 presents the results of the T-tests for the wholesale activities of the firms and Table 4.29 presents the results for their manufacturing activities.

The information presented in Table 4.28 indicates that for the IIT industries there was a large (but not statistically significant) increase in the wholesale activities of the subsidiaries between 1974 and 1979. This is in contrast to the wholesale activities of the subsidiaries in the non-IIT industries and the Canadian-controlled firms in both the IIT and non-IIT industries. The increase in wholesale activities by the subsidiaries in the IIT industries is consistent with them specialising horizontally over the 1970s (perhaps through the use of world product mandate strategies), but continuing to offer a full product line to their domestic customers by importing products from affiliates. A similar pattern would not exist for the Canadian-controlled firms because they lack affiliates from whom to purchase dropped product lines. Also, unlike the subsidiaries, the whole-sale role is usually performed by specialist firms in the wholesale rather than the manufacturing sector.

The increase in the wholesale activities of the subsidiaries between 1974 and 1979 results in a difference in this activity between the sectors of control by 1979 (at a level of significance of 0.08). In 1974, the two sectors had similar ratios, but by 1979 the ratio for the foreign sector was almost three times that for the Canadian sector of control. This is also consistent with the evidence presented above in which it was shown that the Canadian-controlled firms are more specialised than the sub-sidiaries and that the subsidiaries import a substantially greater amount of finished goods. However, the comparison is incom-plete because the data are not comparable between the sectors with respect to the treatment of their wholesale activities.

Within the foreign sector of control, the subsidiaries in

131

Table 4.29: Results of T-tests on Ratio of Purchased Material to Value-added Manufacturing Activity between Sectors of Control and Years 1974 and 1979, for 159 Industries by Industry Categories (Manufacturing Sector)

Description	IIT		non-IIT		IIT		non-IIT		IIT		non-IIT		IIT		non-IIT	
	Fgn.9	Fgn.4	Fgn.9	Fgn.4	Cdn.9	Cdn.4	Cdn.9	Cdn.4	Fgn.9	Cdn.9	Fgn.9	Cdn.9	Fgn.4	Cdn.4	Fgn.4	Cdn.4
Number of industries	79	79	80	80	44	44	115	115	70	70	89	89	70	70	89	89
Unweighted averages (per cent)	155	175	124	134	174	163	131	124	161	173	123	120	189	156	123	118
Significance of T-test	0.57		0.29		0.35		0.03		0.39		0.81		0.32		0.53	
R^2 of correlation	0.18		0.71		0.76		0.87		0.57		0.23		0.45		0.24	
Slope of correlation	0.20		0.76		1.01		0.95		0.80		0.99		1.72		0.97	

Note: IIT = MINDF, MINDC and MINDT >0.10; non-IIT = MINDF, MINDC and MINDT <0.10. Where: MINDF, MINDC and MINDT apply to the appropriate intra-sector comparisons of the statistic and MINDT applies to the inter-sector comparisons.

Source: See text and Appendix.

industries that are allocated to the IIT category have a wholesale activity that is about twice as great as that for subsidiaries in the non-IIT industries, reflecting the greater specialisation of IIT enterprises and their high level of cross-trade as opposed to the diversified tariff factory enterprises in the non-IIT industries. However, there is no appreciable difference in the statistic between IIT and non-IIT industries for the Canadian-controlled firms nor between them and the subsidiaries in non-IIT industries. This suggests that Canadian-controlled firms (and especially the small ones) who wish to offer a wide variety of products to international markets yet achieve the cost benefits of being specialised producers, should form consortia of producers to act as trading houses such as the Japanese have done to market their products internationally.

Table 4.29 presents the results of the T-test on the statistic for just the manufacturing activities of the enterprises. This statistic is interpreted as a measure of both domestic IIT and the degree of vertical specialisation by manufacturers.

With the exception of the comparison in the statistic between 1974 and 1979 for the Canadian sector of control in the non-IIT industries, none of the tests are significant. Yet, the pattern of the change in the statistic is so different between the sectors of control that it leads one to the view that the two sectors did perform differently between 1974 and 1979 in terms of their make-or-buy decision. Therefore, it is of interest to explore these relationships even though definite assertions cannot be made.

The unweighted average of the statistic declined for the foreign sector of control between 1974 and 1979 in both the IIT and non-IIT industries. This is in contrast to the Canadian sector of control for which the statistic increased in the same time period and the increase was significant for the non-IIT industries. In contrast to Canadian-controlled firms, the subsidiaries appear to have moved towards greater contracting-in (i.e. greater diversification in production activities through increased vertical integration) across both the IIT and non-IIT trade categories which led to a reduction in their ratio of purchased material to value-added. Increased contracting-out and production specialisation by the Canadian-controlled firms as evidenced by the increase in their ratio of purchased material to value-added is consistent with their greater increase in product specialisation between 1974 and 1979, and their greater increase in export activities as specialist exporters (both of these points were noted previously).

133

An increase in vertical integration by the subsidiaries is consistent with information in another study which, based on interviews with a sample of firms, showed that the subsidiaries were somewhat slower than their Canadian-controlled counterparts in responding to the changing trade environment with increased specialisation.[10] In that study, some of the subsidiaries were more resistant to changing their role from that of a tariff factory to being more specialised producers and exporting, which would increase their utilisation of capacity. Instead, they were attempting to increase use of capacity as market share and plant load were being lost to competitors, through increased vertical diversification in production activities. Such a response, while perhaps just a short-run adaptation, perpetuated the subsidiaries as high-cost tariff factories and is counter-productive. It increases costs and would further add to longer-term losses in market share and rate of capacity utilisation. It should be noted, however, that some subsidiaries in the sample ultimately did respond appropriately with strategies to increase their scale and specialisation so that in the longer run their originally perverse short-run behaviour would not be a problem.

The greater variation, compared to their Canadian-controlled counterparts, in the response by subsidiaries to increases in competition would be the cause of the statistically weak results in Table 4.29. Over the time period covered, some subsidiaries would be moving towards increased vertical specialisation while others would be moving towards greater diversity. The effect of these different reactions would be to create 'noise' in the data and a higher level of unexplained variance. The time period of 1974 to 1979 covered by the data was a period of uncertainty and confusion for the MNEs as they attempted to work out and put in place longer-term missions and strategies for their plants in Canada. These replaced their historical strategy which is no longer appropriate to the changed economic environment of being tariff factories. Therefore, it would be prudent to put minimum emphasis on the interpretation of the movement in the statistics between 1974 and 1979 until the longer-term direction for the subsidiaries is established. On this basis, it may be appropriate to conclude only that the Canadian-controlled firms were at a lower level of production specialisation in 1974 than the subsidiaries, and that by 1979 the Canadian-controlled firms had caught up with them. As a result, no significant difference now exists between the sectors of control in terms of their degree of vertical specialisation.

The different pattern of change evident between the sectors of control in the ratio of purchased material to value-added for the IIT industries does not exist for the non-IIT industries. Nor is there an appreciable change in the statistic for the non-IIT industries between 1974 and 1979 for either sector of control. The non-IIT industries also have a lower level for the statistic, which suggests they are more vertically integrated than firms in the IIT industries, although it may reflect, too, the mixing of both import- and export-oriented industries in the non-IIT industry category, with the high-cost, import-oriented ones that are vertically integrated pulling down the average for the statistic.

SUMMARY

Small markets and diverse, high-cost producers resulted in the structure of the manufacturing sector in Canada being dominated by a large number of small enterprises. However, in terms of production, exports and imports the manufacturing sector is dominated by a relatively small number of larger firms, of which a significant proportion are foreign-controlled. And even this trade is dominated by a small number of foreign MNEs in the transportation industries. The small subsidiaries are extensively involved with importing minor and major product lines as well as components. Many of these items are imported by the subsidiaries on a wholesale basis from their foreign affiliates. This allows the subsidiaries to offer a wider variety of products to their customers without incurring the costs of small scale and diversity which would otherwise be associated with their production in Canada for just the domestic market. The Canadian-controlled manufacturers tend to leave the wholesale function to specialised importers in the wholesale sector.

It is the larger subsidiaries in Canada that are actively involved in IIT and a major part of it is intra-firm related to wholesale activities, fostered by the easy access the subsidiaries have to the products and markets of foreign affiliates. The Canadian-controlled enterprises, in comparison with the subsidiaries, tend to be relatively more involved in inter-industry trade. That is, they are more oriented to being just exporters and have a much lower propensity to import components and finished products.

While the subsidiaries do have higher import propensities than

135

their Canadian-controlled counterparts because of their extensive wholesale activities, if the distribution role performed by firms in the wholesale sector were integrated with the Canadian-controlled manufacturers then it is doubtful that there would be a significant difference on import performance for finished goods between the sectors of control. This would be especially so for the larger Canadian-controlled enterprises for whom the difference on import performance with their foreign-controlled counterparts is much narrower than for the small enterprises. Part of the reason for the narrowing in import performance between the sectors of control as enterprises become larger is due to the subsidiaries displacing imports of finished goods with domestic production.

The subsidiaries, after allowing for the difference between the sectors of control in wholesale activity, have higher import propensities for components because of their more extensive use of foreign suppliers. The difference in this propensity between the sectors narrows for the larger firms, as the larger Canadian-controlled enterprises increase their contracting-out activities and use of foreign suppliers.

The extent of IIT in major products is not as great as prior studies that use a relative measure of it would indicate. Also, when the tendency for subsidiaries to import and the Canadian-controlled firms to export are aggregated to the level of an industry, the indices measure the overall effect as IIT when in fact the trade is of the HOS type. However, when the imports of minor product lines and components are included in the definition of IIT, then it becomes more pervasive. But there still appears to be considerable room for increased specialisation, scale and IIT.

The export propensities of the small Canadian-controlled enterprises are about one-half those of their counterpart subsidiaries. They also tend to use foreign suppliers much less than the subsidiaries and less than the larger enterprises in both sectors of control. The lower export propensities may reflect the difficulty that small firms have in accessing the export market because they lack the aid provided by a large, mature marketing organisation such as that available to most subsidiaries. The low import propensities reflect to some extent inefficient purchasing procedures and also a lack of access to foreign suppliers that limits the search for competitive components to just domestic suppliers and internal production. The development and use of trading houses, for both exports and imports, by the small enterprises in the Canadian sector of control would help to overcome these problems.

The source of supply for components imported by subsidiaries (as well as minor and major product lines) is mainly affiliates, or the same suppliers as those used by the affiliates. This extensive tied trade, whether intra- or inter-firm, raises the question of the appropriateness of the transfer prices used to price the goods. This is not meant to imply that the transfer prices of imported goods *per se* are incorrect or that the practice of intra-firm sourcing is undesirable. A case can also be made for the other extreme in which small Canadian-controlled firms do not search globally for efficient suppliers. As a result, they too are involved in tied trade, but it is tied exclusively to domestic suppliers. This behaviour could have as deleterious an impact on competitiveness, income and employment in Canada as the tied trade between subsidiaries and their foreign suppliers. Indeed, it may be that the higher propensity of the small subsidiaries as well as the large enterprises in both sectors of control to use foreign suppliers is an indication that there are cost and availability problems associated with using many Canadian suppliers. No doubt the transfer price issue is important, but it is a general problem related to more than just the purchases by subsidiaries from affiliates since it is also a problem for firms tied to high-cost domestic suppliers. What is required is an increased awareness by all firms that efficient prices will prevail only if adequate global search procedures are employed to find efficient, low-cost suppliers wherever they are domiciled.

While some industries do have high import propensities, those identified as being involved in IIT tend to also have high export propensities. In particular, there is a tendency for import propensities to rise as the subsidiaries and Canadian-controlled firms increase their degree of specialisation and engage in increased contracting-out to more efficient foreign suppliers. But, at the same time, there also is a tendency for the firms to increase their export propensities, perhaps because of the greater international cost-competitiveness which accompanies increased specialisation. The net result is a rise in cross-trade of the IIT type with the higher level of imports being offset by increases in exports.

The relatively greater response by Canadian-controlled firms in the IIT industries, compared to the subsidiaries, in terms of

137

increased scale and levels of product and production specialisation, may explain their greater improvement in export performance between 1974 and 1979 relative to the foreign sector of control. Such responses would improve their unit costs and make them more competitive internationally. On the other hand, the relatively weaker response by the subsidiaries, even though they started from higher levels of IIT, production specialisation and export performance, is of concern and needs further investigation.

A major policy problem exists in relation to those firms that are continuing in their tariff-factory role and have not adjusted to the changing environment by increasing their degree of specialisation. In this case, imports increase on a one-way basis without the benefit of increased scale and exports. There appears to be a relatively larger group of subsidiaries than Canadian-controlled firms that are acting in this fashion, whether one looks at the non-IIT industries in which they tend to be, or at the ratio of purchased material to value-added. This may just be a temporary problem while the subsidiaries sort out their new role in relation to the changing trade environment and also with their parents and affiliates. But it is of concern that in some cases the problem may be longer-term in nature. Unlike the case of firms that increase imports but also increase exports as they specialise, it is not possible to be as sanguine with respect to subsidiaries that mainly increase their imports from affiliates to remain competitive rather than increasing their specialisation and scale through exports as trade protection declines. In such cases, the subsidiaries will eventually become just wholesalers, importing the products of affiliates. In terms of government policy in the host countries of MNEs that seek higher levels of employment and production in their manufacturing sectors, it is the specialised subsidiary engaged in IIT that is viable in the longer run and such a pattern of development should be encouraged by government policy. At the same time, it should be recognised that some industries and firms may have to contract in accordance with the HOS model of comparative disadvantage.

The most desirable form of adaptation by the subsidiaries would be if they were to develop a long-run comparative advantage that would allow them to become specialised on a full-mission basis with a world product mandate. This requires the subsidiary to have an aggressive management that can build on some firm- or country-specific advantage and export. The subsidiaries would then no longer produce products identical to those of their affiliates. This would increase their propensity to source from domestic suppliers (as well as from affiliates), some of whom may have to be developed by the subsidiaries. This will especially be the case as the movement towards 'just-in-time' production and delivery systems develops and the need increases for local suppliers. No doubt, as the subsidiaries specialise they will increase their imports of minor products and components from affiliates. But so also will their competitiveness improve and their ability to increase exports.

The Canadian-controlled enterprises appear to now be at least as specialised, if not more so, than the subsidiaries in their production activities as well as in the products they produce. This will help to make them more competitive with the subsidiaries and other competitors at home and abroad. However, the subsidiaries do have the advantage of being able to offer a wider variety of products because of their ability to wholesale the different products of affiliates. Therefore, it is important for Canada to have an efficient wholesale and trading-house sector for exports as well as imports that can bring together the different products of several Canadian-controlled producers and offer the final customer the same product variety as can the MNEs.

The subsidiaries do not appear to have increased their degree of production specialisation to the same extent as the Canadian-controlled firms over the 1970s, and may even have become more diverse in some cases. This may reflect a propensity to continue as tariff factories even when such a role is no longer appropriate because of internal rigidities in the MNE to adopt new strategies. This would not help to make them competitive with imports or in export markets. The subsidiaries account for a significant share of Canadian employment and exports so that any cost inefficiency arising from their inability to become more specialised raises some concern. So also does the general lack of increased production specialisation in both sectors of control between 1974 and 1979 by firms in the non-IIT category of industries.

There are large flows of foreign direct investment moving internationally to countries that are competitive. This creates considerable impact on trade flows and manufacturing employment in both the host and home countries. The next chapter will turn to some of the policy issues related to trade and MNEs that have been raised by this study.

NOTES

1. The reader is referred to the relevant publications by Statistics Canada for further details on the methods used for collecting and reporting the data used in this study. The concepts and definitions relating to establishments, enterprises and other reporting units are contained in Catalogues 31−528 and 31−203. The ICC and SIC classification procedures are outlined in Catalogues 12−501 and 12−541. The definition and determination of sector of control, BRID code and inter-corporate structures are contained in Catalogues 61−517. The determination of destination of shipments for export purposes is discussed in Catalogues 31−522 (1974) and 31−530 (1979). Other catalogues may also be relevant in describing the data and their sources.

2. Export values, by commodity group, were available from the responses on the 1974 and 1979 Census of Manufactures form to the question asking for the first destination of an establishment's shipments for its largest five commodity groups. A ratio of total exports to total shipments was calculated from this information and used to prorate all the commodity groups for an establishment between domestic and export destinations. While this average export propensity does not provide the true value of exports for each of an establishment's commodity group, it should be close to the actual value. However, the extent of any bias in the estimate is unknown.

In total, the export values used in this analysis are close to those reported elsewhere by Statistics Canada for the trade data on manufactured goods (with one exception for imports, as noted in the Appendix). There are, however, two difficulties that arise from the way Statistics Canada collects export data on the Census form. First, an establishment could report the first destination as an export point even though the goods had been sent to a head office for transhipment as an export. Both the establishment and the head office could then report export sales and create a double count in the data. An adjustment was made for this by allocating exports reported by head offices on their short Census forms back to the establishments from which shipments originated. This adjustment covered about 80 per cent of such exports (which were mainly by the automobile producers) and it largely corrected for this major problem in the export data. Second, firms in the wholesale sector could export manufactured goods, but they would not be reported on the Census of Manufactures because wholesalers do not fall under its purview. No attempt was made to correct for this problem because of its intractable nature. However, the two difficulties with the export data are to some extent offsetting in total, but the amount of any net bias is unknown.

3. The values for imports came from sources different than the Census reports which were used for the information on shipments and exports. Also, import data were available only for 1979 rather than the two years of 1974 and 1979 for which data on exports and shipments were available. The source documents used to determine the value of imports were invoices of foreign exporters and Customs forms. Invoices are normally prepared by firms shipping goods, while Customs forms

140

are normally prepared by Canadian brokers on behalf of their importing clients. The complete sets of documents are reviewed by Customs staff at the port of entry. Customs personnel allocate a five-digit Import Commodity Classification code (MCC) to the documents and a firm-specific identifier called a PD number. The PD identifier is used by Revenue Canada (Taxation) to identify firms remitting payroll deductions and taxes so that it is accurate and complete. Import transactions are largely automated for the major ports of entry.

Revenue Canada audits every import transaction over $10,000 that enters through a major port for its declared fair market value. Statistics Canada also audits the source documents for their consistency and accuracy in the use of codes. All import values are stated FOB with no freight costs included in the fair market value. This is consistent with the valuation of shipments and exports on the Census form.

An algorithm is used to convert the MCC code on the entry documents to a Producer's Standard Industrial Classification code (PSIC), disaggregated to the four-digit level of industry identification. The PSIC code is based on the concept of identifying the industry that would have produced the goods had they been made in Canada rather than imported. The algorithm restates the PSIC code so that it is conformable to the SIC code used by Statistics Canada for analysis of the Census of Manufactures data on shipments and exports by commodity class and industry.

4. The firm-specific PD number (see note 3 above) is cross-referenced to a separate code used for determining the ownership of enterprises (i.e. BRID code number). The BRID code was developed by the Business Finance Division of Statistics Canada to trace the ownership of individual enterprises through to the larger consolidated enterprise of which they are a part. Initially this was done to develop comparative financial information on the two sectors of control under the Corporations and Labour Unions Returns Act (i.e. CALURA reports). The BRID code was used in this study to aggregate exports, which are collected on an establishment basis, to the level of the unconsolidated enterprise where it could be matched with the data on imports. The BRID code was also used to aggregate data on imports, exports and shipments up to the level of the consolidated enterprise.

5. Daly and MacCharles, *Canadian Manufactured Exports*.

6. The noticeable improvement in the export propensities of subsidiaries could be accounted for by the greater number of industries included in the intra-sector, as compared to the inter-sector, test. The major reason for this relates to how the tests were performed. In the inter-sector test, the foreign and Canadian sectors of control were matched by industry. But the Canadian sector is not as actively involved in IIT because its enterprises lack the same degree of international affiliations, compared to the subsidiaries. Consequently, the index used to select IIT industries for the inter-sector tests identified fewer IIT industries in the Canadian than in the foreign sector. Those IIT industries for which there were no data for the Canadian sector of control were then put into the non-IIT category. Also, the different mix of industries between the IIT and the non-IIT categories partly explains

why the export performance of the non-IIT industries increased in the foreign sector of control between 1974 and 1979 for the inter-sector tests but decreased for the intra-sector tests.

For the intra-sector comparison on IIT industries, the variability in the export propensities between 1974 and 1979 is less (i.e. the R^2 is greater) and the correlation between the propensities is larger (i.e. the slope of the correlation is 1.0) for the foreign sector than for the Canadian sector of control. The opposite is the case on the T-tests for the non-IIT industries, although the significance of this is weaker than for the tests on the IIT industries. This is due to the greater variability in the data created by the larger increase in the export propensities by firms in the IIT industries and in the Canadian sector of control between 1974 and 1979.

7. The following table shows the results of the T-tests already discussed in relation to Tables 4.17 and 4.18, but using the wide-market rather than the narrow-market definition in the denominators of the import propensities. Only the results for IMSH1 and IMSH5 are presented because IMSH3 and IMSH7 are not affected by this change in market definition and the results for the total import propensities (IMSH13 and IMSH57) are so dominated by IMSH1 and IMSH5 that the results are almost identical for both sets of variables. The results are presented only to assess whether there is any difference in them because of the use of a particular definition of the market.

It does not appear to make much difference in the T-tests whether the narrow-market or wide-market definition is used to calculate the import

Table 4.30: Results of T-tests on Import Propensities (Based on Wide-market Definition) between Sectors of Control for Unconsolidated Enterprises that Import Only, by Size Classes and Trade Categories (Manufacturing Sector, 1979)

| Description | <$10 million in shipments | | | | >$10 million in shipments | | | |
| | IIT | | non-IIT | | IIT | | non-IIT | |
	IMSH1	IMSH5	IMSH1	IMSH5	IMSH1	IMSH5	IMSH1	IMSH5
Number of industries	77	77	69	69	42	42	22	22
Unweighted averages (per cent)	41.7	23.7	31.9	9.4	9.2	10.2	12.4	13.5
Significance of T-test	0		0		0.74		0.67	
R^2 of correlation	0.25		0.29		0.01		0.87	
Slope of correlation	0.49		0.98		0.05		0.69	

Note: IIT = MINDT >0.10; non-IIT = MINDT <0.10.
Source: See text and Appendix.

propensities. The major difference is that the propensities based on the wide definition are marginally lower, as would be expected because of the larger value for the market that is included in the denominators of the propensities. The above table does, however, reinforce the result already discussed that the import propensities of the subsidiaries decline as they become larger for both the IIT and non-IIT industries and become similar to those for the larger enterprises in the Canadian sector of control. This is attributed partly to a relative increase in foreign sourcing by Canadian-controlled firms and partly to import substitution behaviour by the subsidiaries as they become larger and increase their use of Canadian suppliers along with more internal domestic production of components and minor product lines.

Some of the difference in import propensities between the small and large firms for those enterprises that import only (IMSH1 and IMSH5) is accounted for by the way the data were collected. That is, imports by larger enterprises were often allocated to the small size category simply because the imports were minor product lines and components that were not associated with the larger enterprises' major product lines. It is also of interest that the larger enterprises in IIT industries tend to import different products in each sector of control (i.e. $R^2 = 0.01$) while the two sectors import similar products in the non-IIT industries (i.e. $R^2 = 0.87$).

8. A caveat is noted here on the information in Table 4.24. It is a matter of interpretation as to whether the imports of minor product lines and components represent IIT or inter-industry trade. The definition of IIT developed earlier was based on the concept that it is a result of firms both importing and exporting products similar to those manufactured as part of their major product line. Clearly, the imports of minor products and components in trade groups 1 and 5 ('M only') are not similar to the major products of the importers. In many cases these products have been allocated to industries only distantly related to the major industries of the firms. It could be argued, however, that it is not material whether the trade in similar products is by the same or separate firms in an industry with one group of firms importing and another group exporting. The specialisation by some firms in an industry in exports (perhaps because of specialisation in major products differentiated from imported goods) and the imports by other firms (because of production specialisation and increased contracting-out of components and minor product lines to foreign suppliers) are each a response to increased international competition. The resulting impact on trade flows is to create inter-industry trade. However, the important point is that there is cross-trade in similar goods for the industry. Nevertheless, this latter type of cross-trade is suggestive of specialisation in exports by some firms with import competition being provided by others, which is similar to an inter-industry pattern of trade. No particular view on this issue is taken here, except to present the results for the combined imports of firms in trade groups 1 and 5 ('M only') and trade groups 3 and 7 ('Both X and M'). Readers can draw their own conclusions.

9. Baldwin, J. R. and P. K. Gorecki, *Trade, Tariffs, Product Diversity and Length of Run in Canadian Manufacturing Industries:*

1970–1979 (Economic Council of Canada, Ottawa, August 1983), Discussion Paper no. 247; and, by the same authors, *The Relationship Between Plant Scale and Product Diversity in Canadian Manufacturing Industries* (Economic Council of Canada, Ottawa, August 1983), Discussion Paper no. 237.

10. Daly and MacCharles, *Canadian Manufactured Exports.*

5

Policy Issues

INTRODUCTION

Historically, infant industry arguments led governments in countries with small domestic markets to adopt protectionist policies. Canada and individual countries in Western Europe are examples. However, the tendency has been for the infants to have high costs rather than to grow up and become internationally efficient. Protection fostered the development of inward-looking attitudes on the part of managers, constrained firm sizes and led to high levels of diversity in products and production activities. The result was lower productivity and higher unit costs than for more specialised counterparts in larger economies and in smaller economies that had export-led development policies. The US, and more recently Japan and other Pacific-Rim countries, are examples, respectively, of countries with these latter situations. High costs, in conjunction with the attitudes of managers, inhibited protected manufacturers from selling into export markets which denied them a major opportunity for specialising, growing and becoming competitive.

The development of freer trade and increased manufacturing capacity worldwide has led to higher levels of competition which now dictates that managers of small and diverse manufacturers without natural protection must rationalise their operations in order to reduce costs and survive. Small-country governments can aid this process of adaptation by joining larger common market groups. Indeed, many governments had followed this route and the EEC is a case in point. Canada has been late in doing so and is only now engaged in discussions with the US to form a North American free trade area. However, while appropriate government policy is important in terms of negotiating access to international markets and providing a stable and low-cost economic environment, informed managers form the key element in survival strategies. They must be outward-looking and understand that the route to cost reduction is through increased scale, specialisation, contracting-out and niche marketing based on product differentiation using large export markets to achieve these objectives. The impact of such rationalisation on production conditions in smaller countries, carried out on an international basis, has resulted in intra-industry trade.

This analysis, using Canada as a case study, has reviewed the interrelationships between international trade flows, direct foreign investment and rationalisation using the IIT paradigm as a guide to the analysis. It has shown the major role played by MNEs in Canada's international trade, especially in the transportation industries. It has also shown a strong association between MNEs, intra-firm trade and IIT. There are several policy issues arising from these findings that have application generally to small, open economies that must cope with a world of increasing international interdependence, competition and exposure to changes, often volatile, in economic circumstances.

One policy issue is the kind of adaptive behaviour used by subsidiaries as barriers to trade are lowered. Many foreign subsidiaries exist because of initially high barriers to trade since they were convenient substitutes for exports from home countries as a way to access protected foreign markets. MNEs could now reverse this process as barriers to trade are reduced, substituting home-country exports for production in host countries. Such behaviour would have significant policy implications for host country governments because of its impact on domestic income, output and employment in manufacturing.

Other policy issues also arise when firms rationalise under the pressure of increased competition. They pose questions about whether the consequent resource reallocation and changes to trade flows resulting from the transition to freer trade will create major adjustment costs and whether transfer prices on the large trade flows transacted by MNEs on an intra-firm basis are efficient. Policy issues of this kind will be addressed by this chapter. First, however, the empirical findings on Canadian IIT will be reviewed, some caveats noted on the extent of IIT and the evidence reviewed on changes to scale and specialisation in Canada over the 1970s as competition increased.

EXTENT OF IIT

In terms of the sub-categories of trade making up total trade undertaken by firms, the subsidiaries are relatively more involved than the Canadian-controlled firms in cross-trade of major products and in one-way trade as importers only of components and minor product lines from affiliates and third-party suppliers. The Canadian-controlled firms are relatively more involved than the subsidiaries in one-way trade as exporters and in having no international involvement whatsoever. But the bulk of international trade is by the larger firms in both sectors of control and it is largely of the IIT type. The larger enterprises account for over two-thirds of Canadian imports (excluding the auto industries), with the subsidiaries being responsible for almost 70 per cent even though they account for only about 45 per cent of non-auto shipments. The larger firms also account for the major portion of exports, with only 20 per cent of them by enterprises that export only and the balance of 80 per cent by enterprises that both import and export their major product lines on a cross-trade basis.

On a cross-section basis, for the trade in major products of the IIT industries, there is a relatively high R^2 and high correlation between import and export propensities. That is, as import propensities increase across these industries, so also do the export propensities. These results are supportive of the hypothesis that firms engaged in IIT do tend to move resources into the production of exportables and rely on imports to replace the production of products and components that have been displaced as the firms specialise. This resource reallocation is largely within firms and industries. However, this is not the case for the non-IIT industries. In these industries, the firms tend to be specialised in either imports or exports on an inter-industry basis and any increase in exports would have to be accomplished by drawing resources from outside the industry while resources released from any increase in imports (relative to market size) would release resources to other industries. But a high proportion of Canada's international trade in manufactured products is associated with the IIT industries and firms, especially the subsidiaries.

147

Over 80 per cent of manufacturers are small and Canadian-controlled (excluding the double-count created by enterprises that import only), although they account for only about 10 per cent of manufactured shipments. They also have very little involvement with international trade. In addition, the small subsidiaries tend to be tariff factories with significant imports. These small firms in both sectors of control are high-cost and vulnerable to import competition. Some of them enjoy natural protection in the form of freight-cost advantages and local-purchase preferences and will continue to exist because of this. But a large number could benefit from increased scale through export sales to make them competitive. However, many of them are incapable of making the transition from being suppliers to local and regional markets to growing into larger, cost-competitive, export-oriented firms. Many of them are bound to exit from their industries over time for lack of competitiveness or else, in the case of subsidiaries, move out of manufacturing completely and become just wholesalers.

However, it is these smaller firms, and especially those in the Canadian sectors of control, that in total have created most of the growth in employment over the last decade. Furthermore, it is these firms that offer the largest opportunity for increased exports, income and employment. It is difficult to see how policy can be used to identify the winners ahead of time in order to promote their growth. For this reason, all that can be done is to ensure there is a favourable cost environment that will attract new foreign industries and allow the winners in both sectors of control to grow and succeed. Government-sponsored information and management education programmes would also be appropriate so as to reinforce the point that the longer-term success of smaller manufacturers depends on them becoming specialised exporters.

It is the larger enterprises in both sectors of control that account for the major portion of the international trade in manufactured products (excluding imports of manufactured goods by non-manufacturers in the wholesale sector). These larger enterprises, while representing only 5 per cent of the total number of manufacturing firms, account for over 50 per cent of the shipments of manufactured products. They are extensively involved in the international trade of their major product lines on a cross-trade basis, which is consistent with IIT. This suggests that both sectors of control are responding in a major way to the changing trade environment through increased scale, specialisation and export activity.

One policy implication of this information is that subsidiaries should be encouraged to seek world product mandates and plant specialisation agreements with their parents. Ideally, they should be based on comparative advantages held by or accessible to domestic firms. This would avoid the problem of having them abandoned or turned into just wholesalers because they are not competitive. This is particularly appropriate in the case of the small subsidiaries that are continuing in their traditional role as unspecialised tariff factories even when the trade environment has changed and this role is no longer justified. Also, the small Canadian-controlled firms should also be encouraged to engage in more contracting-out to efficient suppliers at home and abroad and to export more.

CAVEATS ON IIT

This study has emphasised that IIT is a function of firms responding to increased competition by increasing their degree of specialisation and scale through exports. It has also shown IIT to be extensive (when it includes trade in both final goods and components) based on the traditional Grubel and Lloyd index as the basis for measuring it. However, two major caveats must be expressed on the accuracy of the G&L index. One is its lack of sensitivity to the significance of IIT relative to total activity in an industry. For many industries, the index measured high levels of IIT flows, but they were not significant in relation to total output and employment in these industries.

The other caveat is evidence that the index overstates IIT when it is measured at the level of the industry. Disaggregating the data to the level of sectors of control within an industry, as was done for this study, indicates that in some industries what is measured as IIT by the index is really not IIT but the effect of combining two different types of inter-industry trade. The foreign sector tends to be relatively import-oriented, especially because of its extensive wholesale activities, while the Canadian sector of control tends to be relatively more specialised in exports of related goods. When these two different types of trade activity are aggregated across the sectors of control in order to arrive at industry level data, it gives the appearance of

149

cross-trade in the related goods of an industry. In fact, the firms are often specialised by type of trade as either importers or exporters. In this study, a variant of the G&L index was used (i.e. the MIND index) which reduces this problem to some extent in the data. But, other studies have not done so and consequently have upwardly biased their estimates of the extent of IIT for many countries and especially for Canada because of its large foreign sector of control and its impact on the trade data.

SCALE AND SPECIALISATION

The above-mentioned caveats, along with other evidence presented in this study, are that cross-trade in just major products by Canadian manufacturers is not as widespread as indicated by other studies. It is even less widespread in the Canadian sectors of control than in the foreign sector. While the extent of IIT is increased if imports of components and minor product lines are taken into account, there is still considerable room for increasing it since much more can be done by smaller producers to increase their scale and by larger manufacturers to increase their specialisation. These adaptations, achieved by increased contracting-out and exports, would lead to further increases in IIT and many firms across a wide range of industries still have to make such adjustments to freer trade in a significant way. When they do, import propensities will increase, as will export propensities. But this should not be considered ground for concern. It is part of an adaptation process that improves production conditions which must be entered into by manufacturers. Attempts to prevent import penetration of domestic markets through increased protection will only retard the movement of the manufacturing sector to a more competitive position and improvements to longer-term employment and incomes.

The export propensities of the subsidiaries and domestically controlled enterprises have increased significantly in IIT industries. Also, the export propensities of domestically controlled firms in non-IIT industries increased significantly over the 1970s, but declined for the subsidiaries. For IIT industries, the domestically controlled firms started from a lower level of export performance and improved it more quickly than the subsidiaries so that by the 1980s they had caught up with the subsidiaries. This is consistent with the domestically controlled enterprises adapting to the changing trade environment more quickly than the subsidiaries and confirms at a more general level similar findings based on a recent study using a small sample of firms.[1]

Since the export propensities do not differ between the sectors of control for the larger enterprises, this suggests that the larger Canadian-controlled ones do not have any greater difficulty gaining access to foreign markets than do the subsidiaries. The policy implication of this is that size is important in achieving success in export markets and that the small firms would benefit from combining into trading-house consortia to market their products internationally.

Small enterprises, even if they are specialised, suffer from cost penalties associated with their lack of scale. Larger firms can also have significant unit cost disadvantages if they have achieved their size through diversification of products and components produced internally instead of purchasing them from suppliers. The product-specific diseconomies of scale associated with diversity can be substantial. One form of adaptation by manufacturers in an era of increasing competition is to increase diversity as market share declines. While this increases plant utilisation levels, it raises costs and adds to longer-term problems with productivity and competitiveness. The evidence from this and other studies indicates that increases in scale and specialisation were at work in the data, as were increases in diversity. The latter were especially prevalent among the subsidiaries. While initially more specialised, they are no longer so compared to their domestically controlled counterparts.[2] This behaviour on the part of subsidiaries is understandable since they traditionally imported minor product lines and components along with some major lines from affiliates for which there was a small domestic demand while manufacturing in Canada those major products that had a larger market demand. Consequently, they were diverse in their wholesale activities (along with having high import propensities for components) but more specialised in production than their Canadian-controlled competitors. The subsidiaries had a competitive advantage in being able to offer a wide product line to meet the needs of their customers without incurring the same level of product-specific cost disadvantages as their Canadian-controlled counterparts who had to produce these items internally or else acquire them from Canadian suppliers at high cost because of the small scale of their production in Canada. It is only natural for the subsidiaries to extend their diversification when market share is lost to increased competition since this is consistent with their past behaviour as tariff factories and was a viable strategy in the past. Also, their higher level of specialisation initially would allow them greater latitude to diversity than their Canadian-controlled counterparts. As a result of this increased contracting-in of the manufacture of products and components, the subsidiaries are no longer more specialised in production (and may even have become more diversified) than their Canadian-controlled counterparts, as well as continuing with high levels of imports as wholesalers of finished goods and consumers of components. This behaviour helps them to remain competitive since they get the cost advantages of the more efficient affiliates from whom they import. However, ultimately it would transform the subsidiaries from being manufacturers to being wholesalers. This has implications for income, output and employment in the host country's manufacturing sector.

Other evidence from this study is also consistent with this type of adaptive behaviour by the subsidiaries. Firms in non-IIT industries in the Canadian sector of control that are specialised as exporters and those in IIT industries in both sectors engaging in two-way trade increased their scale more than the subsidiaries engaged in one-way trade. This indicates that subsidiaries in the non-IIT industries (and in some cases those in the IIT industries) operating as import-oriented tariff factories have not experienced the same growth as have firms in both sectors of control in the IIT industries and firms in the Canadian sector of control in the non-IIT industries that tend to be specialised as exporters only.

To summarise the evidence on scale and specialisation, it appears the subsidiaries are no longer more specialised in their manufacturing activities than their Canadian-controlled counterparts, either horizontally or vertically. In fact, the subsidiaries may even have increased their degree of vertical diversity, which in the longer run would increase their costs and make them even less competitive. This type of response is perverse and would be harmful to Canadian incomes and employment. And by extension, it would be similarly harmful in other small countries with large foreign sectors. However, this could be a temporary situation until the subsidiaries identify a new mission that would move them from being just tariff factories to more specialised and competitive manufacturers. However, this requires conscious planning efforts. The alternative, if this is not done, would be a regression by default on the part of the subsidiaries to wholesaler status. On the other hand, relatively more domestically controlled firms have responded appropriately to the changing trade environment by increasing their degree of specialisation and scale through exports, resulting in a higher growth rate in exports over the 1970s for them than for their counterparts in the foreign sector of control. But, generally, given the lack of widespread IIT along with the large number of small manufacturers and the relatively high degree of diversity by the larger firms in both sectors of control, there is still considerable room for increased scale, specialisation and cross-trade in similar goods for many industries.

POLICY IMPLICATIONS OF THE IIT AND HOS PARADIGMS

The analysis in Chapter 4 indicates that the HOS as well as the IIT models are needed to explain satisfactorily Canada's trade flows of manufactured goods. The HOS model is also useful for explaining trade flows of materials and semi-finished goods because of Canada's comparative advantage in resources. In the case of manufactured goods, the two paradigms are complementary rather than acting as alternative explanations. The HOS model is more appropriate for explaining the trade behaviour of domestically controlled firms, especially the smaller ones, whilst the IIT model best explains the trade behaviour of foreign-controlled firms and larger firms in both sectors of control. Thus the IIT paradigm extends, rather than replaces, the HOS model for understanding international trade flows of manufactured goods. It has particular application to smaller countries with high levels of direct foreign investment in their manufacturing sectors and that are adapting to increased competition.

However, the differences in the two models do lead to different commercial and industrial policies and to different understandings of the adjustment in resource allocation and trade flows as competition is increased. The policy emphasis flowing from the HOS model is on picking potential winners based on assumed prior knowledge of which are the industries with comparative advantages. Generally, subsidies are offered for the firms in these industries to promote exports and to assist them in becoming international 'stars'. However, the policy emphasis flowing from the IIT model is to let market forces sort out the winners from the losers. The reason for this is that policies to identify potential stars are difficult to apply, particularly in small countries because of their relatively large number of small firms. The likelihood of a significant number of these firms surviving and growing is not high. While their birth-rate is high, and they provide the potential source of tomorrow's 'stars', their death-rate is also high. This situation is further complicated because governments do not have access to the type of knowledge at the micro level that is required to predict with some accuracy those firms which are most likely to succeed and are worthwhile candidates for subsidies. The information required on such items as the marketability of products and the capability of management in firms likely to survive does not exist even among the firms' bankers who have a day-to-day working relationship with them. And once product differentiation enters the analysis, it is even more difficult to predetermine which products and firms will be successful. It is unlikely that government planners, who are further removed from first-hand knowledge on such matters than bankers, would be able to identify the winners ahead of time. Only the test of profitable market acceptance in competitive world markets can sort out this issue.

The IIT paradigm, therefore, suggests governments should not try to pick winners ahead of time. Instead, since only the firms themselves know their firm-specific strengths and comparative advantages, each should be allowed to develop the necessary strategies to take advantage of them in international markets. This is in contrast to the HOS model which would identify winning industries and provide help to all firms in them on the basis that all firms in an internationally competitive industry should thrive. The main policy role in cases where rationalisation is needed should be for government to reduce protection and limit itself simply to advising manufacturers on the reasons for their high costs so they can more quickly see the route to cost-reduction through increased exports, scale and specialisation.

This policy role for government is different than the emphasis which flows from the HOS model of identifying industries with comparative advantages based on present factor endowment ratios and its inherent short-range viewpoint. Such a role emphasises short-range issues and detracts from more appropriate longer-run public policies that should be directed at *changing* areas of comparative advantages such as remedying deficiencies in the supply of key inputs. This would include better management training, improved labour training, increased funding of the social and management sciences and encouragement of faster adoption of new technologies in use elsewhere in the world.

COMPETITIVE ADAPTATIONS IN RESOURCE ALLOCATION AND TRADE FLOWS

The type of adjustment in resources and trade flows that takes place as protected economies are subjected to increased compeition is all-important. There are two competing hypotheses that suggest very different adjustments. In the HOS paradigm, resources are reallocated to exporting industries from different import-competing ones. Costs for a product would differ from country to country, depending upon the resources that were relatively abundant and cheap in each country and the relative amount of them used in a product. Cost differences arising from these influences would lead to trade between countries, with each country specialising in industries that export products in which it has an advantage and importing the products of other industries from other countries in which there is a domestic cost disadvantage. Industries in which producers are internationally competitive would have increasing export propensities as output expanded and resources were attracted from declining industries that were not competitive. At the same time, import propensities would increase and export propensities decline for producers in uncompetitive industries. The result would be inter-industry shifts in trade flows and resources.

These inter-industry changes are different than those predicted by the IIT model in which uncompetitive firms, instead of going out of business, rationalise their operations. Resource reallocation takes place within the firms in an industry as they drop high-cost products, contract-out production activities, retrain their labour force and improve production facilities. At the same time, both import and export propensities increase for the industry.

The major reason for the different resource reallocation between the two models is a result of them having different emphases. The HOS model emphasises disaggregation of

155

economic activity to the level of the industry only, whereas the IIT model carries the disaggregation to the level of the plant. The HOS model assumes all firms produce efficiently using latest state-of-the-art technologies, even in high-cost industries. International cost differences for a product only arise because of differences between countries in the relative domestic availability and prices for the key inputs of an industry. And these cost differences apply to all firms in an industry within a country. Firms are also assumed to be price-takers and if the prices for key inputs were higher than in other countries because of their relative scarcity, then all firms in such an industry would not be competitive and would be forced to close. Labour and other inputs would move from industries and regions to those that were competitive, exporting and growing. No recognition is generally given, as it is in the IIT model, to the possibility that production conditions, or efficiency, can vary in the same industry between countries or even between firms within an industry, creating intra-firm cost differences within an industry. Nor is recognition generally given to the possibility that over time increased competition can lead to adaptation and improvements to production conditions in a country and in individual firms.

The HOS model can be adapted to allow for changes in production conditions through economies of plant scale as output is increased to reduce unit costs. It can also be adapted to allow for changes in the relative availability of key inputs, which would lead to lower prices for them and reductions in unit costs. But, again, such changes are generally assumed to affect uniformly all firms in an industry so that resource reallocation remains on an inter-industry basis as trade is liberalised. Also, the import and export propensities still change in opposite directions for an industry rather than in the same direction. The difficulty with the HOS model is that these predictions are inconsistent with actual developments. First, there has been an increased flow internationally of resources, people, technology and knowledge that has narrowed the gap between countries in the availability of the key inputs to production, especially for the production of exports in many countries. Second, trade patterns have changed such that there have been simultaneous increases in both import and export propensities in the smaller countries.

Adaptation of the HOS model to allow for industry-wide improvements to efficiency and costs, by allowing for plant- and firm-level economies of scale and increased availability of key inputs over time, has made it more dynamic. Indeed, this variant of the model is termed the dynamic model of comparative advantage. It has been used by many countries, especially the smaller countries in the Pacific-Rim, as the basis for industrial policy. They target for rationalisation those industries which have unexhausted scale economies and aid firms in the targeted export industries. Such policies help to explain the success of the planned economies in penetrating the international markets for high-technology goods in recent years.[3]

However, the HOS model is not appropriate for explaining changes in resource allocation and trade flows that emanate from factors at work in firms which require information disaggregated to a level below that of an industry. It is the changes within firms, rather than industries, that often determine which products will be exported and imported. Firm-specific comparative, or natural, advantages do exist that can be both developed and acquired by individual firms and that are not available to the industry as a whole. These advantages include such items as technological leads spun off from R&D efforts, differences in marketing expertise and unique management skills. International trade determined by which firms have specific advantages results in intra-industry rather than inter-industry resource reallocation and trade as some firms become 'winners' even if they are in a 'losing' industry.

The resource reallocation in the IIT model is mainly within firms in an industry as they reduce their inefficiency and become internationally competitive. As a result, both the import and the export propensities increase for an industry in which this rationalisation process is going on. One of the dominant features of international trade over the past twenty years has been the simultaneous increase in both imports and exports, across a wide range of industries in the manufacturing sector, between the industrialised nations which have relatively similar factor endowment ratios.[4] At the same time, there has been an absolute decline in the level of employment in manufacturing. The IIT model not only explains the increase in both propensities but also explains the reduction in manufacturing employment through the improved efficiency that accompanies the increased scale and specialisation which underlies increases in IIT. Therefore, the IIT paradigm appears to have some relevance in explaining actual trade flows which are not handled as well by the HOS model.

157

The major national exception to the simultaneous growth in both propensities across a wide range of industries is Japan. One explanation of this is the Japanese insistence on reliability in suppliers because of their use of 'on-time' production and inventory control methods. This precludes imports from distant suppliers in the industrialised nations and a consequently higher propensity to use domestic suppliers. At the same time, Japanese purchasing practices help to ensure domestic suppliers are internationally competitive. Therefore, Japanese imports have not risen commensurately with exports as they have elsewhere, even though there has been significant rationalisation through increases in specialisation, scale and exports along intra-industry lines.

It is the firms in the IIT model that undertake the cost of retraining labour as rationalisation takes place. This is in contradistinction to the HOS model which implies considerable public assistance to help labour retrain and relocate on an inter-industry and inter-region basis. As a result, in the IIT model, resource reallocation would be quicker and smoother, thereby considerably reducing the costs of dislocation and unemployment and lessening the need for government assistance to smooth the transition process. This should help to allay the fears of those affected by increased competition since the resource reallocation associated with it is considerably less traumatic than would be associated with inter-industry resource shifts. In the case of Canada, it has been estimated that the total cost, in terms of unemployment and relocation costs, of moving to complete unilateral free trade would be about 6 per cent of the total resources involved in the reallocation.[5]

This is not meant to suggest that it will be easy to undergo the transition through increased specialisation, scale, contracting-out and exports as rationalisation takes place. The North American automobile industry is a case in point. The movement towards increased rationalisation since the early-1980s as a result of increased competition has forced producers to reallocate resources internally into specialised production facilities and to engage in greater contracting-out to efficient suppliers. Some auto workers that were laid off will never be re-employed in the industry and they may have to be retrained and seek opportunities in other industries. Nevertheless, many of the workers have been continuously employed in the industry as it went through the adjustment period and others have been re-employed as the firms became more competitive. Had the auto industry been abandoned in line with the principles of the HOS model of inter-industry trade all these workers would have been required to seek employment in other industries that were internationally competitive, which would have proved far more traumatic. The major difficulty with rationalisation lies not so much in the disruption costs associated with resource reallocation, but in getting access to and implementing the new skills and technologies that are needed to be efficient in a world where large and rapid technical changes are taking place.[6]

MNEs, INTRA-FIRM TRADE AND IIT

The MNEs are particularly well positioned to engage in rationalisation. They can make available to their subsidiaries significant advantages through their control of large pools of management expertise and state-of-the-art knowledge on new production technologies and products. This knowledge flows readily on an intra-firm basis and provides foreign subsidiaries with comparative advantages over their counterparts, especially the smaller ones, in host countries. They also have more flexibility in rationalising production through specialisation because of the access subsidiaries have to products of affiliates and the marketing channels of parents. As a result, the subsidiaries are better able to reduce costs and gain access to export markets and this creates international intra-firm and intra-industry trade and resource reallocation.

The evidence from this study, and also from the literature survey, is that IIT and direct foreign investment (DFI) are strongly related through intra-firm trade flows. Some estimates have put the level of intra-firm trade at 70 to 80 per cent of Canada's total trade, although this seems high in the light of the evidence from this study. But certainly a large portion of trade is on an intra-firm basis. Studies by other researchers indicate that about 80 per cent of the exports of Canadian subsidiaries go to affiliates with over 80 per cent of them being materials and components meant for further processing by the receiving affiliates. Imports from foreign affiliates are also extensive. Other studies have estimated these to be about 10 per cent of shipments by Canadian subsidiaries with approximately two-thirds of them being finished goods (i.e. major and minor products) with the balance being components and capital equipment used in manufacturing. The data from this study indicate imports by subsidiaries are now higher than when the earlier estimates were calculated, at about 25 per cent of shipments (excluding the auto industries). The present higher import propensities may reflect increased IIT since the original research was done. Disaggregating the estimate of imports to shipments of this study into the type of goods imported suggests about 20 per cent of these are minor products (i.e. about 5 per cent of shipments), 40 per cent are major products and 40 per cent are components (i.e. about 10 per cent of shipments each). The imported components divide about equally into those from affiliates and those from third-party suppliers. The imports from third-party suppliers do not directly constitute intra-firm trade, but a proportion of it arises because of the relationships the foreign suppliers have with the foreign affiliates of the subsidiaries in Canada. Consequently, some of this trade could be classified as semi-tied. These estimates indicate that combined imports of finished goods (i.e. both minor and major products) comprise about 15 per cent of shipments by Canadian subsidiaries. These are items imported from affiliates mainly for resale without further processing, with the subsidiaries acting as wholesalers. On this basis, wholesale activities represent over one-half of imports by the subsidiaries and account for a large part of the difference between the sectors of control in their import propensities.

The connection between intra-firm trade and MNEs exists because the multinationals can specialise plants internationally and utilise their marketing organisation in each country as wholesalers to distribute the products of their plants on an international basis. Also, they can establish plants as specialist suppliers of components to affiliates. The specialisation of products and production activities across nations allows them to overcome the problems of small-scale production and diversity of activities that would otherwise exist if the plants were producing all products and components for just the domestic markets of the nations in which they reside. Such specialisation is particularly important for the smaller countries such as Canada because firms owned by nationals do not have as ready an access to management skills and technologies and to large domestic markets, thereby constraining their ability to be large, specialised and efficient producers. Subsidiaries owned by multinationals help to make the domestic manufacturing sector more

efficient. In addition, the spill-over of their methods and knowledge to smaller domestically controlled firms is an important
benefit to countries hosting the subsidiaries of MNEs.

However, to benefit from the increased efficiency and competitiveness that results from international specialisation by
MNEs, it is necessary to accept that much international trade by
the smaller countries will be in the form of intra-firm transactions as MNEs trade products and components among themselves on a two-way basis. The MNEs, through their ability to
specialise internationally, create benefits in an era of increasingly freer trade which would not otherwise be as readily
available to the smaller countries in which they invest. The
MNEs give their subsidiaries access to world markets which
provides an opportunity for them to specialise and increase their
scale and exports (provided they are in a hospitable cost environment and can show they are competitive with other suppliers and
plants). They also give subsidiaries access to efficiently produced
components and minor product lines that would otherwise have
to be produced at a higher cost either by local suppliers or
through internal production by the subsidiaries themselves. This
is why, given the high level of DFI in Canada, there is a high
elasticity of exports with respect to imports. The subsidiaries
provide greater opportunity for rationalisation as competition
increases, which has made easier the process of adaptation to
increased competition. The flexibility to carry out rationalisation strategies creates two-way flows of products and components between affiliates. The result is a strong relationship
between the number of MNEs in a country that are adapting to
increased competition and the level of IIT. For smaller countries, the net impact of having high levels of DFI is a greater
potential to adapt to increased competition with increased cross-
trade on an international basis as both exports and imports
increase with rationalisation. As a result, the subsidiaries help to
stabilise income and employment during the transition to
increased competition.

It is important to point out, however, that the achievement of
these benefits from DFI in an era of increasing competition
assumes the subsidiaries do adapt to the changing environment
by becoming large, specialised manufacturers that are internationally cost-competitive and capable of exporting. This is less
of a problem for the large subsidiaries but more serious for the
small tariff factories. But, based on the evidence for Canada,

subsidiaries of all sizes are slower in adapting than domestically controlled firms because of various rigidities encountered by them in reallocating resources. This is partly related to the lack of awareness by local managers of the need to develop a new role for their subsidiaries as the trade environment changes. Local managers are also not aggressive in pursuing the adoption of new missions with corporate-level management, partly because they are relying on the natural advantages of the larger corporation and its deeper purse to provide continuing protection. But such behaviour is no longer appropriate in a world where new competitors also have similar advantages. Nor may corporate-level managers, either, be enlightened about the need for a new role for the subsidiary. Other factors also intervene to prevent the foreign-controlled firms from adapting as quickly as might be desired, such as regulation or the creation of barriers to international investment and trade flows.

PURCHASING PRACTICES AND TRANSFER PRICES

The value of major product lines imported, as a ratio of shipments, declines as the subsidiaries become larger, indicating that they produce internally relatively more of their major product lines as they become larger. This is not the case for domestically controlled enterprises. Also, the subsidiaries do not undertake to acquire domestically or produce internally relatively more of their minor product lines and components as they become larger. Instead, they continue to use foreign sources of supply for them. This suggests Canadian suppliers are high-cost, due in part to their small size and diversity, so that it is not beneficial to switch purchases for components from foreign domestic sources of supply. However, the domestically controlled firms do appear to change their source of supply for minor products and components as they become larger, increasing them from virtually nothing for the small enterprises to about 9 per cent of shipments for the larger ones, which is about 75 per cent of the value for the larger subsidiaries. This suggests that the domestically controlled firms purchase relatively more components from foreign suppliers as they become larger, mainly at the expense of domestic suppliers. Clearly, there is a significant difference in the purchasing practices between the smaller and the larger domestically controlled enterprises. It appears that the larger domestically controlled firms engage in improved search procedures for more efficient suppliers on an international basis than do the small ones.

What emerges from this information on import performance is that Canadian-controlled firms, especially the smaller ones, do not engage as much as might be desired in adequate search procedures for low-cost sources of supply internationally. This could harm their competitiveness if they are tied to high-cost domestic suppliers or to internal sources of supply. On the other hand, given the changing trade environment which makes tariff factories less relevant, it appears that the subsidiaries, especially the smaller ones, could undertake to source more of their requirements for components and products domestically which would help to improve the efficiency and costs of domestic suppliers.

It is generally assumed that small, open economies are price-takers in competitive markets for imports and exports. The extensive trade by large firms on an intra-firm basis in both imports and exports does raise the issue of whether or not the transfer prices of the transactions are equivalent to the prices that would be set by efficient, free markets. Since the trade is tied, this allows prices to be set by fiat decisions based on tax avoidance and other income-redistribution criteria. If this is the case, then to what extent is there resource misallocation from the use of fiat-determined transfer prices? Prices set by fiat may also pose a problem for purchases by subsidiaries from third-party foreign suppliers because of their supply relationships with foreign affiliates (semi-tied trade). The estimates derived from this study are that approximately one-half of imports are on a tied basis and a considerable portion of the balance are on a semi-tied basis. The extent to which exports are to affiliates or third parties is unknown. But, clearly there is a potential for a significant part of the pricing of international trade in manufactured goods to be set by non-market factors that might not be in the best interests of subsidiaries or a nation as a whole.

It is known that intra-firm international trade is less price elastic than inter-firm trade. That is, exchange rate changes do not reallocate purchases between domestic and foreign suppliers as much if the trade is intra-firm than if it is inter-firm. This has been the experience for Canada and for other countries as well.[7] But the price stability of tied purchases from affiliates may be due to valid factors. No doubt continuity and stability of supply,

163

quality of the goods, and the proprietary nature of some items purchased from affiliates are all involved and would mitigate against changing sources of supply even if relative prices changed. There are also several audit features in the international trade system that prevent transfer prices being too far removed from efficient ones. For instance, customs authorities in most countries audit the declared values at the port of entry and tax authorities audit transfer prices for income tax purposes. The subsidiaries themselves are also auditors. They are profit maximisers and would resist paying prices to affiliates that might harm their profit performance and reduce their reputation in the eyes of corporate-level managers. However, the issue is one that needs further investigation because of its potential significance, its political sensitivity and the strident manner of some in putting forward their nationalist (and often discriminatory) viewpoints on the issue.

Any investigation of transfer prices, however, should not be limited to just those involved with tied international trade. It should also review the 'tied' trade behaviour of firms buying from domestic suppliers even when the structure of relative prices is such that foreign sourcing would be appropriate. This applies primarily to small domestically controlled firms. Such behaviour is just as serious in terms of its implications for domestic resource misallocation and competitiveness as similar behaviour by the subsidiaries with respect to their tied purchases from affiliates. The almost exclusive use of high-cost domestic suppliers by the smaller Canadian-controlled firms, when cheaper sources of supply are available from foreign manufacturers, would make the purchasers less competitive and reduce Canadian incomes, output and employment. It is the *purchasing practices* as well as the transfer prices used by firms in both sectors of control that should be evaluated, not just the transfer prices used by the subsidiaries.

The extent of intra-firm trade in total international trade of manufactured goods also challenges the appropriateness of the models used for commercial and industrial policy by smaller countries. The usual assumption is that they conduct international trade as small, open economies operating in free markets characterised by conditions of perfect competition. More recognition should be given to elements of imperfect competition and their implications for policy. One movement in this direction is the IIT model, which takes into account the impact on trade flows of product differentiation and first-mover advantages by firms wanting access to international market niches. It is the market power acquired by firms arising from their product differentiation and firm-specific comparative advantages that contributes to IIT flows.

SUMMARY

The subsidiaries in IIT industries engaged in cross-trade do not have significantly different import and export propensities for their major product lines, but their import propensities are higher than for domestically controlled firms. This reflects the larger wholesale activities of the subsidiaries and their ability to specialise internationally. However, most studies of MNEs tend to look at just their import propensities and criticise them for this on the grounds that their high imports displace domestic production and employment. This is misleading, since such analyses do not allow for the large wholesale activities of the subsidiaries which make them more efficient and compatititive, thereby creating, rather than reducing, domestic employment. It is also misleading since the higher import propensities, compared to domestically controlled firms, are also offset (after adjusting for differences between the sectors in their wholesale activities) by higher export propensities because of the greater ability of the subsidiaries to access export markets and engage in cross-trade with their foreign affiliates. Proper analyses would adjust for the difference in wholesale activity between the sectors. In this study, once this was done, the import and export propensities did not differ significantly between the sectors of control for the bulk of Canadian international trade in manufactured goods. To the extent any difference remained it was largely offset by higher export propensities. This important point cannot be made without examining imports and exports together and on a consistent basis of calculation.

However, the issue of transfer pricing and efficient purchasing practices generally, in both sectors of control, is one area needing further investigation. And the generally slower response by the subsidiaries noted in this and other studies to the changing trade environment is an area of concern. Subsidiaries had smaller increases in their export propensities, in their degree of contracting-out, and in their scale and specialisation. This

165

may only be a temporary problem arising from short-term rigidities in the MNEs related to their greater financial staying power which gives them time to delay responding compared to their less liquid, domestically controlled counterparts. Also, short-term rigidities arise because of the inability of local managers in subsidiaries to identify the need for change, which combine with rigidities within the MNEs on a worldwide basis that retards their ability to change quickly. But, their slower response is a matter of concern and warrants further investigation.

Small domestically controlled enterprises suffer cost penalties from their disadvantages of scale. Many of them are not involved in any way with international trade either as importers of low-cost components or as exporters of products. They have higher unit costs than counterpart subsidiaries of the same size because of their shortcomings in the areas of management expertise and attitudes as well as in plant and product-specific economies of scale. Yet, these small firms account for a significant share of output in most economies and their impressive growth over the past decade suggests they can materially affect employment opportunities. Policies directed at informing and educating management would be helpful in improving their competitiveness and growth as exporters. They should consider combining their resources to develop centralised research facilities, greater involvement in employee and management training programmes, more foreign sourcing, improved methods for fostering faster transmission and diffusion of new technologies to their plants, and the setting up of trading houses.

But most importantly, it needs to be recognised that about three-quarters of exports are by the larger consolidated enterprises, representing one-quarter of their output. These export propensities are two to four times those of the small enterprises. Scale and specialisation *are* important to productivity and export performance. The smaller enterprises need to become more outward-looking and all enterprises need to consider expanding their specialisation and scale through exports and increased contracting-out. The net result will be improved performance on cost and productivity. There will also be increased IIT which, while bringing about a rise in imports, will at the same time cause exports to increase. This will enure to the benefit of domestic income and employment in domestic manufacturing sectors for the smaller countries on a worldwide basis.

166

NOTES

1. Daly and MacCharles, *Canadian Manufactured Exports*.

2. The data in this study suggest this is happening, as do studies by Baldwin and Gorecki, *Trade, Tariffs, Product Diversity*; see also by the same authors, *The Relationship Between Plant Scale*; and also Daly and MacCharles, *Canadian Manufactured Exports*.

3. Scott and Lodge (eds), *U.S. Competitiveness*.

4. Laroisière, 'Persistent Structural Rigidities'.

5. Harris with Cox, *Trade, Industrial Policy*.

6. Baranson, Jack, 'Trade Liberalization and the New Generation of Manufacturing Technologies: Implications for Canadian Industry in North America's Markets' (Illinois Institute of Technology, Chicago, 1986), mimeograph of a paper for the 4th International Congress of the North American Economics and Finance Association, Montreal, July 1986.

7. Daly and MacCharles, *Canadian Manufactured Exports*; and Goldsbrough, 'International Trade of Multinational Corporations'.

Appendix

Description and Treatment of Issues Related to Data

IMPORT PROPENSITIES AND DOUBLE-COUNT OF ENTERPRISES

The use of the four categories of unconsolidated enterprises, based on the type of involvement they had with international trade as discussed in the introduction to Chapter 4, created some complexities as to the data and its analysis. In particular, imports could not be as readily related, as could exports, to domestic shipments of similar goods by producers in order to calculate import propensities. The values for shipments and exports come from the same Census of Manufactures document, by establishment, so they are easily matched to each other and to the establishment and commodity groups to which they belong. But, in the case of imports by enterprises in groups 1 and 5 ('M only'), they cannot always be related to the shipments of an enterprise if the imports are components that have been allocated to an industry unrelated to the output of the establishment. To a lesser extent, this also applies to imports of minor product lines imported for resale if these products are only distantly related to the shipments of the major product lines of an enterprise. These data problems apply mainly to imports by foreign-controlled subsidiaries. Since there would be few or no shipments of these imported items by the importing establishment, the result would be to bias the import propensities upwards for the enterprises in groups 1 and 5 ('M only'), even though these enterprises might have significant levels of shipments in the other industries to which their main products belong.

This bias in import propensities could be overcome by adding together the shipments of each enterprise across all the industries in which it operates (i.e. across all four categories of international trade activity). This was done when appropriate, but such a procedure introduces other difficulties because the shipments of groups 4 and 8 enterprises ('No X or M') are included in the denominator of the propensities in such a case. As will be noted later, this group is chiefly comprised of small, Canadian-controlled enterprises serving purely local, regional and national markets in Canada. There is virtually no counterpart to this group in the foreign sector of control. Therefore, by summing shipments across all trade groups to avoid one bias, another bias is introduced since the import propensities for the 'M only' group of enterprises would be biased downwards for the Canadian sector of control, compared to those for the foreign sector.

In an attempt to determine the boundaries of these biases, two different calculations were made for the import propensities. One included the shipments for enterprise groups 1 and 5, 2 and 6, and 3 and 7 ('M only', 'X only' and 'X and M') for which there is greater comparability in the types of enterprises between the sectors of control. This is referred to in the balance of this chapter as the 'narrow-market' definition for a propensity. The other variation included the shipments for all four groups of enterprises, including the 'No X or M' group, and is referred to as the 'wide-market' definition. The true propensity in an industry for groups 1 and 5 enterprises ('M only') probably lies somewhere in between these two variations. In fact, as is noted in Chapter 4, there is very little difference in the results of the tests for significant variations between the sectors of control, no matter which definition is used.

The problems noted above associated with calculating the appropriate import propensities for 'M only' unconsolidated enterprises do not arise in the case of the consolidated enterprises. In this case, the imports of an enterprise are consolidated across all enterprise groups and industries associated with the overall entity. The total for imports is then related to the total shipments of the entity. The consolidated enterprise is allocated to the industry in which the major portion of its shipments belong. This does create another problem since the consolidated enterprise could be allocated to an industry that is not appropriate for some of its imports of minor product lines and components. But at least the imports are associated with the shipments of each enterprise doing the importing, which is one of the items of interest to this study.

The allocation of imported components and minor product lines distantly related to the main industry of an enterprise also resulted in an inflated count of the number of unconsolidated enterprises in the manufacturing sector as a whole, as well as in individual industries and trade groups. This is because an enterprise could import the products of several different industries. For instance, an enterprise could be a television producer and the shipments of its major product lines would be associated with the television industry. The enterprises would correctly be included in the count of producers belonging to that industry. However, if it also imports transistors and picture tubes, then it would also be counted in this study as being in these different industries as well. Thus, the count of enterprises actually producing in the manufacturing sector would be overstated by the entries in the transistor and picture tube industries, as would also be the count in these individual industries and enterprise groups. This is not a problem, however, when dealing with the consolidated enterprises since they are counted only once and for the industry to which the major products of the enterprise belong. This issue affects the count of enterprises presented in Chapter 4 but it is not a significant problem.

COMPARISONS OF DATA WITH OTHER PUBLISHED SOURCES

The Census data used in this analysis, which was taken from the Census of Manufactures (i.e. MAPID) data bank compiled by Statistics Canada (exports, shipments, value-added and other information from the Census), were cross-checked with publications issued by Statistics Canada to ensure they were consistent in total. No major exceptions were found. However, in the case of imports (which were developed from non-MAPID sources) a significant variation was found and it has major implications for public policy towards MNEs. The total value of imports used for this analysis was about one-quarter higher than the value of imports reported by Statistics Canada in a publication that compared imports and import propensities between the sectors of control.[1] Subsequent investigations determined that the difference arose from the wholesale activity of manufacturers and this is particularly associated with foreign-controlled subsidiaries. Statistics Canada did not include in their analysis the imports of manufactured goods brought in by non-manufacturers who resell items without further processing. An example would be a company with no manufacturing facility which imports furniture or clothes as a retailer or wholesaler. But such imports would be included in the data base used for this study because all manufactured imports were allocated, by enterprise, to the manufacturing industry that would otherwise have produced them in Canada.

The emphasis in this study is on the trade activities of manufacturers. The inclusion of imports related to the activities of firms in the wholesale, retail and other sectors would distort the analysis. Removed from the data, therefore, were the value of imports and their resale value by enterprises with no shipments of goods manufactured in Canada. The following procedure was used: if the shipments for an enterprise were equal to zero (where shipments could be in any of the 159 SIC industries but excluded the manufactured goods imported for resale), then the value of imports and their subsequent resale value were deleted from the data bank. It was necessary to make this adjustment only for the imports and sales of groups 1 and 5 enterprises ('M only'), and it is similar to the one implicitly made by Statistics Canada in its study of import propensities by sector of control.

This adjustment did introduce a bias into the import data which would affect comparisons of import propensities between the sectors of control. The bias would arise because foreign-controlled subsidiaries would tend to be more actively involved in importing goods as wholesalers, because of their access to the products of their foreign affiliates, than would Canadian-controlled manufacturers. As a result, eliminating the imports of manufactured goods by wholesalers with no manufacturing activities would understate the imports and import propensities of enterprises in the Canadian sector of control compared to those of the manufacturers in the foreign sector. This is because the subsidiaries tend to combine both wholesaling and manufacturing into their activities whereas Canadian-controlled manufacturers tend not to wholesale, relying instead on firms in the wholesale sector to perform this function. The significance of this adjustment in relation to total imports of manufactured goods and in relation to each sector of control is shown in

Table A.1: Imports by Trade Group of Enterprises, (Manufactured Goods in $ billions, 1979)

Trade group of enterprises	Imports: this study before adjustment		Imports: this study after adjustment		Imports: Statcan study	
	Foreign sector	Canadian sector	Foreign sector	Canadian sector	Foreign sector	Canadian sector
Group 1 & 5	13.5	14.9	8.4	3.7	n.a.	n.a.
Group 3 & 7	20.5	2.8	20.5	2.8	n.a.	n.a.
Total	34.0	17.7	28.9	6.5	29.7	7.6
Sales	108.4	94.8	102.6	83.2	96.5	81.1

Source: See text.

Table A.1, along with comparisons with the total import values used in the Statistics Canada study of import propensities.

It should be noted that the Statistics Canada study used corporate tax return (CALURA) files as the source for its data, except for imports which came from the same data source as used for this study. CALURA data, in turn, are compiled from the financial statements of firms required to report under an Act of Parliament. Since sales, not shipments, are available from financial statements, the denominator of the Statistics Canada import propensities used sales even though the traditional import propensity calculation uses shipments, plus imports, minus exports (i.e. domestic market disappearance). The MAPID database compiled from Census of Manufactures information used in this study contains data on shipments, imports, and exports, but not sales. The closest measure to sales that could be calculated from the MAPID data was shipments plus imports. This was used as the counterpart to the sales values used for the Statistics Canada study. It is reasonably close, in total, to those values, as is apparent from Table A.1, if the post-adjustment values are compared to the values from the Statistics Canada study.

Table A.1 shows that, based on a comparison of the pre- and post-adjustment values, wholesalers with no manufacturing activities accounted for a significant portion of the value of imports of manufactured goods in 1979. Furthermore, as expected about two-thirds of this activity was by Canadian-controlled firms. One of the conclusions in the Statistics Canada study was that, on average for the manufacturing sector as a whole, the import propensity for the foreign sector of control was over double that for the Canadian sector. However, given the difference in wholesale activities between the two sectors of control and the biased manner in which Statistics Canada adjusted for it, the difference is not that great, especially if allowance is made for the significant imports and shipments by the automobile sector which is mainly in the foreign sector of control. Removing auto sector data would reduce imports and shipments in the foreign sector by about $14 billion and $28 billion respectively (before adjustment for imports by non-manufacturing wholesalers), as well as considerably reducing the difference in the overall average propensity between the sectors of control. The problem is that, given the present methods for determining imports and shipments, it is extremely difficult to adjust accurately for the variations in the level of wholesale activity between the sectors of control. Either goods imported by wholesalers only are removed from the data (as was done for this study), which under-adjusts for wholesale imports by subsidiaries, or no adjustment is possible, which also leaves non-comparable levels of wholesale activity between the sectors of control.

Paired T-tests were carried out on the import propensities between the sectors of control (before the adjustment for wholesaler activity) at the four-digit level of industry aggregation. A propensity was calculated for the importing enterprises in an industry, by sector of control and by type of trade activity within a sector, using the test statistic of imports divided by total sales for an industry. Total sales were calculated using the wide-market definition, which includes the shipments for all four trade groups in the denominator of the propensities. The tests were for significant differences in the propensities between the sectors of control using a two-tailed test. Only industries with observations in both sectors of control were used for the T-tests, thus reducing the number of usable observations to less than the potential full set of 159 industries. The tests were undertaken in order to determine the validity of Statistics Canada's conclusion that there is a difference in the import propensities. The results are presented in Table A.2.

These tests show that, contrary to the Statistics Canada conclusion, there is no significant difference in import propensities between the sectors of control, either overall or for the groups 1 and 5 enterprises ('M only'), if no adjustment is made for

Table A.2: T-tests between Sectors of Control on Cross-section of Import Propensities, by Trade Group of Enterprises and in Total (Manufacturing Sector, 1979)

Trade group of enterprises	No. of industries	Unweighted averages of propensities (per cent)		Significance of difference
		Foreign sector	Canadian sector	
Groups 1 & 5	147	23.7	24.3	0.77
Groups 3 & 7	120	6.1	2.5	0
Total	147	29.0	26.4	0.20

Source: See text.

imports of manufactured goods by non-manufacturers (i.e. wholesalers). There is a significant difference, however, between the enterprises in trade groups 3 and 7 ('Both X and M'), with the foreign sector of control having the higher propensity. But the propensity in this latter case is much lower than reported by Statistics Canada. Further, the difference between the sectors for this group of enterprises is mainly due to the fact that the subsidiaries are far more extensively involved in cross-trade of their products (presumably with foreign affiliates) so that their higher import propensities are offset by higher export propensities. This is an important result since, after allowing for any offsetting exports, it is not supportive of the nationalist position (which found sustenance in the Statistics Canada study) that subsidiaries import significantly more than do Canadian-controlled firms and as a result are harmful to domestic income and employment. The differences between the sectors which were observed by Statistics Canada arise largely because of the wholesale activities of the subsidiaries that have no major counterpart in Canadian-controlled manufacturers. It also arises because the Statistics Canada study focused exclusively on imports and did not allow for the possibility of higher exports by firms with higher imports.

Note, however, that the above conclusions are based on comparing averages for the manufacturing sector as a whole and on T-tests between the individual averages for each industry. These averages do not give weight to the relative importance of the imports by individual industries. This means that dominant industries, such as autos and parts, do not unduly influence the overall and industry averages. But it also means that industries of lesser relative importance have a disproportionate influence on the averages and their comparisons. It is also worth noting here that even though in this study the wholesaler-adjusted values are used for imports solely in order to assess trade in manufactured goods by producers only, it is done with the fore-knowledge that there is a bias in the data as a result of this adjustment. However, the bias, since it is now explicit, can be taken into account when interpreting the results of analyses on the data. This is in contrast to the results of the Statistics Canada study in which the conclusions were largely a result of an undis-covered bias in the data. In addition, T-tests similar to those per-formed above in which the import propensity was calculated by taking imports as a ratio of total sales (i.e. the wide-market definition) were also undertaken using the narrow-market definition of an import propensity (i.e. imports as a ratio of shipments plus imports, minus exports; or what is termed domestic market disappearance). The results of these latter tests were very similar to the tests discussed above and are not reported here because they would add little new information to the analysis.

T-TESTS ON STATISTICS

T-tests of various statistics calculated from data on the 159 industries were undertaken to determine if observed differences in them were significant. The tests presented here relate to the statistics shown in Tables 4.7, 4.11 and 4.14, but the methodo-logy is common to all the tests used for the analysis presented in Chapter 4. The T-tests on the data underlying the overall averages shown in these tables provide a more rigorous basis for the conclusions developed in the discussion on them in Chapter 4. The tests on the statistics were partitioned, depending upon the question of interest, by: size of enterprise; sector of control; trade group; and type of trade predominating in an industry (i.e. IIT or HOS type). The observations on a statistic are paired, by industry, across the partitions used in a test. The purpose of pairing the observations by industry was to ensure that any dif-ference in the averages could be attributed to the influence of the different partitions rather than to the influence of using a

175

different mix of industry observations. The averages presented in the following tables for the various partitions of a statistic are unweighted by the importance of the industries used in each test. The results of the T-tests shown in the tables include its significance, expressed as the probability that the averages are the same in the two partitions being compared. That is, for a significance level of 0.05, there is one chance in twenty that the means are not different. The author has assumed that the null hypothesis in which the averages are assumed to be the same can be rejected at this level of significance.

The number of industry observations used in a T-test depends upon several factors. For instance, if the test is on a statistic calculated just for the large enterprises, then several industries that have no such enterprises would have null observations. Since the tests reported on here do not use null observations, any counterpart observations in the other part of the partition were not used. This results in fewer than the full 159 potential industry observations being used in many of the tests. One of the consequences of this is that the proportion of exports, imports and other variables are less than their total values in some cases. For instance, for the larger enterprises in groups 3 and 7 ('Both X and M') in Table 4.3, total sales were $74,095 million and $36,894 million, respectively. The respective values for total exports were $18,819 million and $10,549 million (Table 4.4). In the case of imports they were $19,919 and $2,436 millions (Table 4.5). But, if only pairable, non-zero value observations are used then the number of industry observations falls from 159 to 80 and the values also fall, in the foreign and Canadian sectors of control, respectively, to: $55,039 and $34,894 for sales; $11,224 and $10,279 for exports; and $14,181 and $2,372 for imports. In this case it is the Canadian sector of control (group 7) that is the major limiting factor because of its less extensive involvement in international trade which reduces the number of industries with non-zero observations. This is especially so for trade groups 3 and 7. A good example of this is the auto industry which has a null observation for the Canadian sector of control, yet this industry represents a significant amount of the manufacturing sector's sales, exports and imports for the foreign sector of control.

One test was on the comparison of the size of enterprises between the sectors of control in order to establish if the differences noted for them in Table 4.7 are, in fact, significant. The results of this test are presented in Table A.3.

Table A.3: Results of T-tests on Average Shipments per Unconsolidated Enterprise; for 159 Industries between Sectors of Control, by Trade Group and Size of Enterprise (Manufacturing Sector, 1979)

Description	Trade group of enterprises							
	M only		X only		Both X and M		No X or M	
	<$10M	>$10M	<$10M	>$10M	<$10M	>$10M	<$10M	>$10M
Number of industries	146	64	100	30	102	80	134	23
Average for industries ($000)								
foreign	113	30,236	2,160	36,697	2,602	65,368	1,649	34,446
Canadian	312	24,458	1,784	45,498	2,430	64,664	735	16,459
Significance of T-test	0	0.42	0.06	0.27	0.48	0.96	0	0.01
Percentage of sales in sample								
foreign	99	76	99	72	96	74	n.a.	n.a.
Canadian	99	91	87	46	95	95	n.a.	n.a.

Source: See text.

The results of the T-tests presented in Table A.3 are generally consistent with those commented on when discussing Table 4.7. There are, however, some differences. In the case of the larger enterprises in groups 2 and 6 ('X only'), there was a difference in average shipments with the subsidiaries having the lower average. But, given the variability from industry to industry in the size of enterprises, this difference between the sectors is not significant. Also, the apparent large difference in firm size for the larger enterprises in groups 3 and 7 ('Both X and M') that is shown in Table 4.7 (with the subsidiaries having the smaller size) is not supported by the tests presented in Table A.3. The difference shown in Table 4.7 probably results from the influence of a few large industries dominating the overall average, since the T-tests on comparable industries show virtually no difference in the average firm size between the sectors of control for this group of enterprises. The results shown in Table A.3 do support the results noted for Table 4.7 that the subsidiaries are significantly larger than their Canadian-controlled counterparts for those enterprises in groups 4 and 8 ('No X or M').

Table A.4 presents the results of the tests for significant differences between the sectors of control on the statistics of: major product line shipments to total shipments; major product line exports to total exports; and major product line imports to total imports. Consolidated enterprises were the economic units for which these ratios were calculated and the results are useful for comparing with those in Table 4.14.

Table A.4: T-test Results on Major Product Lines to Total Shipments, Exports and Imports between Sectors of Control; Using Data Collected on a Consolidated Enterprise Basis for 159 Industries by Size of Enterprise (Manufacturing Sector, 1979)

Description	Size of consolidated enterprises (Sales $)					
	<$10M		$10–50M		>$50M	
	Foreign	Cdn	Foreign	Cdn	Foreign	Cdn
Number of industries	134		77		40	
Shipments						
Unweighted average						
(per cent)	90	93	81	83	65	68
Significance of T-test	0.01		0.41		0.56	
Exports						
Unweighted average						
(per cent)	51	80	64	68	61	65
Significance of T-test	0		0.41		0.42	
Imports						
Unweighted average						
(per cent)	26	41	31	30	30	21
Significance of T-test	0		0.65		0.07	

Source: See text.

The results presented in Table A.4 are similar to those already discussed in relation to Table 4.14. The small enterprises in the Canadian sector of control are significantly more specialised in all three activities. The small subsidiaries have a much larger proportion of their imports in the form of minor product lines and components than do the Canadian-controlled enterprises. And, for the large enterprises in the Canadian sector of control, the import propensity for major products decreases, which reflects an increasing level of diversification by these enterprises as they increase their imports of minor product lines and components. This could be accomplished by greater contracting-out of products and production activities as well as by switching from domestic to foreign suppliers as the enterprises become larger and are more specialised and more aware of the need for increased cost-competitiveness. In the case of exports, the small subsidiaries export a much more diverse array of products than do their Canadian-controlled counterparts. However, there is no significant difference between the sectors for all three activities in the case of the intermediate size firms. Nor is there any significant difference between the sectors for the large firms in their shipments and exports. In summary, the chief differences between the sectors of control for their major activities are mainly for the small firms (who account for a small part of total activity) and in the import activity of firms of all sizes. This latter point is the important one and is drawn upon in Chapter 4.

Table A.5 compares trade balances between the sectors of control (using the statistics of exports minus imports as a proportion of the sales for the consolidated enterprises). The trade balances were calculated for the 159 industries in the data bank, by sector of control. This test provides a more rigorous examination of the information discussed in relation to Table 4.11. Note that the imports and exports are collected by consolidated enterprise and allocated to the industry to which its major output belongs. This may not necessarily be the industry to which all of the imports and exports belong.

The results presented in Table A.5 are clearly supportive of the conclusions reached earlier based on Table 4.11. There is a significant difference between the sectors of control for all size classes, with the foreign sector consistently having negative

Table A.5: Results of T-tests on Net Trade Balances between Sectors of Control; Using Data Collected on a Consolidated Enterprise Basis, for 159 Industries by Size of Enterprise (Manufacturing Sector, 1979)

Description	Size of consolidated enterprises (Sales $)					
	<$10M		$10–50M		>$50M	
	Foreign	Cdn	Foreign	Cdn	Foreign	Cdn
Number of industries	134		77		40	
Ratios						
Unweighted average (per cent)	(10.5)	2.0	(10.3)	(1.0)	(3.9)	3.6
Significance of T-test	0		0		0.02	

Source: See text.

179

trade balances. This result, as has already been discussed in relation to Tables 4.5, 4.10, 4.11, 4.13, and 4.15, primarily comes about because of the greater propensity of the subsidiaries to import minor product lines and components from foreign suppliers.

THE IIT INDICES

This section describes the various indices, based on the Grubel and Lloyd index, that were used to allocate industries to either the IIT category or the non-IIT category. It will be recalled that the Grubel and Lloyd index is a measure of the proportion of total trade in an industry that is represented by IIT. Several variations of it were developed to meet the requirement in this study of determining the extent of IIT in the different data sets on which T-tests were carried out. The major variations in the index that had to be taken into account depended on whether the trade data being analysed were for a particular group of enterprises in an industry, for a particular sector of control in an industry or for the industry as a whole.

One variation of the Grubel and Lloyd index has a micro orientation. It was calculated for each *enterprise* in an industry and weighted by its shipments in the industry. The weighted index was then averaged over all the enterprises in the industry to arrive at the value for the industry as a whole. This index, calculated at the level of the firm, is in contrast to the usual method used to calculate the Grubel and Lloyd index in which total imports and exports are used for the industry, rather than the imports and exports at the more disaggregated level of individual firms in the industry. Because of this distinction the index is called the micro index. One of the variations on this index was to calculate it separately for the two sectors of control in an industry, using only the enterprises in groups 3 and 7 ('Both X and M'). Another variation was to calculate it at a higher level of enterprise aggregation that included the data for all four enterprise groups within each sector of control of an industry. Yet another variation was to calculate the index for an even higher level of aggregation that included all the enterprises in an industry in both sectors of control. The acronyms for these various indices are, respectively, MIND3, MIND7, MINDF, MINDC, and MINDT. The derivation of the acronyms is from the term *m*icro *ind*ex with the suffix representing the level of aggregation of the enterprise groups included in it (i.e. for group *3* enterprises, group *7* enterprises, *f*oreign sector enterprises, *C*anadian sector enterprises, and the *t*otal number of enterprises in an industry).

A different calculation of the index has a more aggregated, or macro, orientation. It is consistent with the traditional calculation of the Grubel and Lloyd index, since it is based on the total values for imports and exports in an industry, rather than on the imports and exports of the individual enterprises. The acronyms used for it are GIND3, GIND7, GINDF, GINDC, and GINDT. The acronyms are based on the words *g*ross (or macro) *ind*ex with suffixes representing the level of aggregation of the enterprise groups in an industry, as outlined for the micro index.

In summary, several indices were used to allocate industries to the IIT or non-IIT categories, which are related to the level of the enterprise aggregation used to calculate them. The levels of aggregation associated with each index are: total imports and exports for an industry (MINDT or GINDT); imports and exports for a particular sector of control in an industry (MINDT, MINDC, GINDF or GINDC); and the imports and exports of particular groups of enterprises within an industry such as groups 3 and 7 (MIND3, GIND3, MIND7 and GIND7).

The use of a particular index depended upon the T-test being undertaken. If the test was between, say, an import and export propensity for the same sector of control then the index for just that sector would be used (e.g. MINDF or GINDF). Further, if the test was on the same propensities but for a particular trade group of enterprises in the foreign sector of an industry (e.g. those that both import and export), then the appropriate indices would be MIND3 or GIND3. Counterpart indices would be used if the tests were on the propensities for the Canadian sector of control (i.e. MINDC, GINDC, MIND7 or GIND7). If the tests were performed on propensities in which the comparison was between sectors of control, then MINDT and GINDT indices were used for categorising the industries to their respective trade categories.

As would be expected, the use of indices based on different levels of enterprise aggregation sometimes resulted in the same industries being put into different categories of trade. An example for one of the industries in the study will be presented here to explain this point. The industry was partitioned into two sectors of control and the three trade groups of enterprises involved with international trade (groups 1 and 5; 2 and 6; and 3 and 7). The trade performance of the enterprises measured by the indices was different in each of the cells created by the partitioning.

The subsidiaries in group 3 ('Both X and M') had a value for GIND3 of 0.81 and for MIND3 of 0.59. Clearly, they were in the IIT category with imports of \$20 million and exports of \$29 million. The subsidiaries in trade group 1 ('M only') were major importers of components and minor product lines, and often not in the industry to which their major product lines belonged. These subsidiaries imported \$138 million and had no exports of products belonging to this industry. The aggregation of the group 1 and the group 3 enterprises resulted in a value of 0.32 for the GINDF index and 0.21 for the MINDF index, both of which were substantially lower than for GIND3 and MIND3 indices. On the basis of the GINDF and MINDF indices, the foreign sector of control would now barely qualify as an IIT industry.

The Canadian-controlled enterprises in trade group 7 were mainly specialised exporters that had only a low value of imports. The GIND7 index had a value of 0.14 and the MIND7 index had a value of 0.05, indicating the significant export orientation of the firms and which would classify them to the interindustry (or non-IIT) category of trade. The enterprises in trade group 5 were active as importers with imports worth \$74 million. These enterprises, like their counterpart subsidiaries, were importing components and minor product lines distant from the industry to which their major product lines belonged. Moreover, the enterprises in trade group 6 that are exporters only, shipped exports worth \$25 million. The aggregation of the imports and exports across groups 5, 6 and 7 increased the value of the GINDC index to 0.69, which would classify the Canadian sector of control in the industry to the IIT category. However, the MINDC index remained low at 0.03. The enterprises in group 5, with their low value of shipments (that are used to weight the index) relative to imports in this, their non-major-product-line industry, did not dominate the index. Consequently, the low value for the MINDC index reflected the specialised export orientation of the industry's international trade and was the more reliable indicator of the type of trade taking place. This index correctly allocated the Canadian sector of the industry to

the non-IIT category which reflected the strong export orientation of the enterprises in this sector of control.

When the trade data are aggregated across all groups of enterprises and both sectors of control in this industry, the GINDT
index has a value of 0.88, which would classify the industry
unequivocally to the IIT category. In fact, the industry as a
whole is very export-oriented with inter-industry trade dominating. The high GINDT arises because the export orientation by
the enterprises in the Canadian sector of control is combined
with the import orientation of the enterprises in the foreign
sector of control to give the appearance of IIT. However, the
MINDT index remains at a low value of 0.07, which is a truer
indication of the type of trade in the industry which is inter-
industry in nature. Again, the micro index is the better measure
because it uses weighted shipments which are very low for the
enterprises importing items removed from the industries of their
major product lines.

The micro indices were the more frequently used ones in this
study for two reasons. One is that they reflect the viewpoint
underlying this study that IIT is a result of actions at the level of
firms as they individually adjust to increased competition. This
view is consistent with the use of the micro indices since they are
calculated from micro-level data. In addition, as has already
been discussed above, the micro indices provide a truer measure
of the predominant type of trade when large imports of components and minor product lines are brought in by one sector of
control while the other sector is export-oriented.

The disaggregated indices (GIND3, MIND3, GIND7 and
MIND7) were used whenever tests were performed on statistics
for enterprises in groups 3 and 7 ('Both X and M') within a
sector of control. GINDF, MINDF, GINDC and MINDC were
used on tests at the overall level within a sector of control, with
the preferred indices being MINDF and MINDC. And GINDT
and MINDT were used on tests between sectors of control, with
MINDT being the preferred index. However, there were situations in which the macro index was more appropriate and the
justification for using it is noted in Chapter 4 when it is used. It
is also worth noting that the tests, whether using the MIND or
GIND series, produced very similar results.

The preference for either a micro or macro index is not an
issue that has been identified as yet in the literature. However, it
is an important issue for countries such as Canada that have

high levels of foreign direct investment because the subsidiaries often have a different orientation on international trade than domestically controlled enterprises. The aggregation of trade data across the sectors of control can obscure this difference and lead to an interpretation of the trade data that is inconsistent with the actual facts, as has been noted in the case study presented above for one industry.

This aggregation of trade performance is a major problem for the Grubel and Lloyd index which is traditionally calculated at the macro level for an industry and does not allow for the different trade performance by different sectors of control or trade group of enterprises within an industry. Canadian trade data are dominated by subsidiaries that import extensively and Canadian-controlled firms that are often specialised in exports. The combination of their behaviour gives the appearance of cross-trade flows in similar goods by firms in the industry, when in fact the two trade flows are distinctly separate and undertaken by different sets of firms. This, in part, no doubt explains some of the relatively high Grubel and Lloyd indices for IIT that have been recorded for Canada by other researchers, as noted in Chapter 3. It may be that in the case of Canada the conceptual problems related to the measurement of IIT are not so much those noted in Chapter 3 of incorrect industry identification (i.e. categorical aggregation and overlapped trade) as they are the problem of aggregating over sectors of control within an industry that perform differently on international trade.

CRITICAL VALUES FOR THE INDICES

A critical value was developed for each index that reasonably and accurately allocated industries to the IIT and non-IIT categories. Two different procedures were used to establish the appropriate critical values. One evaluated the frequency of the values for an index and then used the median value. The other procedure used a sensitivity analysis in which different values of the index were used to allocate the industries and the resulting categorisations were inspected to establish the value that most appropriately allocated them.

A critical value of 0.30 for the gross index and 0.10 for the micro index separated between one-third and one-half of the industries (depending upon the particular index used) into the inter-industry trade category with the balance being in the IIT category. Hence, this test, which is based on the use of frequency distributions, suggested these were the most appropriate critical values to use.

The results of the sensitivity tests are presented in Tables A.6 and A.7. Four statistics were tested for their sensitivity to different values for the indices. They were: exports by enterprise groups 3 and 7 as a ratio of their shipments (EXSH3 and EXSH7 for the foreign and Canadian sectors of control, respectively); and imports as a ratio of the domestic market for enterprise groups 3 and 7 (IMSH3 and IMSH7 for the foreign and Canadian sectors of control, respectively). Table A.6 shows the statistics for the various values of GINDT and Table A.7 shows them for various values of MINDT.

Table A.6: Results of Sensitivity Tests on Export and Import Propensities for Various Values of GINDT; 159 Industries Using Unconsolidated Enterprises (Manufacturing Sector, 1979)

	GINDT value				
Description	0	0.25	0.30	0.35	0.40
Number of IIT industries	120	72	63	57	52
Propensities (per cent)					
EXSH3	20.9	24.0	25.1	23.8	25.0
EXSH7	21.6	23.3	25.2	23.5	24.2
IMSH3	16.6	17.8	17.9	16.8	17.6
IMSH7	12.4	10.0	8.7	8.0	8.4

Source: See text.

Removing non-IIT industries from the total pool of 159 industries should cause the weight of the IIT industries to increase and, in turn, to cause the import and export propensities to increase. This is because of the propensity for IIT enterprises to have high levels of both imports and exports. A continued removal of industries would result in an increasing number of IIT industries to be extracted from the pool. This would result in the propensities stabilising and perhaps even declining. Table A.6 shows rising propensities up to a value of 0.30 for the gross index, after which they start to decline. This is the same critical value that was established above using the frequency method.

In the case of the micro index, MINDT, the criterion outlined above provides a less clear rationale for selecting a particular critical value because all the propensities, except EXSH7, increase across all the succeedingly higher values for MINDT (Table A.7). However, a slight variation in the criterion suggests an acceptable critical value. That is, the difference between the export and import propensities should continue to narrow as industries with predominantly inter-industry trade are removed from the pool. This is because IIT is associated with more balanced propensities while inter-industry trade is associated with unbalanced ones. The narrowing of the propensities, as shown in Table A.7, stops at a value of 0.10 for the MINDT index. This critical value is also associated with the approximate value at which EXSH7 reaches its maximum value and is also the value established above by using the frequency method.

Table A.7: Results of Sensitivity Tests on Export and Import Propensities for Various Values of MINDT; 159 Industries Using Unconsolidated Enterprises (Manufacturing Sector, 1979)

Description	MINDT value				
	0	0.05	0.10	0.15	0.20
Number of IIT industries	120	87	63	44	35
Propensities (per cent)					
EXSH3	20.9	21.4	19.7	24.6	27.1
EXSH7	21.6	22.2	21.7	14.8	16.3
IMSH3	16.6	18.6	21.7	24.6	27.1
IMSH7	12.4	11.5	13.7	14.8	16.3

Source: See text.

On the basis of the above results, the critical value of 0.30 was selected for the gross indices to allocate industries to either the non-IIT category (i.e. those with an index value <0.30), or the IIT category (i.e. those with an index value of >0.30). A value of 0.10 was selected as the critical value for the micro indices (i.e. <0.10 for non-IIT indices and >0.10 for IIT industries).

DATA RELATED TO TABLES 4.21 AND 4.22

The critical values of the IIT indices that were used to allocate the industries to either the IIT or non-IIT categories utilised

186

both the GIND and MIND series as has been discussed in the preceding section. However, for Tables 4.21 and 4.22, for trade groups 3 and 7 ('Both X and M' enterprises), the MIND indices using the critical value of 0.10 did not adequately discriminate between IIT and non-IIT industries since it allocated too many of them to the IIT category. Rather than increase the critical value, the GIND indices were used instead. It has been noted in this appendix that both the MIND and GIND indices are reliable measures of IIT when tests are performed within a sector of control, by enterprise group (as is the case for the data related to Tables 4.21 and 4.22), and can be interchanged. On this basis, the GIND series of indices was used for allocating industries to the appropriate IIT and non-IIT categories. The use of this series was used only for comparisons of the import and export propensities within a sector of control for trade groups 3 and 7 (i.e. IMSH3 and EXSH3 for the foreign sector, and IMSH7 and EXSH7 for the Canadian sector of control). The MIND series of indices continued to be used when the comparisons were between the total import and export propensities (i.e. IMSH13 and EXSH23 for the foreign sector of control, and IMSH57 and EXSH67 for the Canadian sector of control).

In addition, the import and export propensities used for the tests presented in Tables 4.21 and 4.22 were calculated using the narrow-market definition of shipments. This definition excludes shipments for trade groups 4 and 8 ('No X or M'). Also, in the case of the larger enterprises, it is not material whether the narrow- or wide-market definition is used to calculate propensities. Shipments by larger enterprises in both sectors of control for trade groups 4 and 8 are small in comparison to shipments in the other trade categories because most of the larger enterprises are involved in international trade activities so they do not fall into groups 4 and 8. For the larger enterprises in both sectors of control, shipments in trade groups 4 and 8 tend to be a constant proportion of total shipments across all trade groups. Consequently, using the narrow-market definition of shipments does not introduce a significant bias, either between the sectors of control or otherwise, in the import propensities. Indeed, the narrow-market definition may not be as biased as the wide definition. The relatively small value of shipments by the larger enterprises in trade groups 4 and 8, in relation to their total shipments, results in the import propensities based on the wide-market definition being only marginally lower than those based

187

on the narrow-market definition.

It could, however, make a significant difference which market definition is used in the case of the small enterprises. As has already been noted when discussing the overview of the trade data, the enterprises in trade group 8 (i.e. enterprises in the Canadian sector of control not involved in international trade) represent a significant portion of the total shipments in the Canadian sector and which is greater than in the foreign sector of control. This would tend to bias any comparisons of import propensities between the sectors of control. But, it should not influence the tests for Tables 4.21 and 4.22 because they are all done within a sector of control. Moreover, by performing the T-tests on propensities that are based on just the narrow-market definition, any difference between the sectors of control is minimised since the major reason for the variation is shipments by trade groups 4 and 8 and they are not included in the calculation for the narrow-market definition.

In fact, it is not material whether the narrow or wide definition is used for calculating the import propensities used in Tables 4.21 and 4.22. Nevertheless, the tests were performed using both definitions and the results are basically the same. This is because variation in the propensities between the two definitions is insignificant in relation to the variation between industries. Given this, the narrow- rather than the wide-market definition was chosen for the tests presented in Tables 4.21 and 4.22 because the import propensities based on the narrow-market definition conform more closely than those based on the wide definition to the export propensities with which they are being compared. The reason for this is that export propensities include in their denominators the shipments of just the enterprises in the trade groups for which the propensities are calculated. That is, only the shipments of enterprises for those trade groups that export are taken into the calculation, excluding the shipments of trade groups 4 and 8.

For all the above reasons, only the results for the import propensities based on the narrow-market definition are presented in Tables 4.21 and 4.22. It should be recognised, however, that there is not complete uniformity between the calculations for the import and export propensities being compared. While the shipments of trade groups 4 and 8 are excluded from the denominator of the import propensities, some of the enterprises in these groups could be importing minor product lines and components in trade groups 1 and 5. But these enterprises would still be treated as belonging to groups 4 and 8 in spite of their import activity because the imports are of items only distantly related to their major products and cannot be related to the enterprises and their major products in trade groups 4 and 8 because of the way in which the data were collected. Thus, the shipments of these enterprises in trade groups 4 and 8 are not included in the denominator of the import propensities for enterprises in trade groups 1 and 5 and would bias the import propensities upward in comparison to the export propensities. This could only be adjusted for by including the shipments of all enterprises in groups 4 and 8 in the denominators of the import propensities. But, such a correction for one bias, in which shipments are understated, creates another in which shipments would be overstated for enterprises in trade groups 1 and 5. Since shipments by enterprises in trade groups 4 and 8 that do not import and/or export are probably much larger than the shipments of those enterprises that do import minor product lines and components, a smaller bias is introduced by excluding the shipments of trade groups 4 and 8 from the calculation of the import propensities.

NOTE

1. Statistics Canada, *Canadian Imports by Domestic and Foreign Controlled Enterprises* (Minister of Supply and Services, Ottawa, 1981).

Bibliography

Abernathy, W. J., Kim. Clark and Alan Kantrow, *Industrial Renaissance* (Basic Books, New York, 1983).

Alchian, A., 'Costs and Output' in M. Abramovitz (ed.), *The Allocation of Economic Resources* (Stanford University Press, Stanford, 1959).

—— and W. Allen, *University Economics* (Wadsworth Publishing Company, Belmont, Calif., 1972).

Aquino, A., 'Intra-Industry Trade and Inter-Industry Specialization as Concurrent Sources of International Trade in Manufacturers', *Weltwirtschaftliches Archiv.*, vol. CXIV (1978), pp. 90–100.

Astwood, D. M., 'Canada's Merchandise Trade Record and International Competitiveness in Manufacturing, 1960 to 1979', in K. C. Dwhan, H. Etemed and R. W. Wright (eds), *International Business: A Canadian Perspective* (Addison-Wesley Publishers, Ontario, 1981), pp. 48–73.

Baldwin, J. R. and P. K. Gorecki, *Entry and Exit to the Canadian Manufacturing Sector* (Economic Council of Canada, Ottawa, 1983).

—— and P. K. Gorecki with J. McVey and J. Crysdale, *The Relationship Between Plant Scale and Product Diversity in Canadian Manufacturing Industries* (Economic Council of Canada, Ottawa, August 1983), Discussion Paper no. 237.

—— and P. K. Gorecki with J. McVey, *Trade, Tariffs, Product Diversity and Length of Production Run in Canadian Manufacturing Industries: 1970–1979* (Economic Council of Canada, Ottawa, May 1983), Discussion Paper no. 247.

—— and P. K. Gorecki with J. McVey and J. Crysdale, *Trade, Tariffs and Relative Plant Scale in Canadian Manufacturing Industries: 1970–1979* (Economic Council of Canada, Ottawa, May 1983), Discussion Paper no. 232.

Baranson, Jack, 'Trade Liberalization and the New Generation of Manufacturing Technologies: Implications for Canadian Industry in North America's Markets' (Illinois Institute of Technology, Chicago, 1986), mimeograph of a paper for the 4th International Congress of the North American Economics and Finance Association, Montreal, July 1986.

Bergstrand, J., 'The Scope, Growth, and Causes of Intra-Industry International Trade', *New England Economic Review* (September/October 1982), pp. 45–61.

Bradshaw, M., 'U.S. Exports to Foreign Affiliates of U.S. Firms', *Survey of Current Business* (May 1969), pp. 34–51.

Britton, J. M. H. and J. M. Gilmour, *The Weakest Link, A Technological Perspective on Canadian Industrial Underdevelopment* (Minister of Supply and Services, Ottawa, 1978).

190

Brown, W., 'Market Segmentation and International Competitiveness: Trade Theory and Practices Reexamined', *Nebraska Journal of Economics and Business* (Summer 1972), pp. 33–48.

Buckley, P., 'The Modern Theory of the Multinational Enterprise' in *Management Bibliographies and Reviews* (1979), pp. 171–85.

Cacnis, D. G., 'The Sources of Total Factor Productivity Growth in Canada, 1950–1976' (Adelphi University, New York, 1985), mimeograph.

Canada, *Canada's Trade Performance, 1960–1977, Volume 1, General Developments* (Industry, Trade and Commerce, Economic Intelligence Group, Ottawa, 1978).

—— Department of Extrernal Affairs, 'Background Paper on International Trade' (National Economic Conference, Ottawa, 1985).

—— Department of External Affairs, 'Effect of Enhanced Trade on Investment: Survey Evidence' (Ottawa), mimeograph.

—— *Manufacturing Trade and Measures 1966–1982: Tabulations of Trade, Output, Canadian Market, Total Demand and Related Measures for Manufacturing Industrial Sectors* (Department of Industry, Trade and Commerce/Regional Economic Expansion, Ottawa, August 1983).

Caves, R. E., *Diversification, Foreign Investment and Scale in North American Manufacturing Industries* (Economic Council of Canada, Ottawa, 1975).

Daly, D. J., *Canada's Comparative Advantage* (Economic Council of Canada, Ottawa, 1979).

—— 'Canadian Management: Past Recruitment Practices and Future Training Needs' in Max von Zur-Muehlen (ed.), *Highlights and Background Studies* (Canadian Federation of Deans of Management and Administrative Studies, Ottawa, 1979).

—— 'Natural Science and Human Science Research — Does Research Funding Match Canada's Problem Areas?' in Social Science Federation of Canada, *Cahiers No. 9* (Ottawa, 1983).

—— *Rationalization and Specialization in Canadian Manufacturing* (York University, Toronto, 1984), a survey paper for the Royal Commission on the Economic Union and Development Prospects for Canada, mimeograph.

—— 'The Empirical Applicability of the Alchian-Hirshleifer Modern Cost Theory' (York University, undated), mimeograph.

—— and S. Globerman, *Tarrif and Science Policies: applications of a model of nationalism* (University of Toronto Press, 1976).

—— B. A. Keyes and E. T. Spence, *Scale and Specialization in Canadian Manufacturing* (Economic Council of Canada, Ottawa, 1968), Staff Study no. 12.

—— D. C. MacCharles and W. Altwasser, 'Corporate Profit Drop Worst Since 1930's', *The Canadian Business Review* (Autumn 1982), pp. 6–12.

—— and D. C. MacCharles, *Canadian Manufactured Exports: Constraints and Opportunities* (The Institute for Research on Public Policy, Montreal, 1986).

—— and D. C. MacCharles, *Focus on Real Wage Unemployment*

191

(The Fraser Institute, Vancouver, 1986).

Dunning, J., 'Explaining the International Direct Investment Position of Countries: Towards a Dynamic or Developmental Approach', in *International Production and the Multinational Enterprise* (George Allen & Unwin, London, 1981).

Economic Council of Canada, *Au courant*, vol. 4, no. 2, (1983).

—— *The Bottom Line* (Minister of Supply and Services, Ottawa, 1983).

Finger, J., 'Trade Overlap and Intra-Industry Trade', *Economic Inquiry* (December 1975), pp. 581–9.

Giersch, H., *On the Economics of Intra-Industry Trade* (J. B. Mohr, Tübingen, 1979).

Globerman, S., 'Foreign Direct Investment and "Spillover" Efficiency Benefits in Canadian Manufacturing Industries', *Canadian Journal of Economics*, no. 12 (1979), pp. 42–56.

Goldsbrough, D., 'International Trade of Multinational Corporations and Its Responsiveness to Changes in Aggregate Demand and Relative Prices', *IMF Staff Papers*, vol. 28, no. 3 (September 1981), pp. 573–99.

Greenaway, D. and C. Milner, 'On the Measurement of Intra-Industry Trade', *Economic Journal*, no. 93 (December 1983), pp. 900–8.

Grubel, H. and P. Lloyd, *Intra-Industry Trade: The Theory and Measurement of International Trade in Differentiated Products* (John Wiley & Sons, New York, 1975).

Harris, Richard G. with David Cox, *Trade, Industrial Policy, and Canadian Manufacturing* (Ontario Economic Council, Toronto, 1983).

Helleiner, G., 'Transnational Corporations and Trade Structure: The Role of Intra-Firm Trade', in H. Giersch (ed.), *On the Economics of Intra-Industry Trade* (J. B. Mohr, Tübingen, 1979), pp. 159–81.

—— and R. Lavergne, 'Intra-Firm Trade and Industrial Exports to the United States', *Oxford Bulletin of Economics and Statistics*, vol. XLI, no. 4 (November 1979), pp. 297–311.

Hirschleifer, J., 'The Firm's Cost Function: A Successful Reconstruction?', *Journal of Business*, vol. XXXV, no. 3 (July 1962), pp. 235–54.

Johnson, H. G., 'The Efficiency and Welfare Implications of the International Corporation', in C. P. Kindleberger, *The International Corporation* (MIT Press, Cambridge, Mass., 1976).

Keachie, E. and L. Preston, 'Cost Functions and Progress Functions: An Integration', *American Economic Review* (March 1964), pp. 100–7.

—— *Manufacturing Cost Reduction Through the Curve of Natural Productivity Increase* (University of California, Institute of Business and Economic Research, Berkeley, 1964).

Lall, S., 'The Pattern of Intra-Firm Exports by U.S. Multinationals', *Oxford Bulletin of Economics and Statistics*, vol. 40, no. 3 (August 1978), pp. 209–22.

Lancaster, K., 'A New Approach to Consumer Theory', *Journal of Political Economy*, vol. 74, no. 2 (April 1966), pp. 123–57.

192

Laroisière, J. de, 'Persistent Structural Rigidities Must be Tackled For Industrial World To Break Grip of Stagflation', *IMF Survey* (February 1982).

Lermer, G., 'Evidence from Trade Data Regarding the Rationalizing of Canadian Industry', *The Canadian Journal of Economics*, vol. 1, no. 2 (May 1973), pp. 248–56.

MacCharles, D. C., 'Knowledge, Productivity and Industrial Policy', *Cost and Management* (January–February 1983).

—— *Note on the Updating of Lermer Data* (York University, 1982), mimeograph.

—— *Summary of Ownership and Performance Differences: Non-Production Costs and Manufacturing Productivity* (University of New Brunswick, Saint John, 1982), mimeograph.

—— *The Cost of Administrative Organizations in Canadian Secondary Manufacturing Industries* (University of Toronto, Department of Political Economy, 1978), dissertation.

—— *The Performance of Direct Investment in the Manufacturing Sector* (University of New Brunswick, Saint John, 1981), mimeograph.

McCulla, D., *Evaluating Measures of Canada's Industry Trade Performance: Comparative Advantage and Competitiveness* (Department of Industry, Trade and Commerce, Ottawa, 1980), mimeograph.

MacDougall, G., 'British and American Exports: A Study Suggested by the Theory of Comparative Costs', *Economic Journal* (December 1951).

Machlup, F., *The Production and Distribution of Knowledge in the United States* (Princeton University Press, 1962).

Owen, R., *Trade and Investment: A Disaggregate Study for Canadian Manufacturing* (University of Wisconsin, Madison, 1982), mimeograph.

Palda, K. S., *Industrial Innovation* (The Fraser Institute, Vancouver, 1984).

Rugman, A., *Inside the Multinationals* (Croom Helm, London, 1981).

—— (ed.), *Multinationals and Technology Transfer: The Canadian Experience* (Praeger, New York, 1983).

Safarian, A. E., *Foreign Ownership of Canadian Industry* (McGraw-Hill, Toronto, 1966).

—— *Governments and Multinationals: Policies in the Developed Countries* (British-North American Committee, Toronto, 1983).

Scherer, F., 'Economies of Scale and Industrial Concentration', in H. Goldschmid *et al.*, Industrial Concentration: The New Learning (Little, Brown & Co., Boston, 1974).

—— *et al.*, *The Economics of Multi-Plant Operation: An International Comparisons Study* (Harvard University Press, Cambridge, Mass., 1975).

Statistics Canada, *Canadian Imports by Domestic and Foreign Controlled Enterprises* (Minister of Supply and Services, Ottawa, 1981).

—— *Manufacturing Industries of Canada* (Minister of Supply and Services, Ottawa, various years).

193

——— *Survey of Intentions on Business Investment Spending* (Minister of Supply and Services, Ottawa, 1985).

US Department of Labor, *Report of the President on U.S. Competitiveness* (US Government Printing Office, Washington, September 1980).

Wilkinson, B., *Canada's International Trade: An Analysis of Recent Trends and Patterns* (The Private Planning Association of Canada, Montreal, 1968).

Williamson, O., *Markets and Hierarchies: Analysis and Antitrust Implications* (The Free Press, New York, 1975).

Williamson, Peter J., 'Multinational Enterprise Behaviour and Domestic Industry Adjustment Under Import Threat', *The Review of Economics and Statistics*, vol. LXVIII, no. 3 (1986), pp. 359–68.

Wolf, B., *Canada–US Free Trade: Lessons from the European Experience* (York University, May 1981), mimeograph.

Wonnacott, P. and R. Wonnacott, *US–Canadian Free Trade: The Potential Impact on the Canadian Economy* (The Private Planning Association of Canada, Montreal, 1967).

Index

data
  cross-checking of 60–2, 170–5
  problems of
    see categorical aggregation,
      overlapped trade,
      measurement problems
  sources 50–1, 55–6, 60–2,
    73–5, 140n2, 140n3, 170
    see also Census of
      Manufacturers
  unit of analysis 72–3, 96
developing countries 2–3, 4, 21–5,
  35
  see also Pacific Rim countries
differentiated products 4, 6–8, 67
  in IIT Model 41–2, 45–6
  resulting in cross-trade 46, 107
  see also cross trade, intra-
    industry trade, similar goods
diminishing returns to scale and
  specialisation 48, 49
direct foreign investment
  and high levels of trade 62–5,
    139
  and intra-industry trade 68,
    159–61
  flows of 5, 19, 139, 162
  high levels of 5, 44, 161, 183–4
  in Canada 5, 11, 28, 52, 62,
    161
  historical incentives for in
    Canada 28–9
    see also protected markets,
      tariff factories, trade
      barriers
  see also multi-national enter-
    prises (MNEs), subsidiaries
    (foreign controlled)
diseconomies of scale 10, 26–7,
  40–1, 92, 151
  see also diversification
disincentives
  to nationalisation in Canada
    26–37, 33, 145
  to trade 10, 145
    see also protected markets,
      tariff factors, trade
      barriers
diversification
  creating inefficiencies 10, 26,
    40–2, 59, 145, 151
  historical reasons for in Canada
    25–7
  horizontal 26, 92, 96
  vertical 26, 91–2, 132–5,
    151–3

  see also diseconomies of scale,
    internal production of
    supply
domestic consumption 1, 3, 20, 52
domestic market
  Canadian 9–11, 25–7, 33, 148,
    169
  European 9, 20, 25
  Japanese 10, 20, 25
  production for 75, 95, 128, 135,
    151
    see also Canadian-controlled
      firms, tariff factories
  share of Canadian 54, 59, 134
  small 9–11, 25, 160
  US 10, 20, 25
  see also intra-industry trade,
    domestic
domestic production growth 1, 3,
  20
  see also employment
dynamic model of comparative
  advantage 156–7

economies of scale
  and increased intra-industry
    trade 7, 51
  firm-specific 6–7, 83, 96
  government aid targeted for 157
  plant-specific 5, 7, 166
  product-specific 4, 7, 46, 69n8,
    166
  see also rationalisation, scale of
    production
economies of scope 25–6
  see also diversification
education 23, 36, 148, 155
  see also training
EEC (European Economic
  Community) 11, 21–5, 69n8,
  145
EEC countries 22, 63, 23–4
  see also European countries
elasticity
  of exports to imports 51, 52, 62,
    68, 161
    see also exchange rate
  of intra-firm prices 163–4
    see also transfer prices
employment
  by small Canadian-controlled
    firms 148–9, 166
  created by MNEs 139, 158, 165
  growth from free trade 21
  implications of IIT Model 45,
    166

and world markets 4, 22
capacity growth 4
development of modern trade
structures 10, 145
factor endowment ratios 23–4,
48
level of cross-trade 50, 51
rationalisation in 158
see also 'just-in-time' inventory
control, and use of domestic
suppliers
'just-in-time' inventory control 27
and use of domestic suppliers 10,
139, 158

knowledge
see intellectual capital

labour
see employment, factor
endowment ratios, retraining,
skilled labour, training
large firms
advised to increase specialisation
150–3
dominating manufacturing
production and trade 135,
147, 148–9, 166
export propensity 80–1, 84–6,
88–9, 108–10
import propensity 104–5
imports of intermediate goods
and minor product lines 114
relative size 76–7, 95
see also Canadian-controlled
firms, large and subsidiaries
(foreign-controlled), large
learning curves 40–1
licensing 40–1

major product lines 33–4
imported by subsidiaries 102–5,
135, 147, 151, 178–9
intra-industry trade 34, 119–21,
122, 147
propensity to import 116–17
share of shipments 162, 178–9
share of total imports 103,
178–9
trade by large firms 148
see also finished goods,
wholesalers, wholesaling
activity
management
firm-specific advantage in 3, 83,
157

flows of practices 2
improvements by Canada's
competitors 22–5, 35, 96,
159
intra-firm transfers 5, 13–19,
96, 159
lag in practices 9, 11, 25, 27, 35,
145, 166
spillover of practices to other
firms 29–30, 161
subsidiaries 13–19, 83, 96, 159,
162
see also intellectual capital
managers
Canadian 27, 30, 35, 83, 145,
162
key to adaptation 146, 162, 164
see also training, management
manufacturing activity
in purchased materials/value-
added ratio 129, 132–5
marketing skills
firm-specific advantage in 3, 157
measurement
of absolute level of intra-
industry trade 117–21
of import propensity 142n7
of intra-industry trade 44, 50–1,
55–62, 120–1, 129, 149–50,
180–9
see also categorical aggregation,
Grubel and Lloyd index,
intra-industry trade, tests
for overlapped trade
of scale of production 123–4
of specialisation 125–6
see also data sources
measurement problems
absolute level of intra-industry
trade 149
allocation of imports to
industries 90, 112–13,
168–70
see also categorical aggregation,
overlapped trade
bias in export propensity 140n2
double count of imports 33,
77–8, 82–4, 89, 140n2,
148, 170
effects of automobile trade data
76, 89
effects of excluding distribution
sector 170–5
import propensities 89, 90,
112–13, 168–70
inter-industry trade masked as

results of increasing 5, 6–7,
9–11, 39, 47–9, 146
small firms 150–3
see also rationalisation
search procedures 65–7, 87, 90, 92,
136, 162–4
costs of 66
see also purchasing practices,
suppliers
self-sufficiency ratio 52, 68
semi-tied trade 65, 160, 163–4
shipments 64, 79–85, 90–2, 96,
142n7, 176–7
see also measurement problems,
varying definitions of
market
similar goods 3, 4, 6–8, 20–36
see also cross-trade, differentiated
products
size of firms 74, 76–84, 91–5, 151,
176–7
see also Canadian-controlled
firms, large; Canadian-
controlled firms, small;
large firms; small firms;
subsidiaries (foreign-
controlled), large;
subsidiaries (foreign-
controlled), small
skilled labour 22–5
see also factor endowment ratios,
managers, training
small economies 9–11, 44, 46, 67,
145, 146
small firms
advised to increase scale 150–3
dominant in Canadian manufacturing 77, 78–9, 95, 135,
148–9
export propensity 84–6, 87–9,
104–9, 136–7
import propensity 85–6, 88,
89–90, 102–5, 114
see also Canadian-controlled
firms, small; subsidiaries
(foreign-controlled), small
social and management sciences
155
specialisation 6, 9–11, 39, 55–62,
123–8
and comparative cost advantages
6–7, 59
Canadian lag in increasing 11,
20–1, 25–7, 35
effects on intra-industry trade
34–5, 51, 137–8, 149

historical disincentives in Canada
26–7
horizontal and vertical 4, 5, 9,
128–35
increased by large firms 149,
150, 179
increasing in Canada 32–6, 62,
133–5, 139
in IIT model 41–2
results of increasing 47–9, 122,
146
subsidiaries 89, 91–2, 103,
138–9, 151–3, 165
former tariff factories 70n17,
161–2
see also product mandates
see also rationalisation
specialist importers 135, 148–9
and resource reallocation 147
association with non-IIT
industries 110–12, 113, 147
see also wholesaling activity,
distribution sector
specialist exporters
and resource reallocation 147
association with non-IIT
industries 110, 111–12, 113,
128, 147
Canadian-controlled firms
111–12, 121–2, 133–5, 147
Standard Industrial Classification
(SIC) System 43, 50, 74,
141n3
Standard International Trade
Classification (SITC) System
43–5, 50
subsidiaries (foreign-controlled)
76–7
subsidiaries
access to intellectual capital
28–30, 35
adjustment to changing trade
environment 70n17, 138–9,
123–4, 126–8, 150–3
cross-trade 69n8, 110, 121–2,
124, 147
ease of rationalisation 52
see also multinational
enterprises, role in
adjustment process
subsidiaries (foreign-controlled)
export of major product lines
92–4
exports 62–5, 88, 89, 97–9,
136–7, 159
subsidiaries